THE ULTIMATE
NASCAR
INSIDER'S
TRACK GUIDE

ALSO BY LIZ ALLISON

The Girl's Guide to NASCAR

The Girl's Guide to Winning a NASCAR Driver

Available from Center Street wherever books are sold.

THE ULTIMATE
NASCAR
INSIDER'S
TRACK GUIDE

Everything You Need to Plan Your Race Weekend

LIZ ALLISON

CENTER
STREET®

NEW YORK BOSTON NASHVILLE

The information provided in this book is based on sources that the author believes to be reliable. All such information regarding individual products and companies is current as of January 2009.

This book is intended to be a general guide for all of the 22 tracks on the NASCAR Sprint Cup Circuit. Unless otherwise noted, the author and or publisher does not personally endorse any of the listings and it should not be deemed as such.

Center Street
Hachette Book Group
237 Park Avenue
New York, NY 10017

www.centerstreet.com

Center Street is a division of Hachette Book Group, Inc.
The Center Street name and logo are trademarks of Hachette Book Group, Inc.

Printed in the United States of America

First Edition: January 2010

1   3   5   7   9   10   8   6   4   2

Library of Congress Cataloging-in-Publication Data
Allison, Liz.
The ultimate NASCAR insider's track guide : everything you need to plan your race weekend / Liz Allison.
p.   cm.
ISBN 978-1-59995-711-1
1. Racetracks (Automobile racing)—United States—Guidebooks.   2. Automobile racing—United States.
3. NASCAR (Association)   I. Title.

GV1033.A49 2009
796.7206'873—dc22

2009010971

This book is dedicated to the millions of NASCAR fans
who have an undeniable need for speed.

ACKNOWLEDGMENTS

It never ceases to amaze me how many different people it takes to write a book. I am so blessed that I have a wonderful support team behind me that allows me to do one of the things that I love the most—write about NASCAR racing.

This book in particular called for an enormous amount of man-hours to gather info for each one of NASCAR's Sprint Cup Series tracks. A great big loving thank-you to my brother, Grey, who took on the task like a true champion. Your hard work and dedication was and is such a gift. An extra special thanks goes out to Russ Thompson and Walter Cox for your insight and desire to assist this ole racing girl, no matter what the situation. Walter, you need your own show on the Food Network!

I cannot believe this is my third book with my Hachette/Center Street family. Thank you to my awesome editor, Christina, who is not only a fine editor but an even finer individual. A special thanks to Jana for giving this series the wings to fly. I feel so fortunate to have you steering the way for my books but even more so for the friendship we have developed over the *Girl's Guide* years. Rolf, Meredith, Whitney, Preston, Laini, Lori, and Amy, thank you for your continued support and enthusiasm for my books.

Alden and Pamela, you both are undeniably the best attorney and agent anyone could ever dream of. I value not only your guidance but more importantly your friendship.

As always, my support system is no doubt what keeps me going. Mom, Dad, Wendy, Donna, Georgia, Pandora, Ads, Connie, Linda R., Linda H., Jack H.,

Nisey, Mother Jane, Kimmie, Bethie I., Beffie J., Kim W., Joy, Theresa, Patti, Kelly, and Lori, I am so blessed to have each of you.

To Lesa France Kennedy, Catherine McNeill, Becky Darby, Mike Helton, and Kerry Tharpe at NASCAR for all you do for me personally and professionally.

I would not do what I do without the blessing of my family. To my precious children, Robbie, Krista, and Bella, who continue to allow me to follow my dreams. I am the luckiest mom in the world. I love each of you very much. And of course to my husband, Ryan, who wears many hats. You are my rock, and I love you!

CAUTION

Traveling the NASCAR circuit can be hazardous
to your health.... If you haven't caught the
racing bug yet, you will.

CONTENTS

PART TWO: THE TRACK GUIDE

INTRODUCTION

I f anything, I have learned over my twenty years in the sport that NASCAR racing is a lifestyle. NASCAR fans live, breathe, and sleep their sport, and I am proud to say I am one of those fans.

Thirty-eight weekends out of the year (counting the two all-star events), NASCAR's finest make their way into cities all across America, while the exuberant fans fill the stands, selling out the majority of the events on the packed schedule.

A NASCAR race weekend is much more than just the race—it's the sights and sounds, the excitement in the air, the carnival-like atmosphere. It is the common bond that ties the estimated 75 million NASCAR fans together.

This track guide is intended to give you every piece of information you could possibly need for your next NASCAR road trip. Each track chapter will give you ticket and track information, hotel listings, restaurant listings, shopping spots, hospitals, airports, rental car agencies, area churches, camping info, area attractions, and special events. I have also included chapters on what you need to know before you get there and how to go NASCAR racing with the kids.

The best part about a NASCAR weekend is there is truly as much excitement off the track as there is on. There is nothing else like it, period. If you haven't experienced the rush of a race event before, you'll soon see why NASCAR fans keep coming back for more.

Enjoy!

Liz

PART ONE

RACE DAY OVERVIEW

CHAPTER ONE

PLANNING YOUR TRIP

Before You Get Started

One of the toughest things to decide before you get started on your trip is what track to select as your NASCAR destination. I always recommend selecting the track closest to you, especially if this is your first race. With twenty-two tracks to choose from scattered across the United States, you should not have a problem finding one within a few hours' drive.

You might want to decide what type of track you would like to attend as well. NASCAR Sprint Cup racing hosts several different types of races, including superspeedway, short track, and even road racing. If you are looking for good old-fashioned racing, road racing might not be up your alley, but if you like the longer courses with lots of twists and turns, then Watkins Glen is the place for you.

Another thing to consider is whether or not your favorite driver will be racing at a certain race. Most of the full-time Cup drivers race every race on the NASCAR Sprint Cup schedule, but there are a few top name drivers who are not racing full-time anymore. For example, if you are a Kyle Petty or Sterling Marlin fan, you will want to check their websites for their race schedules. You would hate to drive all the way to an event only to be disappointed because your favorite driver is not there.

For those of you who have already attended a race near you and now want to venture out to a new venue, you can never go wrong with tracks like Bristol, Darlington, Daytona, and Talladega. These tracks are known for their great racing, but take note: these tracks also tend to sell out their tickets so always purchase in advance.

How to Purchase Tickets

Because of the intense popularity and the jaw-dropping growth of the sport, the number of fans choosing to view NASCAR races live has increased tremendously. The impressive television ratings also help grow the number of fans worldwide. All of this popularity, however, has made it a battle getting tickets to a live race event.

A large number of tracks hosting the Cup series events sell out each race, making it even harder for the novice race fan to purchase tickets. The key to ticket purchasing is *purchase early*! Most tracks put the tickets for an event on sale for the next season the day after the event in the current season—basically about a year in advance. If you can plan that far ahead, guarantee yourself a seat in the house by purchasing then. Certain events, like the night race at Bristol and the Daytona 500, actually have waiting lists for prospective ticket buyers.

CAUTION FLAG
Children in reserved seat areas must have a reserved seat ticket.

Almost all of the tracks require children to have a ticket to attend the event. Some tracks allow babies to enter without a ticket, but you might want to think twice before taking a little one to the racetrack. Always call in advance to the track you are attending to inquire about their admittance guidelines for kids. These guidelines tend to change from year to year and track to track.

WAYS TO PURCHASE TICKETS

1. Call the track ticket office. (Always ask for discounts and package specials.)
2. Check the track's website for ticket availability. Some tracks set aside a certain number of seats for online requests.
3. Check your local newspaper's classified section for individuals selling tickets. This is most helpful with "sold out" events like Bristol.
4. Check the track host city's classified section of their newspaper for individuals wanting to sell tickets.

5. Purchase tickets at the race venue from scalpers or fans with unused seats (if you don't mind the risk of not finding a ticket once you've traveled there).

6. Another great source for race tickets as well as hard-to-find tickets like Bristol, Indy, and Daytona is eBay.

CAUTION FLAG
Be careful when purchasing tickets from unknown sources.

There is no sure way of knowing whether the ticket you are purchasing is legit unless going through the official track ticket office. Web sales and scalpers are a sure thing, but the tickets might not be.

Tickets from Internet sites and scalpers may be counterfeited. Ticket counterfeiting is a problem in all sports, and NASCAR is not immune.

HELPFUL HINTS WHEN PURCHASING TICKETS

1. Always ask for discount information.

2. Ask about weekend ticket packages. Many times you can get a better rate if you buy the package deal that usually has a few bells and whistles. For instance, if you purchase a weekend pass versus a one-day ticket, the track may throw in pit and garage passes.

3. Ask for the last row cutoff on a certain ticket price. You can save money by sitting one row back from the higher dollar ticket just by sitting in the first row of the cheaper ticket area.

4. If you are planning to attend with children or if you have to use the bathroom more often, request seats at the end of the row.

5. If you are purchasing four tickets, request two seats on one row and two in the row behind, same seat numbers. This option keeps your group together, just not side by side. It is much easier to buy two and two than four in a row together.

6. If phoning in your ticket purchase, be very nice to your ticket operator—you would be surprised what they can help you with!

Where to Sit

NASCAR racing is best viewed "from the top," as they say. In many other sport arenas the better seats are close to the ice or field. Not with NASCAR. In most cases, the higher the seat, the better. The lower seats do not offer a full view of the racetrack, making it hard to see what happens at all times.

Many tracks have made ticket buying easy by adding an interactive option to their websites. This added bonus actually allows you to see what your view is like from the seats available. The virtual ticket experience is surprisingly accurate.

All tracks on the NASCAR circuit have reserved seating for wheelchairs and other special needs. Each track provides special handicapped parking areas to further accommodate visitors.

When traveling with someone who is handicapped or has other special needs, make sure you request track-specific information *in advance* to ensure the full advantage of all the services available to you or someone traveling with you. (See more on specific track special needs in Part Two.)

CAUTION FLAG
Beware of extremely high seats.

Some of the newer grandstands at different tracks like Talladega, Bristol, and Daytona are actually built on top of existing grandstands, making the older sections once referred to as "nosebleed sections" look like front-row seats. Seating such as this can be quite difficult for senior citizens and children to access. Always check with the ticket agent on other options available.

Where to Stay

HOTELS

In many cases the hardest part of your road trip is securing a hotel room. Rooms book up months in advance with some fans returning to their hotel of choice year after year. The ever-growing number of race team members is also to blame for the shortage of hotel rooms.

There are many hotel choices in the track section, but you also may want to check with the area chamber of commerce for accommodation listings. Make sure you inquire about private home, condo, and apartment rentals. This works especially well for families traveling together or families with children.

CAUTION FLAG
Stay in hotel chains you are familiar with.

Just because a motel has a business license does not mean you would want to lay your head on their pillow.

If you cannot secure reservations in the racetrack host city, try the closest larger city. I always tell people to check the closest airport location for the tracks that are farther away and make reservations in the city where the airport is located. You may have to drive a little longer, but you will have a place to sleep. For example, if you cannot find a room in Talladega, try Birmingham. You will have to drive forty minutes, but the rates should be lower and you will have more choices.

CAUTION FLAG
Beware of the dreaded "minimum night stay."

Many hotels gouge the race fans by insisting they buy multiple nights, even if they only stay for one. You can get around the minimum night stay and expensive rooms in most cases by just staying a little farther away from the track. Usually hotels twenty or more miles from the track will not have a minimum night stay. It is worth the extra drive time to save money on hotels.

Once you secure hotel accommodations you are pleased with, make sure you ask about holding your reservation for the next year. Many hotels give their current guests a courtesy "hold" for the next event. This is exactly why hotels are so hard to find. But make sure you find out the cancellation policy before you agree . . . just in case!

CAMPING

Most of the tracks on the NASCAR circuit have areas in which camping is allowed and, quite frankly, welcomed. Many retired senior citizens make their way from track to track throughout the course of the season. Some never walk through the gates of the track but are still proud just to make the NASCAR Cup rounds.

Most tracks have several camping options, from back to the basics with a tent to special RV spots with hookups. Depending on your price range you can get campsites with a view to kill but know you will pay the price. VIP camping areas range in price from event to event and also fill up very quickly. Your best bet is to call the track office in advance for your best rates and availability.

All tracks on the circuit have a variety of camping options available both on-site and off. The farther you move from the track, the less you can expect your overnight camping fee to be. The camping fees vary and tend to change from race to race. If you find a spot you like on a certain campground, always make your reservations for the following event if you plan to return. Many campsites are booked solid from year to year with the same folks who have been camping there for years.

When trying to decide what campground to stay in, first check location. The infield camping areas are wild and crazy and quite fun but maybe not the best place for kids under twelve. Most tracks on the circuit offer family camping areas just for the familes with kids. Take note and seek these areas out if you are traveling with kids. These areas are made available for a reason.

One other thing to keep in mind when booking your camping site is how crowded is too crowded for you and your family. Many of the tracks have both large and small camp areas to choose from. The larger the area, the more people to deal with. This also means more campfires (lots of smoke) and rowdier behavior. In fact, Talladega is known for being one of the smokiest campgrounds on the circuit. If you have a smoke allergy, you might want to stay clear of the infamous Talladega campgrounds.

It is a great idea to always contact the track you plan to visit in advance for fees, locations, and availabilities as these change from event to event. (See Part Two for more on track camping.)

INSIDER TIP—With non-track-owned camping you are taking your camping into your own hands. You might want to take a quick drive through the campsite before signing on the dotted line. If you are looking for a more family-friendly setting, always ask for curfew and family areas.

What to Wear and Pack

When going to a race, think *comfort*! You will be doing a lot of walking, so comfortable shoes are a must. Weather conditions change from track to track; whatever the case may be, dress in layers. *Always, always* check the local weather report before heading out for any race. Leave a few degrees on both sides for padding. There is nothing worse than being too hot or too cold at an outdoor sporting event.

It is a good idea to take along a fanny pack or small backpack to carry all of your track essentials. Always check the track's website for any current backpack or cooler stipulations as the rules pertaining to these tend to change from race to race. Cooler sizes are in place for various reasons, including safety, storage in seating areas, and the fact that tracks make a huge amount of money off of concessions, which means they will allow you to bring a cooler but they also want you to make your way to the concession stand. (Also, see Part Two.)

Seat cushions are very handy and comfy for a long afternoon on the hard grandstands. Many race cushions have a handy clip to hook onto your bag or pants. Keeping your hands free is a must. You do not want to get caught carrying items around all day.

Remember . . . pack light, but *do not cut back on your race day essentials.* You won't be sorry!

TRACK CHECKLIST
- ❏ Race tickets
- ❏ Cash (always carry some cash for parking, etc.)
- ❏ Credit card
- ❏ Binoculars
- ❏ Seat cushion
- ❏ Sunblock
- ❏ Hat
- ❏ Earplugs
- ❏ Sunglasses
- ❏ Hand sanitizer
- ❏ Cell phone
- ❏ Race scanner—rent or buy at tracks
- ❏ Rain poncho
- ❏ Backpack

❏ Extra toilet paper (just in case)
❏ Wet wipes—to wash hands, face, etc.

THE DOS AND DON'TS OF SURVIVING A DAY AT THE TRACK

Do drink *lots* of water to stay hydrated.

Do remember . . . water, beer, water, beer, water, beer, water (you get the idea).

Do use sunscreen (even if you think you don't need it).

Do wear a hat to block the sun from beaming down on you all day.

Do pack the poncho . . . just in case (a wet day at the track is not fun . . . trust me!).

Do wear comfortable shoes (your little puppies will thank you later).

INSIDER TIP—There are many activities to do on race weekend besides the race itself. Many of the cities plan special events and festivals to coincide with the race. Cities like Talladega, Charlotte, and Daytona have special museums and exhibits for the fans to experience while visiting their tracks. It is a good idea to contact the local chamber of commerce (see Part Two) before taking a road trip. You won't want to miss out on anything going on, from driver autograph sessions to festivals.

CHAPTER TWO

AT THE TRACK

Traffic

Traffic for NASCAR Sprint Cup Series races gives a new meaning to the phrase *hell on wheels*! Anytime 100,000 to 250,000 fans pile into one race venue, be ready to hurry up and wait.

INSIDER TRAFFIC TIPS
1. Leave early—the highest traffic time is within four hours of the race.
2. Leave late—the lowest traffic time is an hour before the start of the race.
3. Check highway listings for alternate routes, back roads, etc.
4. Check with your hotel for area maps and alternate routes.
5. Make sure you fill up with gas the night before.

If you just cannot stand to sit in traffic at the end of the day, park farther away when arriving at the track. This will make for a little longer walk, but the traffic moves more quickly farther away from the main parking areas. Another tip is to leave the race with about fifty laps to go. Most people wait until the end of the race; leaving early will almost guarantee a light traffic situation. If you hurry, you can catch the last few laps on the radio coverage.

Top Five Worst Traffic Jams

1. Pocono
2. Texas
3. Atlanta
4. Dover
5. Michigan

Top Five Smoothest Departures

1. Daytona
2. Indy
3. Kansas
4. Richmond
5. Charlotte

Tailgating

Tailgating has become a favorite pastime of NASCAR fans. Devout tailgating fans live for the experience and show up hours before not only to beat the race day rush but more importantly to enjoy great food, company, and the race day excitement in the air!

Tailgating takes place in the infield, camping areas, and general parking areas before and after a race. What used to be the same old fare of fried chicken has now found its way to steaks on the grill. Serious tailgaters plan far in advance for where they want to park and what the menu will hold.

Some of the best food at racetracks is served off the tailgate.

The Grandstands

The grandstands seat more fans than any other area during any given race. This is where the fan action is. Most tracks seat close to 50,000 enthusiastic fans in the grandstands, while tracks like Indy seat 250,000. Nowhere can the sights and sounds be experienced as they are here!

FIVE WAYS TO FIT IN WITH THE CROWD:
  1. Wear your favorite driver's name or likeness on a T-shirt.
  2. Stand up and cheer for your driver.
  3. Be respectful of others and their choice of drivers.
  4. Don't get up every two laps to go to the bathroom.
  5. Dress accordingly—wear casual, comfortable clothes and shoes.

The Infield

The infield is what many consider to be the danger zone. The "gut" of the race-track would be more appropriate. The infield is located inside the track. Not all tracks allow general admission infield privileges (see box), but the ones that do are fan favorites to the "infield crowd."

The infield is basically an "enter at your own risk" area set up for tents, RVs, and campers. The biggest party on any given race weekend is in the infield, but it certainly does not provide the best seat in the house. Many fans who stay in the infield see very little of the race.

Tracks Offering Infield Access

Atlanta	Indy	Pocono
California	Kansas	Richmond
Chicagoland	Las Vegas	Talladega
Darlington	Lowe's	Texas
Daytona	Michigan	Watkins Glen
Dover	Phoenix	

The tracks have only a certain number of infield tickets. Driving miles in a camper only to find out the infield is full would not be a good start to your race weekend! Always check with your track of choice in advance for details and availability. California, Chicagoland, Kansas, Richmond, and Texas all have long waiting lists. The best way to get on the list is to contact the speedway office and ask to be added. Waiting to clear a waiting list can take anywhere from one month to several years.

Listening In

Live NASCAR events can be extremely loud due to the roar of the cars. Take a track like Bristol—it's basically a half-mile bowl, so the roar of forty-three cars has nowhere to go but into the stands. The sounds of a track bounce from one grandstand to another. During a race it is very hard to talk with the person sitting next to you, much less hear the track announcers reporting what is happening on the track. Luckily, there are a few ways to keep up to speed during a NASCAR race.

> **Headset-style radios** allow you the opportunity to listen in to the national radio coverage of the race. The announcers do a great job of giving you information as it happens on the track. The announcers also give expert analyses of car problems, wrecks, and more.

> **Racing scanners** allow you to basically eavesdrop in on the driver/team conversations. Scanners are available to rent at all tracks. Rental prices range from $20 to $50. Scanners are available to purchase at tracks as well. When renting a scanner, you will be given a driver frequency list so that you can track your favorite driver. Even though kids love the scanners, be aware that inappropriate language is used at times.

Potty Breaks

"Potty breaks" during the day at a race can be quite an experience . . . at best! (Especially if you bring the kids!) One tip is to beat the "caution flag sprint" to the bathrooms by running to the restrooms as soon as the caution flag waves. Most people wait in their seats to see what happened to bring out the caution flag. The track overhead announcer always reports what is happening on the track, which means you will have to hear what happened instead of seeing the action, *but* you will beat the crowd to the restroom.

POTTY TIPS

1. Always pack extra toilet paper . . . just in case.
2. Hand sanitizer is a must.
3. Insist your kids use the restroom when you do regardless of whether they feel the need.
4. For female fans—bring tampons/feminine products (no machines in restrooms at most tracks).

Concessions

Track concessions, like food and beverages at most sporting events, are quite expensive. Concessions are believed to produce more revenue than any other track source, including ticket sales. While concessions are certainly easier than bringing your own, the price you have to pay is something to take into consideration. My kids love to eat racetrack food, but they like to "graze" all day, which runs up a hefty food tab. I always let my kids pick one or maybe two things to ward off any concessions grumblings.

Many race fans choose to bring their food, which can prove to be the cheaper route, but *always* check with the track *prior* to race day for any updated cooler restrictions. Coolers on wheels are the route to go. You do not want to carry around a heavy cooler all day at a hot, long race. You will be wishing you had paid for the $5 hamburger at the concession before the green flag waves. Also remember, you have to park that baby at your feet once you find your seat.

FOOD TIPS FOR RACE DAY

1. Pack sandwiches in individual bags to keep them from sticking together.
2. Stay away from items that can spoil easily, such as turkey, eggs, mayonnaise, etc.
3. Pack individual bags of chips and snacks. Look for lunch box–size bags available in grocery stores.
4. Pack fresh fruit . . . apples and oranges.
5. Stay away from chocolate chips, marshmallows, and other items that can melt.
6. Pack drink boxes and bottled water—stay away from glass items.
7. Soft drinks are not a good idea as they do not quench thirst.
8. Freeze water bottles the night before the race, pouring a little out first so the bottles don't crack. It will keep your drinks (and the food you pack with it) cold.
9. Pack protein snacks like nuts and trail mix with dried fruit and nuts.

INSIDER TIP—Store wet washcloths in cooler for every member of your family to cool off their faces later in day.

Souvenirs

Souvenir Alley is the grandest NASCAR shopping experience you will ever encounter. Whatever a NASCAR race fan wants . . . Souvenir Alley delivers!

Every track has an area (usually near the main grandstands) where they line up the dozens of haulers to sell driver and team goods like T-shirts, hats, etc.

These haulers have a convenient pop side that opens up to display a full view of all the merchandise each carries. The haulers accept all forms of payment from good ole cash to check cards and major credit cards. Some tracks even provide cash machines conveniently positioned near Souvenir Alley.

Shop for NASCAR souvenirs either early in the day, so you can take your purchases back to your car before the race starts, or on the way back to your car after the race is completed. Lugging around anything extra on race day is not worth the effort.

In the Pits

Many tracks on the NASCAR circuit are now offering prerace "pit" tours. The prerace tour is basically a behind-the-scenes look into the area that comes to life during the race. The pit tours are usually conducted starting as early as 7:00 a.m. on race day, with the final tours concluding about one hour before the start of the race.

These tours are usually sold as a part of the weekend race packages to entice the fans to participate in all of the track's events all weekend long. Some tracks do, however, offer pit tickets separately from the package deals. Most tracks only offer a certain number of the prerace pit passes, making it imperative to inquire about the pit opportunities at the earliest possible date.

THE DOS AND DON'TS IN THE PITS

1. **Do** stay with your tour guide if you are a part of a tour group or special group. They know how to make your trip to the pits enjoyable as well as informative.
2. **Don't** touch any equipment in the pit stall areas. The teams are very particular about where items are placed. NASCAR officials do not have a problem with asking someone to leave who they feel steps out of line.
3. **Do** remember the crew members are working! Race morning is very busy for the drivers and team members, only allowing a certain amount

of time to get many jobs completed. The crew members are not there to answer your race questions; they are there to do their job.

4. **Do** be respectful of NASCAR officials' requests at all times. The officials are there to "police" not only the race but everything to do with the race.

5. **Do** take pictures; you might not have another chance to get that close again. Most crew members do not mind having their picture taken while working. It is, however, a nice gesture to always ask before taking a crew member's picture.

6. **Do** ask for rules and regulations pertaining to children before buying pit tour tickets for them. Some tracks do not allow anyone under the age of eighteen in the pits. Always check in advance.

The Garage

The garage area is the eye of the storm for racing. This is a secured area where the team haulers are parked, the race cars are kept, and the teams work their magic. This is also the workplace for the drivers, an office of sorts. There is no other place at the racetrack where more official racing business takes place than in the garage area.

Because of the nature of the garage area, not everyone is allowed in. In order to enter the garage area you must have a hard card credential, a paper temporary credential, or a onetime walk-through pass. These passes are distributed by NASCAR very selectively. NASCAR will allow sponsors and teams only a certain number of passes per event to keep the total number of non-working bystanders to a minimum. The onetime walk-through garage pass was designed to reduce the number of fans hovering around the garage area throughout race morning.

The garage area can be a very dangerous place to be. The race cars are driving in and out of the secured area, teams are hustling tool carts, and wrenches are flying. Everyone must be careful and, most importantly, stay alert.

THE DOS AND DON'TS IN THE GARAGE

1. **Do** be alert! Always look around you and be aware of your surroundings.

2. **Don't** cross from one side of the garage area to the other without abiding by the rules of the road . . . stop, look, and listen!

3. **Don't** bring anyone under the age of eighteen into the garage area, unless the individual is a child of one of the drivers . . . NASCAR rule.

4. **Don't** touch anything! The teams will not appreciate you tampering with or even touching any equipment.

5. **Do** keep your garage pass visible at all times. Do not be insulted if you are questioned by a security officer or NASCAR official. Their main focus is to keep everyone safe and within the guidelines, which NASCAR has set for the garage area.

6. **Don't** approach drivers while they are with their team members (more about autographs later). Remember this is their office, and they are working.

7. **Do** ask for an autograph if a driver is clearly not working and is standing near his team hauler. Most drivers have autograph cards readily available (free of charge) for the fans. The cards can be found near the back of the hauler. Quickly ask for the autograph and then move on. Do not linger to chat.

8. **Don't** enter any team hauler . . . you will be asked to leave immediately.

9. **Don't** stand closely to the car or work area for the cars.

10. **Do** take lots of pictures.

11. **Don't** consume alcohol while in the garage area or enter while under the influence. Because of the danger factor involved in the garage area, NASCAR is very specific about what behavior will be tolerated.

"GARAGE AREA" ATTIRE

NASCAR will only permit people to enter the garage area who are wearing:

1. Long pants. No shorts or skirts are allowed in the garage area.
2. Shirts with sleeves. The rules state that all shirts must cover the shoulder, so tank tops and sleeveless shirts aren't permitted.
3. Covered-toe shoes. No open-toed shoes such as sandals or flip-flops.

Autographs

NASCAR driver autographs are heavily sought after but probably not as hard to get as you may think. It is a known fact that NASCAR drivers are more accessible than any other professional sport athlete. The timing and approach are everything.

TIPS ON GETTING AUTOGRAPHS

1. Check Souvenir Alley to find out when drivers will be signing autographs at their souvenir haulers on race day or even the day before the race. The drivers are set up in front of their respective trailers in order to sell merchandise and meet fans.
2. Contact the track before race weekend to find out about special events where drivers may be making appearances.
3. Check the driver's website where most drivers keep an updated schedule of upcoming appearances.
4. Read the local newspapers of host cities—some have a special race section with events and other helpful information such as traffic.
5. Check with the chamber of commerce prior to race weekend to find out about special events, which includes driver appearances.
6. When approaching a driver, be courteous by only asking for one autograph. There is no quicker way to get "that look" than to ask for multiple autographs. Also be sponsor sensitive—don't ask Dale Jr. to autograph a Coors hat.
7. Always keep a Sharpie pen (permanent black marker) on hand for quick autographs. If you have to search for a pen, you may lose your chance!
8. Put on your running shoes—be ready to walk along (quickly) with your driver. If he is in a hurry, you better be, too.
9. If you want to have your picture taken with a driver, always ask for permission and make it quick. Make sure the camera is on the right setting in advance and that you are not at the end of the roll of film or, if using a digital camera, out of memory or battery power.
10. Always thank the driver for his or her time.

Driving Schools

Most everyone who tunes in to watch NASCAR races week after week has some level of the need for speed. While very few would ever have the opportunity to race at Daytona against Dale Jr. or Tony Stewart, racing in a real stock car around Daytona is not a far-out dream.

Thanks to the numerous driving schools/experiences made available to fans, more people are living out their driving fantasy than ever before. The Richard Petty Driving Experience, the Andretti Gordon Racing School, and the Dale Jarrett Racing School are a few of the options available to race fans.

Most of the driving schools offer several different ride/drive options to choose from. You can ride along with an instructor or take the driver's seat yourself. All riding experiences are in real stock cars at average speeds of up to 170 mph, depending on the track.

This is a great gift to yourself or to someone else. There are few things a race fan would love more than taking the wheel of a real stock car.

The driving schools schedule riding experiences at different NASCAR tracks across the country on specific dates. The best approach is to select the school you are most interested in and then check their calendar for upcoming events. The Andretti Gordon Racing School has an option of stock cars or Indy-style cars, which is great for fans wanting both experiences.

DRIVING SCHOOLS

- Andretti Gordon Racing School: (877) ANDRETTI
- Buck Baker Racing School: (800) 529-BUCK
- Dale Jarrett Racing School: (888) GO-RACE-1
- Fast Track: (704) 455-1700
- Racing Experience, Inc.: (913) 322-1205
- Richard Petty Driving Experience: (800) BE-PETTY
- SpeedTech Auto Racing Schools: (877) 80-SPEED

Emergencies

You plan all year and then *boom* on the first night of your perfect NASCAR vacation, you (or someone with you) wake up with a temperature of 104. Why is it just when you think you have everything planned, you realize you forgot one thing . . . where is the closest hospital? Life will happen, as they say.

WHAT TO DO IF AN EMERGENCY HAPPENS AT THE TRACK

Every track on the NASCAR circuit has at least one first aid center. The easiest way to find the location is to ask a track official or police officer. It is usually located under the main grandstands. Larger tracks have several centers set up around the facility. The first aid areas are primarily for minor and non-life-threatening situations. The most common requests are for Tylenol, aspirin,

Band-Aids, and other simple over-the-counter items. The more serious conditions are handled by the emergency workers on-site. Ambulances are always readily available to transport patients to nearby hospitals if necessary.

All tracks on the NASCAR circuit have infield care centers, which are state-of-the-art trauma units complete with air transport capabilities. They mainly treat driver injuries, but will certainly treat ticket buyers if the need should arise. These trauma units are located in the infields of each track facility. They are equipped by local hospitals, with a full staff of nurses, doctors, and specialists. If you or someone with you should experience a serious situation at a track, you will be advised to visit the infield care center and be transported to a nearby hospital for further evaluation or treatment.

WHAT TO DO IF AN EMERGENCY ARISES AT THE HOTEL

For non-life-threatening situations, area hospitals are listed in the track guide in Part Two. But if you are staying at a hotel, it's best to call the front desk and ask for the closest emergency room or walk-in emergency clinic. Also ask the front desk attendant to write down directions for you so there is no confusion on which way to go. Emergencies tend to make most of us not as sharp as we would normally be—the more specific the directions, the better.

For more serious conditions or life-threatening situations, call 911 and wait for an ambulance. The time it will take you to drive to the nearest emergency room could be time well spent in an ambulance with the proper personnel who are trained to handle the situation.

Dining Out

The key word here is *patience*! Remember, you and everybody else in town are attempting to eat out. There is an extensive list of restaurants in the track guide but, as with most things, the local area chamber of commerce is also a great source for a full range of restaurants, from high dollar to quick low budget meals. Your hotel is another great source for restaurant info. Many tracks also have a restaurant link on their website with addresses and phone numbers.

TIPS FOR EATING OUT
- Make reservations when you can.
- Eat late—after the race day traffic has cleared.

- Break up in small groups (it is much harder to get larger tables).
- Ask about sitting at the bar (many restaurants have walk-up service available in the bar area).
- Order takeout.
- Have pizza delivered to the hotel.
- Seek out "off the beaten path" restaurants.
- Consider hotel restaurants.
- Use room service when available.

Shopping Offtrack

Shopping around NASCAR events is worth the trip. Some of the best shopping spots in the country are within miles of a racetrack. For an extensive list of shopping, check the track guide in Part Two.

INSIDER TIP—Ask the stores you purchase from to ship your items home, so you do not have to cart around bags all day. Remember, the suitcase will only hold so much, and some airlines charge extra for suitcases over a certain weight. If you are traveling by air, shipping is a must!

CHAPTER THREE

TRAVELING WITH KIDS

Deciding to Bring Your Kids

NASCAR fans under the age of sixteen are the fastest-growing demographic (along with the female fans) in NASCAR today. The younger generation drivers like Kasey Kahne, Casey Mears, Kyle Busch, and Dale Earnhardt Jr. have made the sport more appealing to the younger generation of fans.

The hip factor, along with the fact that NASCAR *really is* a family sport, is making it impossible for kids not to catch the race fever. Besides, where else can you go that virtually every member of your family can pull for someone different? Kids love the fact that they can root for their own driver regardless of who their parents like. It's their declaration of independence.

But *before* heading out for a NASCAR race family-style, you should ask yourself these four questions:

1. Can my child handle a long day at the track—walking, heat, loud noises?
2. Is there a family-friendly area for kids—for example, a Kids Zone?
3. Are my seats good enough for my kids to see?
4. Does my child like racing enough to watch a race all day?

If you answered "yes" to these questions, then by all means take your kids with you.

Another thing to consider is that while NASCAR racing is a family-friendly sport with a family-friendly environment (most of the time), you should always count on a few "oops" factors along the way. Anytime beer is served in the hot sun with an average of 100,000 people in attendance, you have to be ready (if the need should arise) to do some explaining to the kids. The majority of race fans are very respectful of children in the grandstands, but you can never be too sure. Expect the best, but prepare for a slip here and there, particularly when it comes to language.

Atlanta, Bristol, Darlington, Dover, Indy, Lowe's, Pocono, Richmond, and Watkins Glen now offer family grandstands, which are highly recommended for kids under fifteen. These areas are alcohol and tobacco free to better ensure a kid-friendly environment. Always ask for family seating when purchasing tickets for a trip with your kids.

CAUTION FLAG
Leave children under the age of four at home with a family member or babysitter.

The elements of a live race—noise factor, long days, sun exposure, lack of naps—are not conducive for babies and small children.

THE FIVE MOST FAMILY-FRIENDLY TRACKS

1. **Daytona**—Daytona leads the way for kid-friendly tracks with the addition of Fan Walk in 2005 and the Daytona USA exhibit, as well as the beaches and the fact that Disney World is less than two hours away in nearby Orlando.
2. **Lowe's Motor Speedway**—Lowe's was the front-runner in making tracks family friendly by introducing the concept of family grandstands that are tobacco and alcohol free.
3. **Vegas**—The Vegas track is great to bring along the kids to, but the city is the big kid pull. Las Vegas has more attractions and shows geared toward kids than any other city on the NASCAR Cup tour, making this a kid's top choice.
4. **Pocono**—Families (and kids) are important to the Mattioli family, who own and operate this track facility. The Pocono mountain area resorts are a great summer escape for the entire family.
5. **Martinsville**—This short track owns the racing world hospitality vote with its southern-style charm and family-friendly setting. Kids love this track.

What to Do at the Track

Racetracks offer many sights and sounds that only kids can truly appreciate—a big NASCAR Cup event can feel like a carnival. NASCAR understands they are indeed in the entertainment business, which is apparent with all that is going on for the ticket holder on race weekends, particularly for the kids.

"MUST DOS" AT THE TRACK

1. Check with track officials for kid activity areas. Many of these areas have kid-friendly interactive games, races, etc.
2. Always visit Souvenir Alley (allowance will come in handy here).
3. Look for driver autograph postings in the souvenir area.
4. Look for simulators and other interactive games for the kids. (Many need an adult to be with the child to participate.)
5. Slot car racing is scattered throughout the fan area at most tracks. Slot cars are fun for kids and adults.

THE DOS AND DON'TS FOR KIDS

Do make sure your child drinks lots of water—it is easier for a child to get dehydrated than an adult.

Do make sure they eat throughout the day.

Do reapply sunscreen several times throughout the day.

Do dress them in layers as the weather can be tricky . . . cold in the morning, hot in the afternoon, with a rain shower in between.

Do rent a race scanner or take along a radio with a headset so that they can keep up with what is going on trackside.

Don't allow your child to throw anything on the track—you will be escorted right out the front gates.

Do insist your kids splash water on their faces on very hot days as this will help keep them cool. Cold washcloths comes in handy here as well.

Safety

Always, always, always have an emergency plan with your kids on what to do if you are separated from them. Make sure they know where to go, what to do, and who to talk to if they can't find you. It is easier than you think to get separated from someone in large crowds. Point out track personnel and police officers as "safe" people to talk to. A cell phone is a good way to communicate if this happens. If you are a two cell phone family, give one to the kids. Make sure the kids have a ticket stub in their pockets at all times. This will assist them in finding the seats or assist track personnel in locating you.

It is also a good idea to have an emergency meeting place in the event that you do get separated. This designated place should be made clear to all family members at the start of the day. A great place to meet is the main entrance gate. There are many entrances to track grandstands but there is only one main entrance. Walk your kids to the meeting spot to make sure they know where it is located. Even older kids can get fearful when separated in a crowd of 200,000.

PART TWO

THE TRACK GUIDE

ATLANTA MOTOR SPEEDWAY

Start | Finish Line

Pit Road

Garage Area

Infield

Track Information

Inaugural Year: 1960
Owner: Speedway Motorsports,
Inc. (SMI)
City: Hampton, Georgia
Size: 1.54 miles
Banking: 24 degrees in turns,
5 degrees on straightaways
Grandstand Capacity: 124,000

ADDRESS
Atlanta Motor Speedway
P.O. Box 500
1500 Tara Place
Hampton, GA 30228

(770) 946-4211
www.atlantamotorspeedway.com

TICKET INFORMATION
Phone: (770) 946-4211
www.atlantamotorspeedway.com

About the Track

Atlanta is known by the fans for its
race finishes, but it is known by the
competitors as one of the fastest and
scariest tracks on the circuit. The late
Bobby Hamilton Sr. said he was not

afraid of anything in life except the Atlanta Motor Speedway. But while Atlanta might provide fast racing on the track, the traffic flow leaving the race is one of the slowest on the circuit. The track has worked closely with city officials to help traffic flow, but it is still a slow-moving process.

Track History

Ground breaking for Atlanta International Raceway took place in 1958. The building team was made up of a group of young architects. The building process took almost two years and $1.8 million to complete. The track was originally built as a 1.5-mile standard oval, but was rebuilt in 1997 to fit the mold of two other 1.5-mile tracks owned by SMI, Lowe's and Las Vegas. At this time the frontstretch and backstretch of the track surface were swapped and the track was reconfigured to the 1.54-mile quad oval shape. The track name was changed to Atlanta Motor Speedway (AMS) in 1990 to fit in line with the other SMI track names.

Track Records

Most Wins: Dale Earnhardt (9)
Most Top Five Finishes: Dale Earnhardt (26)
Most Lead Changes: 45—on 11/7/1982

Fewest Lead Changes: 6—most recently on 6/30/1963 (total of 3 times)
Most Cautions: 11—most recently on 11/14/1993 (total of 3 times)
Fewest Cautions: 1—most recently on 8/2/1970 (total of 2 times)
Race Record: Bobby Labonte—159.904 mph (3 hours, 7 minutes, 48 seconds) (11/16/1997)
Qualifying Record: Geoffrey Bodine—197.478 mph (28.074 seconds) (11/15/1997)

Fast Facts

- The first NASCAR Sprint Cup Series race at Atlanta was held on July 31, 1960, and was won by Fireball Roberts.
- Morgan Shepherd is the oldest driver to have won at Atlanta—winning in March of 1993 at the age of fifty-one (plus four months and twenty-seven days).
- Atlanta Motor Speedway offers an unpaid internship program that provides hands-on experience in many different aspects of the marketing and promotion of auto racing events.
- Scenes from the movie *Smokey and the Bandit II* were filmed at AMS.
- President Jimmy Carter worked as a race day ticket taker at AMS before he became a U.S. president.

- Mike Helton, NASCAR's president, is the former general manager at AMS.
- Monkey Wrench is the track's mascot.

Parking

Atlanta Motor Speedway has more than eight hundred acres of parking for fans attending the race. All parking is first come, first served. AMS does not allow overnight parking in the general parking areas. For up-to-date parking information, call the ticket office at 770-946-4211 or check out the track's website at www.atlantamotorspeedway.com.

Track Rules

According to the track's official website www.atlantamotorspeedway.com, the track's rules are as follows:

ITEMS ALLOWED IN THE GRANDSTANDS
- ✓ coolers (no larger than 14" × 14" × 14")
- ✓ cameras (no video)
- ✓ scanners
- ✓ seat cushions
- ✓ binoculars

ITEMS *NOT* ALLOWED IN THE GRANDSTANDS
- ✗ glass containers
- ✗ umbrellas
- ✗ strollers
- ✗ firearms
- ✗ pets (unless used by those with special needs)
- ✗ scooters
- ✗ go-carts
- ✗ bicycles
- ✗ Rollerblades
- ✗ skateboards

INSIDER TIP—AMS offers prerace pit packages, which allow fans access to pit road prior to the race. For more info on the packages, contact the track at 770-946-4211.

Special Needs and Services

AMS offers seating and parking for fans needing special assistance or accessibility. One companion is allowed to accompany those with special needs. For up-to-date info call the track office at 770-946-4211 prior to your arrival. Always request your parking to be near your seats.

Track Tours

Atlanta Motor Speedway is open year-round to individuals and groups for speedway tours. Track tours include a brief track history, a visit to Petty

Garden, a tour of one the track's luxury suites, a garage tour including Victory Lane, and two laps in the Speedway van around the 1.54-mile track. Track tours are available daily and run every half hour during operating hours (Monday through Saturday 9 a.m. to 4:30 p.m., Sunday 1 to 4:30 p.m.). Call the track at 770-707-7970 for fees and schedule changes. Group tours are best scheduled in advance. Tours are not conducted on race weekends.

Souvenirs

AMS official track merchandise can be purchased in the Atlanta Motor Speedway's gift shop located in the same building as the ticket office, adjacent to Tara Place, or on the track's website at www.atlantamotorspeed way.com. Driver-specific items can be purchased at Souvenir Alley located at the main entrance of the track. These souvenir trailers carry just about anything your heart desires from your favorite driver.

About the Area

AMS is located about twenty-five miles from downtown Atlanta. Due to the close proximity of the track and downtown, many race fans plan an extra day of travel to visit the area's many cultural and tourist at-

tractions. The average temperature for the spring race is seventy-five degrees; the fall race is sixty-two degrees. Due to the changing seasons for both events, always check the local weather forecast before traveling. AMS has been plagued with rainfall in years past and has seen temperatures drop to coat weather. This is a track where one should always dress in layers and keep the rain gear handy.

CHAMBERS OF COMMERCE

Henry County Chamber of Commerce
Westridge Business Center
1709 Highway 20 W.
McDonough, GA 30253
(770) 957-5786

Metro Atlanta Chamber of Commerce
235 Andrew Young International Boulevard NW
Atlanta, GA 30303
(404) 880-9000
www.metroatlantachamber.com

Transportation

AIRPORT

Hartsfield-Jackson Atlanta
  International Airport (ATL)
6000 N. Terminal Parkway, Suite 4000
Atlanta, GA
(404) 209-1700
(Approximately nineteen miles from
  the track.)

AIRLINES

Air Canada (888) 247-2262
AirTran Airways (800) 247-8726
American (800) 433-7300
America West (800) 327-7810
Atlantic Southeast (800) 221-1212
Comair (800) 221-1212
Continental (800) 523-3273
Delta (800) 221-1212
Frontier (800) 432-1359
Midwest (800) 452-2022
Northwest (800) 225-2525
Spirit (800) 772-7117
United (800) 864-8331
US Airways (800) 428-4322

RENTAL CARS

Airport Rent a Car of Atlanta
  (800) 905-4997
Alamo (800) 462-5266 or
  (404) 530-2800
Atlanta Rent A Car (404) 763-1110
Avis (800) 230-4898 or
  (404) 530-2725
Budget (800) 527-0700 or
  (404) 530-3000

Dollar (866) 434-2226
Enterprise (423) 323-5897 or
  (404) 763-5220
EZ Rent a Car (404) 761-4999
Hertz (800) 654-3131 or
  (404) 530-2925
National (800) 227-7368 or
  (404) 530-2800
Payless Car Rental (404) 766-5034
Thrifty Car Rental (770) 996-2350

Hotels

KEY
⌂ Pet Friendly   ≈ Pool
✕ Restaurant

⌂, ✕ **Americas Best Inns & Suites**
1171 Hampton-McDonough Road
McDonough, GA
(770) 957-5821

⌂, ✕ **America's Best Value Inn**
610 Highway 155 S.
McDonough, GA
(678) 432-6363

≈ **Best Western Inn**
805 Industrial Boulevard
McDonough, GA
(770) 898-1006

⌂ **Budget Inn**
758 Highway 155
McDonough, GA
(770) 957-5801

⟨♿⟩, ≈ **Comfort Inn**
2014 N. Expressway
Griffin, GA
(770) 229-6001

⟨♿⟩, ≈ **Comfort Inn**
80 Highway 81 W.
McDonough, GA
(770) 954-9110

Country Hearth Inn
1078 Bear Creek Boulevard
Hampton, GA
(770) 707-1477

≈ **Country Inn & Suites**
115 East Greenwood Road
McDonough, GA
(770) 957-0082

⟨♿⟩, ≈ **Days Inn**
1719 N. Expressway
Griffin, GA
(770) 229-9797

⟨♿⟩, ≈ **Days Inn**
744 Highway 155
McDonough, GA
(770) 957-5261

≈ **Econo Lodge**
1279 Highway 20 W.
McDonough, GA
(770) 957-2651

≈ **Hampton Inn**
2007 N. Expressway
Griffin, GA
(770) 229-9900

≈ **Hampton Inn**
855 Industrial Boulevard
McDonough, GA
(770) 914-0077

≈ **Holiday Inn Express-Griffin**
1900 N. Expressway
Griffin, GA
(877) 863-4780

≈ **Holiday Inn Express**
1315 Highway 20 W.
McDonough, GA
(678) 782-1100

⟨♿⟩, ≈ **Howard Johnson**
1690 N. Expressway
Griffin, GA
(770) 227-1516

Iris Inn & Suites
1906 N. Expressway
Griffin, GA
(770) 233-4747

⟨♿⟩ **Masters Economy Inn**
1311 Hampton Road
McDonough, GA
(770) 957-5818

&, ≈, ✕ **Quality Inn & Suites**
930 Highway 155 S.
McDonough, GA
(770) 957-5291

&, ≈ **Rodeway Inn**
788 Highway 155 S.
McDonough, GA
(770) 957-5858

&, ≈ **Scottish Inn**
1709 N. Expressway
Griffin, GA
(770) 228-6000

&, ≈ **Sleep Inn**
945 Highway 155 S.
McDonough, GA
(770) 898-0804

& **Super 8 Motel**
2010 N. Expressway
Griffin, GA
(770) 228-1393

Camping

ON-SITE AND TRACK-OWNED CAMPING

AMS offers a variety of camping options for fans attending the race. It is best to call the track's main office number at 770-946-4211 or go to their website at www.atlanta motorspeedway.com for up-to-date camping information and rate information. Make sure you check out the rules specific for the camping area you select, as each camping section has its own set of rules.

East Turn Reserved Camping This all-gravel reserved camping area is located on the front side of the Speedway near turn 4. This area is for RVs only. This is a self-contained campsite.

Infield Camping The infield is one of the most popular camping spots for die-hard fans. Always call the track prior to your arrival for camping options and rate information. It is a good idea to request an updated list of rules and regulations for entering the infield area as these rules tend to change from race to race.

Call the track's main office at 770-946-4211 for information on handicapped camping. It is best to call in advance as these sites tend to fill up.

Legends Camping This area provides grass camping spots for tents, RVs, and pop-ups. It is located across from East Turn Reserved Camping between the main entrance and Entrance E. This area offers access to tram stops as well as the camping shower and restroom facility.

Legends Lakeside Camping These twenty-five gravel spots are located in the front part of the Legends camping area and sold on an annual basis. This area offers full hookups (electric, water, sewer), and the spots surround a small lake.

Mid-State Family Reserved RV Camping This multisectioned camping area located between the main entrance and Entrance C has around-the-clock security and a strictly enforced quiet time (10 p.m.–7 a.m.). This allows for a more relaxed camping experience for the whole family and is *great for kids*. This area has easy access to the large main shower and restrooms.

Mid-State Family Tent/Pop-up Camping One of the sections of the Mid-State Family Camping area is reserved for tent and pop-up camping. This area is adjacent to the main shower and restroom facility for ease of use.

Mid-State Family Premium Reserved RV Currently the newest and closest camping area to the main grandstands and central tram stop. This area offers water and electric hookups.

Premier Camping These asphalt-surface VIP spots are located along the main entrance near the front-stretch grandstands as well as Souvenir Alley. This area offers full hookups.

RAGU Camping RAGU is located outside of turns 1 and 2. The large all-gravel lot offers level spots for RV camping. RAGU camping offers campers easy access to tram stops, grandstands, and the infield.

Speedway Boulevard Reserved RV Camping This is more or less the track's budget camping. This cost-efficient area is located at the intersection of Speedway Boulevard and Highways 19 and 41. The tram service is nearby, which enables campers access to and from all points of interest of the Speedway, including the infield.

OFF-SITE CAMPING

Atlanta South RV Resort
281 Mount Olive Road
McDonough, GA
(770) 957-2610

Campground Texaco Inc.
120 W. Campground Road
McDonough, GA
(770) 898-6654

Elks Honey Creek Campgrounds
2394 Morrison Road SW
Conyers, GA
(770) 761-7800

Restaurants

KEY

🍔 Fast Food   🪑 Sit Down
🍟 Takeout   📞 Reservations

Must Eats

Spondivits
1219 Virginia Avenue
Atlanta, GA
(404) 767-1569
   Known for their great seafood and big drinks. Valet parking is available.

The Swallow at the Hollow
1072 Green Street
Atlanta, GA
(678) 352-1975
   Great food and live bluegrass music.

🪑 **Ballard Southern Style BBQ**
11715 Hastings Bridge Road
Hampton, GA
(678) 479-8690

🍔 **Blimpie Subs & Salads**
108 Woolsey Road
Hampton, GA
(770) 707-2200

🍔 **Burger King**
11170 Tara Boulevard
Hampton, GA
(770) 472-9500

🍔 **Chick-fil-A**
11161 Tara Boulevard
Hampton, GA
(770) 472-6101

🪑 **China Kitchen**
11179 Tara Boulevard
Hampton, GA
(770) 603-8005

🪑 **CT's Fish & Wings**
1544 Tara Road, Suite A
Jonesboro, GA
(770) 472-1065

🍔 **Dairy Queen**
11146 Tara Boulevard
Hampton, GA
(770) 471-6800

🪑 **Dawgs N Jackets**
11768 Hastings Bridge Road
Hampton, GA
(770) 478-1579

🍟 **Domino's Pizza**
11386 Tara Boulevard
Hampton, GA
(678) 479-6468

🪑 **Emperial Buffet**
11341 Tara Boulevard
Hampton, GA
(770) 473-7988

🪑 **Finish Line Cafe**
96 Woolsey Road
Hampton, GA
(770) 897-9111

🍔 **Firehouse Subs**
11348 Tara Boulevard
Hampton, GA
(770) 473-0233

🪑 **Grand Stand Bar & Grill**
11346 Tara Boulevard
Hampton, GA
(770) 210-9180

🪑 **Hog's Pen BBQ & Grill**
2054 Highway 42 N.
McDonough, GA
(770) 954-0434

🪑 **Hong Kong Star**
20 E. Main Street
Hampton, GA
(770) 946-8889

🪑 **Johnny's New York Style Pizza**
11328 Tara Boulevard
Hampton, GA
(770) 210-0001

🍔 **Kentucky Fried Chicken**
11325 Tara Boulevard
Hampton, GA
(678) 479-4011

🍔 **Kickin Chicken of Lovejoy**
11350 Tara Boulevard, Suite B
Hampton, GA
(770) 471-9966

🪑 **Los Avina Mexican**
11332 Tara Boulevard
Lovejoy, GA
(770) 210-1733

🪑 **Lovejoy Wings Cafe**
11169 Tara Boulevard
Hampton, GA
(678) 479-2505

🍔 **McDonald's**
11281 Tara Boulevard
Hampton, GA
(770) 472-7113

🍔 **Pacific Deli**
11363 Tara Boulevard
Hampton, GA
(678) 610-2430

🪑 **Palm Beach Restaurant**
2180 Highway 20 W.
McDonough, GA
(770) 898-6877

Panda Express
11481 Tara Boulevard
Hampton, GA
(770) 478-1005

Papa John's Pizza
11105 Tara Boulevard
Hampton, GA
(770) 477-7775

Pizza Hut
11181 Tara Boulevard
Hampton, GA
(770) 477-7799

Ruby Tuesday
11473 Tara Boulevard
Hampton, GA
(678) 479-2072

Southern Pit Bar-B-Que
2964 N. Expressway
Griffin, GA
(770) 229-5887

Subway Sandwiches & Salads
11135 Tara Boulevard
Hampton, GA
(770) 471-8112

Uncle Sam's American Grill
1 E. Main Street N.
Hampton, GA
(770) 946-4166

Waffle House
1064 Bear Creek Boulevard
Hampton, GA
(770) 707-1109

Wendy's
1072 Bear Creek Boulevard
Hampton, GA
(770) 707-0696

Zaxby's
11131 Tara Boulevard
Hampton, GA
(770) 210-1515

Local Attractions

WORTH THE TRIP

With downtown Atlanta only twenty-five miles away, many race fans make their way downtown for the many area attractions. Here's my must-do list. **The Atlanta Zoo** is one of the few in the country that houses pandas. Due to the spring and fall timing of the races, the outdoor setting of the zoo is perfect, especially if traveling with kids. You can purchase your tickets in advance by visiting their website at www.zoo atlanta.org. **The Georgia Aquarium** is the largest aquarium in the world—a must-see. I recently took my kids to the aquarium. I am not sure who had more fun, them or me. It is recommended that you purchase tickets in advance (www.georgiaaquarium .org) as this is a hot spot for locals and tourists alike. I would also suggest the **CNN Studio Tour** (www.cnn .com/tour/atlanta) and, while you are in the area, **The World of Coca-Cola** (www.worldofcoca-cola.com) and the **Centennial Olympic Park** are easily accessible.

Army Aviation Heritage Foundation and Flying Museum
506 Speedway Boulevard
Hampton, GA
(770) 897-0444

The Atlanta Zoo
800 Cherokee Avenue SE
Atlanta, GA
(404) 624-9453

Centennial Olympic Park
265 Park Avenue West NW
Atlanta, GA
(404) 222-7275

CNN Studio Tour
One CNN Center
Atlanta, GA
(404) 827-2300

Fun Town of Henry County Bowling Alley
300 Highway 155 S.
McDonough, GA
(770) 898-4272

The Georgia Aquarium
225 Baker Street NW
Atlanta, GA
(404) 581-4000

Nash Farm Battlefield
4361 Jonesboro Road
Hampton, GA
(770) 288-7300

Noah's Ark Wildlife Rehab and Zoo
712 LG–Griffin Road
Locust Grove, GA
(770) 957-0888

Panola Mountain State Park
2600 Highway 155 SW
Stockbridge, GA
(770) 389-7801

World of Coca-Cola
121 Baker Street NW
Atlanta, GA
(404) 676-5151

Shopping

KEY

🚗 Automotive $ Discount
⊕ Pharmacy   🏬 Mall
☆ Specialty   🏛 Department store

🏁 **INSIDER TIP**—Lenox
Square and Phipps Plaza,
located about thirty miles from
the racetrack in Atlanta, is a
very popular shopping spot
for the drivers' wives and girlfriends. The shopping is awesome and well worth the trip.
This is a great escape for the
gals on Friday while the guys
attend qualifying at the track.

🚗 **Autozone**
11360 Tara Boulevard
Hampton, GA
(678) 610-0207

☆ **Bed Bath & Beyond**
1898 Jonesboro Road
McDonough, GA
(678) 583-2165

$ **Dollar General**
1112 Bear Creek Boulevard
Hampton, GA
(770) 897-0407

$ **Dollar Tree**
11337 Tara Boulevard
Hampton, GA
(678) 479-1405

$ **Family Dollar Store**
93 Woolsey Road
Hampton, GA
(770) 897-2165

☆ **Fashion To Fashion**
10571 Starling Trail
Hampton, GA
(770) 210-9668

$ **Fred's Store**
80 Oak Street
Hampton, GA
(770) 946-8334

☆ **Jasmine's Apparel**
9361 Sweetbriar Circle
Jonesboro, GA
(770) 472-8951

🏬 **Lake City Commons Shopping
   Center**
5656 Jonesboro Road
Morrow, GA
(678) 422-9751

$ **Marshalls**
1930 Jonesboro Road
McDonough, GA
(678) 583-6122

🚗 **NAPA Auto Parts**
90 Woolsey Road
Hampton, GA
(770) 946-5354

☆ **Peachtree Peddlers Antique Mall**
I-75, Exit 221
McDonough, GA
(770) 914-2269

☆ **Pier 1 Imports**
1784 Jonesboro Road
McDonough, GA
(770) 898-8240

☆ **Radio Shack**
11379 Tara Boulevard
Hampton, GA
(770) 603-6680

✛ **Rite Aid Pharmacy**
11265 Tara Boulevard
Hampton, GA
(678) 610-7733

✛ **Rite Price Store**
1544 Tara Road
Jonesboro, GA
(770) 478-4870

$ **Ross Dress For Less**
1900 Jonesboro Road
McDonough, GA
(678) 432-7556

$ **Sam's Club**
1765 Jonesboro Road
McDonough, GA
(770) 914-0488

🛍 **Southlake Mall**
1000 Southlake Mall
Morrow, GA
(770) 961-1050

🛍 **Step-Ins Outlets**
2948 N. Expressway
Griffin, GA
(770) 229-1949

$ **Tanger Factory Outlet Center**
1000 Tanger Drive
Locust Grove, GA
(770) 957-5310

$ **Terrell's Bargain House**
140 Oak Street
Hampton, GA
(770) 946-4845

$ **Wal-Mart**
11449 Tara Boulevard
Hampton, GA
(770) 471-4451

Churches/ Worship Centers

Berea Christian Church
37 Woolsey Road
Hampton, GA
(770) 946-3127

Calvary Assembly of God
805 Highway 3 N.
Hampton, GA
(770) 946-9860

Calvary Baptist Church
109 Oak Street
Hampton, GA
(770) 946-4181

**Christ Our Savior Lutheran
  Church**
48 Malier Road
Hampton, GA
(770) 227-4082

Church of God of Prophecy
3675 Fayetteville Road
Griffin, GA
(678) 688-5528

Crossway Community Church
700 Upper Woolsey Road
Hampton, GA
(770) 897-2200

First Baptist Church
85 McDonough Street
Hampton, GA
(770) 946-4804

**Hampton United Methodist
  Church**
10 W. Main Street
Hampton, GA
(770) 946-4435

International Bible Church
2701 Highway 3
South Hampton, GA
(770) 707-7912

Nativity Episcopal Church
130 Antioch Road
Fayetteville, GA
(770) 460-6390

Philadelphia Baptist Church
Hampton Locust Grove Road
Hampton, GA
(770) 946-4165

Southside Seventh-Day Adventist
9940 Dixon Industrial Boulevard
Jonesboro, GA
(770) 478-6999

St. Gabriel Catholic Church
152 Antioch Road
Fayetteville, GA
(770) 461-0492

**Summit of South Fayette
  Presbyterian Church**
1373 Highway 92 S.
Fayetteville, GA
(770) 460-3335

**Sunnyside United Methodist
  Church**
5084 Old Atlanta Road
Sunny Side, GA
(770) 228-8243

Medical Centers

Egleston Children's Hospital
2201 Mount Zion Parkway
Morrow, GA
(770) 210-2008

Henry Medical Center
1133 Eagle's Landing Parkway
Stockbridge, GA
(770) 389-2200

Piedmont Fayette Hospital
1255 Highway 54 W.
Fayetteville, GA
(770) 719-7000

Southern Regional Medical Center
11 Upper Riverdale Road SW
Riverdale, GA
(770) 991-8000

Spalding Regional Medical Center
601 S. Eighth Street
Griffin, GA
(770) 228-2721

Pet Medical Centers

Banfield the Pet Hospital
1950 Jonesboro Road
McDonough, GA
(770) 914-1280

AUTO CLUB SPEEDWAY (CALIFORNIA SPEEDWAY)

Infield

Garage Area

Pit Road

Start | Finish Line

Track Information

Inaugural Year: 1997
Owner: International Speedway
Corporation (ISC)
City: Fontana, California
Size: 2 miles
Banking: 14 degrees in turns 1–4,
11 degrees in tri-oval
Grandstand Capacity: 92,000

ADDRESS
Auto Club Speedway
9300 Cherry Avenue
Fontana, CA 92335

(800) 944-7223
www.autoclubspeedway.com

TICKET INFORMATION
Phone: (888) 472-2849
www.autoclubspeedway.com

About the Track

Auto Club (California) Speedway is
known for the celebrities on hand for
any given race. This is due largely in
part to the track's close proximity to

Beverly Hills. Race day is a who's who of Hollywood, with celebs like Pamela Anderson, Nick Lachey, Kid Rock, Gene Simmons, and a cast of others cruising up and down pit road.

Track History

Auto Club (California) Speedway is one of the newer tracks on the circuit even though racing in the Southern California area is not so new. Riverside International Raceway hosted Cup events until the closure of the track in 1988. It was not until 1994 that a public announcement was made of the plans for construction of the California Speedway. The project broke ground a year and a half later at a location that was originally a steel mill. The first stock cars did not make their way around the track until March 1997. The track was built to resemble its sister track, Michigan International Speedway. In February 2008, the Automobile Club of Southern California paid out a whopping $75 million to have the naming rights of the track. Rightfully so, the track is now called the Auto Club Speedway.

Track Records

Most Wins: Jeff Gordon (3)
Most Top Five Finishes: Jeff Gordon (6)

Most Lead Changes: 30—on 9/4/2005
Fewest Lead Changes: 18—on 5/3/1998
Most Cautions: 11—most recently 9/4/2005 (total of 2 times)
Fewest Cautions: 4—on 6/22/1997
Race Record: Jeff Gordon—155.012 mph (3 hours, 12 minutes, 32 seconds) (6/22/1997)
Qualifying Record: Kyle Busch—188.245 mph (38.248 seconds) (2/25/2005)

Fast Facts

- Jeff Gordon won the first NASCAR Sprint Cup Series race held at California Speedway on June 22, 1997.
- Rusty Wallace is the oldest driver to have won at California Speedway—winning in April 2001, he was forty-four years old (plus eight months and fifteen days).
- Kyle Busch is the youngest driver to have won at California Speedway—winning in September 2005, he was twenty years young (plus four months and two days).
- Portions of the movie *Charlie's Angels* were filmed at the track in 2000.

- The Disney remake *Herbie: Fully Loaded* was also filmed at the track.

Parking

Auto Club (California) Speedway has more than 33,000 free paved parking spaces. All parking is on a first-come, first-served basis. ACS does not allow overnight parking in the general parking areas. For up-to-date parking info call the track's main ticket number at 1-800-944-7223 or go to www.autoclubspeedway.com.

Track Rules

According to the track's official website at www.autoclubspeedway.com, the track's rules are as follows:

ITEMS ALLOWED IN THE GRANDSTANDS

- ✓ one soft-sided bag/cooler (no larger than 6" × 6" × 12")
- ✓ one clear plastic bag (no larger than 18" × 18" × 4", may not contain ice)
- ✓ binoculars
- ✓ scanners
- ✓ headsets
- ✓ cameras (not in a bag, worn separately over the neck or on the belt)
- ✓ seat cushions
- ✓ strollers (only in FanZone areas)

ITEMS *NOT* ALLOWED IN THE GRANDSTANDS

- ✗ firearms
- ✗ fireworks
- ✗ alcohol
- ✗ hard-sided coolers
- ✗ thermoses
- ✗ freezer/ice packets
- ✗ insulated cups of any size
- ✗ strollers (except in FanZone areas)
- ✗ umbrellas
- ✗ wagons
- ✗ inline skates
- ✗ skateboards
- ✗ bicycles
- ✗ scooters (motorized or manual)
- ✗ glass, aluminum, and metal containers
- ✗ pets (excluding properly identified ADA escorts)

 **INSIDER TIP**—Auto
Club Speedway offers child ID
wristbands and it is highly recommended that parents take
advantage of this free special
child safety program by signing
up their children (primarily for
those twelve and under) for a
wristband at a Guest Services
Information Booth.

Special Needs and Services

Auto Club Speedway offers seating
and parking for those needing special assistance or accessibility. One
companion is allowed to accompany
those with special needs. For more
info call the track prior to your arrival at the main office number:
(800) 944-7223. Always request your
parking to be near your seats.

 INSIDER TIP—Lost
items can be taken to or claimed
at the Lost and Found Tents/
Information Centers located
throughout the facility.

Track Tours

Currently there are no organized
tours available at the Auto Club
Speedway. Anyone interested in a private tour should call 909-429-5000.

Souvenirs

Official speedway and driver-specific
merchandise can be purchased at
Souvenir Alley located in front of the
main grandstands.

About the Area

The Auto Club Speedway is positioned very close to many favorite
tourist spots in Southern California.
Los Angeles/Orange County, Long
Beach, and Ontario are all less than a
two-hour drive away. This is another
track where an additional day of
travel is needed just to tour the area.
The Southern California weather
is perfect for racing, although you
might need to bring along your rain
gear, as this area tends to get some
passing showers. Sunscreen is a
must!

CHAMBER OF COMMERCE
Fontana Chamber of Commerce
8491 Sierra Avenue
Fontana, CA 92335
(909) 822-4433
www.fontanachamber.com

Transportation

AIRPORT
Ontario International Airport (ONT)
2900 E. Airport Drive
Ontario, CA
(909) 937-2700
(Approximately six miles from the
    track.)

AIRLINES
AeroMexico (800) 237-6639
American (800) 433-7300
ATA (800) 435-9282
Continental (800) 525-0280
Delta (800) 221-1212
ExpressJet (888) 958-9538
JetBlue (800) 538-2583
Southwest (800) 435-9792
United (800) 241-6522
US Airways (800) 235-9292

RENTAL CARS
Alamo (909) 937-3600
Avis (800) 331-1212
Budget (909) 937-6400
Dollar (909) 937-2895
Enterprise (800) 736-8222
Hertz (909) 937-2024
National (909) 957-7555
Rent4Less (909) 635-2600

Hotels

KEY
🐾 Pet Friendly   ≈ Pool
✕ Restaurant

≈ Americas Best Value Inn
16780 Valley Boulevard
Fontana, CA
(909) 822-3350

≈ Ayres Inn & Suites
4395 Ontario Mills Parkway
Ontario, CA
(909) 987-5940

≈ Ayres Suites
4370 Mills Circle
Ontario, CA
(909) 481-0703

≈ Best Western Inn
8179 Spruce Avenue
Rancho Cucamonga, CA
(909) 466-1111

**🐾, ≈, ✕ Best Western Inn Suites
    & Hotel**
3400 Shelby Street
Ontario, CA
(909) 466-9600

Cheryo Motel
15161 Foothill Boulevard
Fontana, CA
(909) 823-6034

🐾, ≈ **Circle Inn Motel**
10227 Cherry Avenue
Fontana, CA
(909) 822-9400

🐾, ≈ **Circle Inn Motel**
9220 Granite Hill Drive
Riverside, CA
(951) 360-1132

≈ **Comfort Inn**
13500 Baseline Avenue
Fontana, CA
(909) 463-5900

≈ **Courtyard by Marriott**
11525 Mission Vista Drive
Rancho Cucamonga, CA
(909) 481-6476

≈ **Econo Lodge**
17133 Valley Boulevard
Fontana, CA
(909) 822-5411

≈ **Fairfield Inn**
3201 Centre Lake Drive
Ontario, CA
(909) 390-9855

Fontana Motor Lodge
16390 Foothill Boulevard
Fontana, CA
(909) 822-4461

≈ **Hampton Inn Ontario**
4500 Mills Circle
Ontario, CA
(909) 980-9888

≈ **Hilton Garden Inn**
11481 Mission Vista Drive
Rancho Cucamonga, CA
(909) 481-1800

≈, ✖ **Hilton Ontario Airport**
700 N. Haven Avenue
Ontario, CA
(909) 980-0400

🐾, ≈ **Homewood Suites**
11433 Mission Vista Drive
Rancho Cucamonga, CA
(909) 481-6480

≈, ✖ **Hyatt Place**
4760 Mills Circle
Ontario, CA
(909) 980-2200

🐾, ≈ **Kings Lodge**
4075 E. Guasti Road
Ontario, CA
(909) 390-8886

🐾, ≈ **La Quinta Inn Ontario
Airport**
3555 Inland Empire Boulevard
Ontario, CA
(909) 476-1112

La Villa Motel
15211 Foothill Boulevard
Fontana, CA
(909) 829-9549

♿, ≈ **Motel 6**
10195 Sierra Avenue
Fontana, CA
(909) 823-8686

≈, ✕ **Ontario Airport Hilton**
700 N. Haven Avenue
Ontario, CA
(909) 980-3420

Rex Motel
1536 W. Foothill Boulevard
Rialto, CA
(909) 822-4211

♿, ≈ **Rodeway Inn**
4075 E. Guasti Road
Ontario, CA
(909) 390-8886

≈ **Sand & Sage Motel**
16364 Foothill Boulevard
Fontana, CA
(909) 822-9507

≈ **Sierra Crossing Motel**
18181 Valley Boulevard
Bloomington, CA
(909) 877-1900

Valley Motel
16762 Valley Boulevard
Fontana, CA
(909) 829-8874

Camping

ON-SITE AND TRACK-OWNED CAMPING

Auto Club (California) Speedway offers a variety of camping options for fans attending the race. Call the track's main office number at 1-800-944-7223 or check the website at www.autoclubspeedway.com for up-to-date camping information and fees. Always ask for the list of rules and regulations for each site, as each camping area has its own set of rules.

RVs.com Camping Area This is a track-owned off-site gravel-pressed dust lot located on Napa Street. Overnight camping is allowed. Restrooms and showers are available as is a tram service to and from the track.

Camping World Infield Camping This reserved camping area is located inside the racing oval.

🏁 **INSIDER TIP**—The Auto Club Speedway does not allow tent camping in any track camping area.

OFF-SITE CAMPING

Mission RV Park
26397 Redlands Boulevard
Redlands, CA
(909) 796-7570

Reche Canyon Mobile Estates
2751 Reche Canyon Road
Colton, CA
(909) 825-4824

Resort Campgrounds International
3546 N. Riverside Avenue
Rialto, CA
(909) 822-2760

San Bernardino RV Park
1080 E. Ninth Street
San Bernardino, CA
(909) 381-2276

Terrace Village RV Park
21900 Barton Road, Suite 170
Grand Terrace, CA
(909) 783-4580

Restaurants

KEY
🍔 Fast Food   🪑 Sit Down
🥡 Takeout   ☎ Reservations

Must Eats

🍔 **In-N-Out Burger**
9855 Sierra Avenue
Fontana, CA
(626) 813-8201
This fast-food restaurant is not hard to find as they seem to be on every corner. If you love a good ole burger, nothing beats the In-N-Out Burger. If you have a man-size appetite, go for the double Animal Style burger. This top-secret burger is the best on the planet.

Rainforest Cafe
4810 Mills Circle
Ontario, CA
(909) 941-7979
The popular chain restaurant is geared for the kids but the adults love it, too. The American food is actually surprisingly good. Make sure you bring your umbrella for the occasional rain shower.

🪑 **Antojitos Mexicanos**
8407 Cherry Avenue
Fontana, CA
(909) 356-5106

Arby's
12749 Foothill Boulevard
Etiwanda, CA
(909) 463-6251

Baker's Burgers
16090 Valley Boulevard
Fontana, CA
(909) 355-3668

Baron's Deli
7373 East Avenue, Suite F
Fontana, CA
(909) 463-0000

The Big Apple Restaurant
18080 Arrow Route
Fontana, CA
(909) 355-2096

Black Angus Steakhouse
3640 Porsche Way
Ontario, CA
(909) 944-6882

Boston's Gourmet Pizza & Pasta
11260 Fourth Street
Rancho Cucamonga, CA
(909) 758-9115

Burger Town USA
7670 Cherry Avenue
Fontana, CA
(909) 854-4999

Carl's Jr.
14454 Valley Boulevard
Fontana, CA
(909) 429-2226

China Cook
16075 Foothill Boulevard
Fontana, CA
(909) 428-2690

Claim Jumper Restaurant
12499 Foothill Boulevard
Etiwanda, CA
(909) 899-8022

Dalia's Pizza
13819 Foothill Boulevard
Fontana, CA
(909) 823-2222

Del Taco
10020 Cherry Avenue
Fontana, CA
(909) 356-1600

Denny's
13479 Baseline Avenue
Fontana, CA
(909) 463-9269

Domino's Pizza
8127 Mulberry Avenue, Suite 101
Fontana, CA
(909) 356-4114

El Lienzo Charro
17264 Foothill Boulevard, Suite M
Fontana, CA 92336
(909) 822-2444

Espinoza's Mexican Seafood
9131 Citrus Avenue
Fontana, CA
(909) 574-3710

Farmer Boys Restaurant
10479 Cherry Avenue
Fontana, CA
(909) 822-2300

5 Star Pizza & Chicken
16105 Arrow Boulevard, Suite B
Fontana, CA
(909) 355-9100

Graziano's Pizza Restaurant
7426 Cherry Avenue
Fontana, CA
(909) 350-0500

Hooters
725 N. Milliken Avenue
Ontario, CA
(909) 989-2209

Jack in the Box
10048 Cherry Avenue
Fontana, CA
(909) 356-0554

Joey's Burger
15324 Merrill Avenue, Suite E
Fontana, CA
(909) 429-1020

Kentucky Fried Chicken
14570 Baseline Avenue
Fontana, CA
(909) 357-1723

La Chiquita
15040 Valley Boulevard
Fontana, CA
(909) 519-1875

Las Playas Restaurant
14451 Foothill Boulevard
Fontana, CA
(909) 822-1584

Logan's Roadhouse
13480 Baseline Avenue
Fontana, CA
(909) 463-2290

Magic Wok-Fontana Inc.
14600 Baseline Avenue
Fontana, CA
(909) 829-6051

McDonald's
14454 Foothill Boulevard
Fontana, CA
(909) 429-7810

Mexico Lindo
9097 Sierra Avenue
Fontana, CA
(909) 822-7747

Panda Express
7376 Cherry Avenue
Fontana, CA
(909) 823-0688

Papa John's Pizza
13655 Foothill Boulevard
Fontana, CA
(909) 463-0660

Patio Burger
13677 Foothill Boulevard
Fontana, CA
(909) 899-4725

Pit Stop Cafe
16005 Valley Boulevard
Fontana, CA
(909) 823-3358

Pizza Connection
16117 Foothill Boulevard
Fontana, CA
(909) 822-7700

Pizza Hut
16075 Foothill Boulevard, Suite C
Fontana, CA
(909) 428-3000

Quiznos Sub
13518 Baseline Avenue, Suite B
Fontana, CA
(909) 899-5545

Red Lobster
4413 Mills Circle
Ontario, CA
(909) 481-5205

Rolling Sushi
12592 Foothill Boulevard
Etiwanda, CA
(909) 899-3441

Rosa Maria's
13451 Baseline, Suite G
Fontana, CA
(909) 463-3882

Saigon Chinese & Vietnamese
12809 Foothill Boulevard
Etiwanda, CA
(909) 899-8606

San Manuel Indian Bingo &
  Casino
5797 N. Victoria Avenue
San Bernardino, CA
(909) 382-2222, extension 240

Sizzler
9680 Sierra Avenue
Fontana, CA
(909) 829-4755

Sons of Italy
9420 Sierra Avenue
Fontana, CA
(909) 357-8149

SS Burger Basket
8535 Cherry Avenue
Fontana, CA
(909) 822-7044

Submarine Express
16120 Valley Boulevard
Fontana, CA
(909) 355-7821

Subway Sandwiches & Salads
12839 Foothill Boulevard, Suite A2
Etiwanda, CA
(909) 899-5255

Sundowners Family Restaurant
8983 Sierra Avenue
Fontana, CA
(909) 823-4515

Taco Bell
12789 Foothill Boulevard
Etiwanda, CA
(909) 899-3319

Up N Smoke BBQ
7373 East Avenue
Fontana, CA
(909) 463-7242

Wendy's
14439 Baseline Avenue
Fontana, CA
(909) 356-8622

Wienerschnitzel
14524 Baseline Avenue
Fontana, CA
(909) 823-7452

Local Attractions

WORTH THE TRIP

With or without the kids, **Disney-land** (www.disneyland.com) and **Universal Studios** (www.universal studios.com) are worth the trip. Where else can you get a day with Mickey and then head over to the track for a weekend of racing? Nowhere—except maybe Daytona.

Claremont Golf Course
1550 N. Indian Hill Boulevard
Claremont, CA
(909) 624-2748

Creekside Golf Course
3151 E. Riverside Drive
Ontario, CA
(909) 947-1981

Disneyland
Disneyland Drive
Anaheim, CA
(714) 781-4565

Knott's Berry Farm
8039 Beach Boulevard
Buena Park, CA
(714) 220-5200

LA Zoo & Botanical Gardens
5333 Zoo Drive
Los Angeles, CA
(323) 644-4200

Legoland California
One Legoland Drive
Carlsbad, CA
(760) 918-5346

Raging Waters
111 Raging Waters Drive
San Dimas, CA
(909) 802-2200

Six Flags Magic Mountain
26101 Magic Mountain Parkway
Valencia, CA
(661) 255-4100

Universal Studios Hollywood
100 Universal City Plaza
Universal City, CA
(800) UNI-VERSAL

Shopping

KEY
🚗 Automotive $ Discount
⊙ Pharmacy   🏬 Mall
☆ Specialty   🏯 Department Store

INSIDER TIP—Okay, for all you shopping fans, here is your chance to shop at one of the most famous shopping spots in the world . . . Rodeo Drive. The ever-popular shopping strip is about an hour's drive from the track. If you are like me, you have to do more window-shopping than true buying, but being there is worth the time and effort. This is a drivers' wives favorite spot.

$ Big Lots
12434 Fourth Street
Rancho Cucamonga, CA
(909) 899-2511

🏬 Carousel Mall
295 Carousel Mall
San Bernardino, CA
(909) 884-0106

☆ Crate & Barrel
12367 N. Main Street
Etiwanda, CA
(909) 646-8668

$ Direct Discount Store
517 W. Holt Boulevard
Ontario, CA
(909) 983-2277

$ **Dollar Store**
9121 Haven Avenue
Rancho Cucamonga, CA
(909) 945-8443

$ **Dollar Tree**
9976 Sierra Avenue
Fontana, CA
(909) 574-6114

☆ **Fashion Plaza**
1153 N. Mount Vernon Avenue
Colton, CA
(909) 370-1255

🏬 **Fiesta Discount Mall**
5700 Van Buren Boulevard
Riverside, CA
(951) 354-8947

🏬 **Inland Center Mall**
500 Inland Center Drive
San Bernardino, CA
(909) 884-7268

$ **Kmart**
17099 Valley Boulevard
Fontana, CA
(909) 822-2004

🏠 **Kohl's Department Store**
1051 N. Milliken Avenue
Ontario, CA
(909) 484-7805

$ **Marshalls**
4377 Mills Circle
Ontario, CA
(909) 484-3291

$ **Mira Discount Store**
9938 Sierra Avenue
Fontana, CA
(909) 428-0240

$ **99 Cent Super Store**
3055 S. Archibald Avenue
Ontario, CA
(909) 673-9000

🏬 **Ontario Mills Shopping Center**
1 Mills Circle, Suite 1
Ontario, CA
(909) 484-8300

☆ **Pier 1 Imports Outlet Store**
985 S. E Street
San Bernardino, CA
(909) 384-1648

○ **Rite Aid**
11673 Cherry Avenue
Fontana, CA
(909) 357-2031

🏬 **Riverside Discount Mall Inc**
Shamrock Avenue
Riverside, CA
(951) 781-7008

$ **Sam's Club**
951 N. Milliken Avenue
Ontario, CA
(909) 476-9259

☆ **That Place**
16405 Merrill Avenue, Suite B
Fontana, CA
(909) 355-4994

$ **T.J. Maxx**
4757 Mills Circle
Ontario, CA
(909) 980-1940

🏬 **Upland Market Place LLC**
1445 E. Foothill Boulevard
Upland, CA
(909) 982-9242

🏠 **Valley Department Store**
245 N. Euclid Avenue
Ontario, CA
(909) 984-8646

🏬 **Village Grove**
1461 E. Foothill Boulevard
Upland, CA
(909) 981-1668

$ **Wal-Mart**
12549 Foothill Boulevard
Etiwanda, CA
(909) 899-1441

Churches/ Worship Centers

Calvary Baptist Church
9444 Mango Avenue
Fontana, CA
(909) 822-9444

Church of Christ
9132 Sierra Avenue
Fontana, CA
(909) 822-1012

Faith Christian Fellowship Church
13819 Foothill Boulevard
Fontana, CA
(909) 822-7100

First Lutheran Church
9315 Citrus Avenue
Fontana, CA
(909) 823-3457

First Presbyterian Church
9260 Mango Avenue
Fontana, CA
(909) 822-6779

First United Methodist Church
9116 Sierra Avenue
Fontana, CA
(909) 822-4105

Sacred Heart Catholic Church
12704 Foothill Boulevard
Etiwanda, CA
(909) 899-1049

Saint Luke's Episcopal Church
16557 Upland Avenue
Fontana, CA
(909) 822-2012

South Fontana Community
  Church
10654 Live Oak Avenue
Fontana, CA
(909) 822-3637

Medical Centers

Riverside Community Hospital
4445 Magnolia Avenue
Riverside, CA
(951) 788-3000

San Antonio Community Hospital
999 San Bernardino Road
Upland, CA
(909) 985-2811

Urgent Care at Sierra
16465 Sierra Lakes Parkway
Fontana, CA
(909) 434-1150

Pet Medical Centers

Fontana Animal Hospital
16153 Foothill Boulevard
Fontana, CA
(909) 355-5600

Sierra Animal Hospital
16736 Arrow Boulevard
Fontana, CA
(909) 350-7807

BRISTOL MOTOR SPEEDWAY

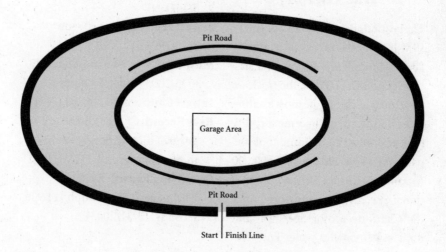

Track Information

Inaugural Year: 1961
Owner: SMI
City: Bristol, Tennessee
Size: 0.533 miles
Banking: 36 degrees in corners, 16 degrees on straightaways
Grandstand Capacity: 160,000

ADDRESS
Bristol Motor Speedway
151 Speedway Boulevard
Bristol, TN 37620
(423) 989-6942
www.bristolmotorspeedway.com

TICKET INFORMATION
Phone: (423) 989-6900
www.bristoltix.com

About the Track

Bristol is short-track racing at its best. The half-mile concrete bowl provides beating and banging like no other track. The competitors love racing at Bristol and the fans love watching racing at Bristol even more. The August night race is said to be the most difficult race ticket on the circuit. The current waiting list is several years long. Legend has it that Bristol race tickets have even made it into divorce court hearings.

Track History

The grounds Bristol Motor Speedway (BMS) now sits on was once a dairy farm. Through the vision of Larry Carrier and R. G. Pope, the track we view today as one of the most exciting races on the circuit became a reality back in 1960. The building took the pair over a year and a hefty $600,000 to construct. The Bristol International Speedway was mirrored after the Charlotte Motor Speedway but on a much smaller scale. The seating capacity for the first event was a mere 18,000, which does not hold a candle to the 160,000 grandstand seating of today. The original asphalt track surface was replaced in 1992 with the current concrete surface, a unique track surface that is used by only two tracks on the Cup circuit. In 1996, Bruton Smith and SMI purchased the track for $26 million from Larry Carrier. The track was named the Bristol Motor Speedway shortly after the sale.

Track Records

Most Wins: Darrell Waltrip (12)

Most Top Five Finishes: Darrell Waltrip and Richard Petty (26)

Most Lead Changes: 40—on 4/14/1991

Fewest Lead Changes: 0—on 3/25/1973

Most Cautions: 20—most recently 8/23/2003 (total of 3 times)

Fewest Cautions: 0—on 7/11/1971

Race Record: Charlie Glotzbach— 101.074 mph (3 hours, 38 minutes, 12 seconds) (7/11/1971)

Qualifying Record: Ryan Newman—128.709 mph (14.908 seconds) (3/21/2003)

Fast Facts

• Jack Smith won the first NASCAR Sprint Cup Series race at Bristol Motor Speedway on July 30, 1961.

• Dale Earnhardt Sr. is the oldest driver to have won at Bristol— winning in August of 1999, he was forty-eight years old (plus three months and thirty days).

• In twenty-one of forty years since Bristol opened, a driver who won a Cup race at Bristol went on to win the series title later the same year.

• Country music star Brenda Lee, who was seventeen at the time, sang the national anthem for the first race at BMS.

- Ryan Newman became the first driver to record a sub-15 second lap at BMS during March 2003. Newman grabbed the Food City 500 pole with a 14.908 second lap at 128.709 mph.
- Atlanta's Jack Smith won the in-augural event, the Volunteer 500, at BMS on July 30, 1961. However, Smith wasn't in the driver's seat of the Pontiac when the race ended. Smith drove the first 290 laps and then had to have Johnny Allen take over as his relief driver. The two shared the $3,225 purse.
- Bristol is known by fans as Thunder Valley and is often referred to as the "world's fastest half mile."
- The track has a hundred-plus person waiting list for grandstand tickets for both of Bristol's Cup series events. The children of the Cup drivers sing the anthem for the August night race, a tradition that started over ten years ago.
- Bristol is one of the few tracks on the circuit that does not have a bad seat in the house.
- Bristol was used as the template for the Motor Speedway of the South in the Disney movie *Cars*.

Parking

Bristol has a variety of parking options, both free and paid. All free parking is on a first-come, first-served basis. BMS does not allow overnight parking in the general parking areas. For up-to-date information on parking availability and fees, call the track at 423-989-6942 or check their website at www.bristol motorspeedway.com.

Track Rules

According to the track's official website at www.bristolmotorspeedway .com, the track's rules are as follows:

ITEMS ALLOWED IN THE GRANDSTANDS
- ✓ cameras
- ✓ stadium seat cushions
- ✓ headsets
- ✓ radios
- ✓ coolers, bags, or backpacks (not to exceed 14″)
- ✓ fanny packs

ITEMS *NOT* ALLOWED IN THE GRANDSTANDS
- ✗ folding stadium seats or chairs
- ✗ umbrellas
- ✗ illegal drugs
- ✗ golf carts
- ✗ fires, grills, or fireworks
- ✗ weapons of any kind

✗ coolers (over 14")
✗ more than one carry-in bag (bag cannot exceed size of cooler)
✗ glass containers
✗ pets (except service animals assisting the disabled)
✗ scaffolds or platforms
✗ bicycles
✗ beer balls
✗ noisemakers, horns, helium balloons, and beach balls

Note: *All bags will be searched upon entry to the track. The track advises race fans to arrive one hour prior to the start of the race to allow ample time for searching. I would advise taking fewer bags and allowing at least two hours prior, so you can enjoy the entire race day experience without being caught up in long security lines.*

Special Needs and Services

BMS offers seating and parking for those needing special assistance or accessibility. One companion is allowed to accompany those with special needs. Contact the Bristol main ticket office at 423-989-6931 for more information regarding special needs and services. Always request your parking to be near your seats.

Track Tours

BMS offers individual and group tours of the track daily except during major Speedway and Dragway events. All peak season tours (May through August) require a reservation. Monday through Saturday, tours begin on the hour starting at 9 a.m. with the final tour of the day starting at 4 p.m. On Sunday, tours begin at noon with the final tour starting at 4 p.m. Call the track at 423-989-6960 for fees and group reservations.

INSIDER TIP—Bristol Motor Speedway hosts **Speedway In Lights** each year beginning in mid-November through early January. The annual event includes more than 1.5 million lights and 200 displays. Holiday light seekers will circle the concrete oval as part of their festive drive and also may visit Christmas Village, which is located in the infield. All proceeds from the event benefit the Bristol Chapter of Speedway Children's Charities.

Note: *The York Ice Skating Rink is situated in the BMS front parking lot adjacent to Volunteer Parkway. The ice rink is open to Speedway In Lights* visitors during evening hours for an additional charge.

Souvenirs

BMS official track merchandise can be purchased in the Bristol Motor Speedway Souvenir Store located just inside the doors of the Bruton Smith Building near the Speedway's turn 2 just off Volunteer Parkway. During event weekends, souvenir and concession stands are located throughout the facility. The race haulers located on Souvenir Alley are driver specific and can be found at the main entrance to the track.

About the Area

Bristol is one of the most unique places the NASCAR Cup Series visits each year. While the track is fast, loud, and lively, the town is anything but. Race weekends by all accounts are the biggest events of the year for the small community. The average temperature for the spring race is sixty-two degrees while the fall race is a hotter and steamier eighty-two degrees. The nighttime running of the fall event helps as the temps fall quite a bit once the sun goes down. Taking along a jacket is always advisable for both events.

Note: *Because this is a rural area, many places listed in this section do not have street numbers. I recommend calling the numbers listed for specific directions.*

INSIDER TIP—The Virginia-Tennessee state line runs right through Bristol race country. Do not be alarmed that Bristol listings have Virginia and Tennessee addresses. The hotels are only blocks apart in many cases.

CHAMBER OF COMMERCE

Bristol Chamber of Commerce
20 Volunteer Parkway
Bristol, TN 37620
(423) 989-4850
www.bristolchamber.org

Transportation

AIRPORT

Tri-Cities Regional Airport (TRI)
2525 Highway 75
Blountville, TN
(423) 325-6000
(Approximately eight miles from the track.)

AIRLINES

Allegiant Air (702) 505-8888
Delta Connection (800) 221-1212
Northwest Airlink (800) 225-2525
US Airways Express (800) 428-4322

RENTAL CARS

Alamo (800) 462-5266
Avis (800) 230-4898
Budget (800) 527-0700
Enterprise (423) 323-5897
Hertz (800) 654-3131
National (800) 227-7368

Hotels

KEY
≈ Pet Friendly   ≈ Pool
✕ Restaurant

≈, ✕ **Best Western**
2406 N. Roan Street
Johnson City, TN
(423) 989-1011

≈, ≈, ✕ **Carnegie Hotel**
1216 W. State of Franklin Road
Johnson City, TN
(423) 979-6400

≈ **Comfort Suites**
3118 Browns Mill Road
Johnson City, TN
(423) 610-0010

≈ **Courtyard by Marriott**
3169 Linden Drive
Bristol, VA
(276) 591-4400

≈, ≈ **Days Inn**
3281 W. State Street
Bristol, TN
(423) 968-9119

≈, ≈, ✕ **Doubletree Hotel**
211 Mockingbird Lane
Johnson City, TN
(423) 929-2000

≈ **Econo Lodge Bristol**
912 Commonwealth Avenue
Bristol, VA
(276) 466-2112

≈, ≈ **Fairfield Inn by Marriott**
207 E. Mountaincastle Drive
Johnson City, TN
(423) 282-3335

≈ **Hampton Inn**
3299 W. State Street
Bristol, TN
(423) 764-3600

≈, ≈, ✕ **Holiday Inn**
101 W. Springbrook Drive
Johnson City, TN
(423) 282-4611

&, ≈, ✕ **Holiday Inn and Suites**
3005 Linden Drive
Bristol, VA
(276) 466-4100

& **Holiday Inn Express**
4234 Fort Henry Drive
Kingsport, TN
(423) 239-3400

& **Knights Inn**
2221 Euclid Avenue
Bristol, VA
(276) 591-5090

&, ≈ **La Quinta Inn**
1014 Old Airport Road
Bristol, VA
(276) 669-9353

&, ≈ **Microtel Inn & Suites**
131 Bristol East Road
Bristol, VA
(276) 669-8164

& **Motel 6**
21561 Clear Creek Road
Bristol, VA
(276) 466-6060

New Hope Bed & Breakfast
822 Georgia Avenue
Bristol, TN
(423) 989-3343

≈ **Quality Inn & Suites**
960 E. Main Street
Abingdon, VA
(276) 676-9090

≈ **Ramada Limited**
2606 N. Roan Street
Johnson City, TN
(423) 282-4011

& **Red Roof Inn**
210 Broyles Drive
Johnson City, TN
(423) 282-3040

& **Sleep Inn and Suites**
202 Franklin Terrace Court
Johnson City, TN
(423) 915-0081

Camping

ON-SITE AND TRACK-OWNED CAMPING

Camping at BMS is about as hard to get as a race day ticket. Many BMS track-owned camping areas are sold out and have a waiting list in place. These are listed as sold out below. To be added to the waiting list, contact the track camping office number at 423-989-6944. Infield access is not available at Bristol.

Campground at Bristol Dragway
Sold out

**The Blue Ox Campground on BMS
property** Sold out

**The Medallion Campground at
BMS** Sold out

The Landing Campground This
recently updated campground is located on Copperhead Road. The lots
are positioned on a flat gravel surface. Restrooms and shuttle service
are offered in this area.

OFF-SITE CAMPING

Cochran's Lakeview Camp Ground
821 Painter Creek Road
Bristol, TN
(423) 878-8045

Lake Front Family Campground
350 Jones Road
Bristol, TN
(423) 878-6730

Lee Highway Campground
2671 Lee Highway
Bristol, VA
(276) 669-3616

Little Oak Campground Host
1051 Little Oak Road
Bristol, TN
(423) 878-6327

Red Barn Camping
191 White Top Road
Bluff City, TN
(423) 538-7177

Thunder Valley Campground
2623 Volunteer Parkway
Bristol, TN
(423) 652-2267

Tri City Tent & Event
1009 Highland Avenue
Bristol, VA
(276) 466-6161

Restaurants

KEY
🍔 Fast Food   🪑 Sit Down
🛍 Takeout   ☾ Reservations

Must Eats

Cootie Brown's
2715 N. Roan Street
Johnson City, TN
(423) 283-4723
    Great steaks and lots of beer.

♞ Atlanta Bread Company
2010 Franklin Terrace Court
Johnson City, TN
(423) 282-8001

♞ Bailey's Sports Grille
2102 N. Roan Street
Johnson City, TN
(423) 929-1370

♞ Brooklyn Grill & Cafe
2125 Euclid Avenue
Bristol, VA
(276) 669-1900

🍔 Burger King
100 Blountville Bypass
Blountville, TN
(423) 323-2745

☎ Cabaret
3005 Linden Drive
Bristol, VA
(276) 466-4100

♞ Casa Mexicana
1020 Volunteer Parkway
Bristol, TN
(423) 844-0063

♞ Cheddar's Casual Café
2004 N. Eastman Road
Kingsport, TN
(423) 230-5851

🥡 China King
1990 Highway 394
Blountville, TN
(423) 323-8828

♞ Chop House
1704 N. Eastman Road
Kingsport, TN
(423) 247-1705

♞ Cracker Barrel
10132 Airport Road
Blountville, TN
(423) 283-4723

**♞ Diamond House Chinese
  Restaurant**
1395 Volunteer Parkway
Bristol, TN
(423) 764-0495

♞ El Chico
Kingsport Highway
Johnson City, TN
(423) 282-4080

♞ Fatz Cafe
1175 Volunteer Parkway
Bristol, TN
(423) 968-4498

♞ Fishtales Pigtales Cafe
2131 Volunteer Parkway
Bristol, TN
(423) 764-3474

🪑 Fuddruckers
2519 Knob Creek Road
Johnson City, TN
(423) 915-1004

🪑 Giovannis
1921 Highway 394
Blountville, TN
(423) 323-4441

🪑 Hooters
2288 N. Roan Street
Johnson City, TN
(423) 610-1484

🍟 Hot Dog Hut
1420 Bluff City Highway
Bristol, TN
(423) 652-0001

🍟 Jersey Mike's Subs
1430 Volunteer Parkway
Bristol, TN
(423) 968-2838

🪑 Levy Restaurants
327 Speedway Boulevard
Bristol, TN
(423) 764-4343

🪑 Logan's Roadhouse
3112 Browns Mill Road
Johnson City, TN
(423) 915-1122

🪑 Mad Greek Restaurant
2419 Volunteer Parkway
Bristol, TN
(423) 968-4848

🍔 McDonald's
220 Century Boulevard
Bristol, TN
(423) 652-2150

🪑 Olive Garden Italian Restaurant
1903 N. Roan Street
Johnson City, TN
(423) 929-0137

🪑 Outback Steakhouse
3168 Linden Drive
Bristol, VA
(276) 466-0100

🪑 Pal's 19
3277 Highway 126
Blountville, TN
(423) 323-3339

🍟 Pardner's Bar-B-Que & Steak
Mount Holston Road
Bluff City, TN
(423) 538-4116

🪑 Pizza Hut
2167 Volunteer Parkway
Bristol, TN
(423) 968-9411

Pizza Plus Inc.
3270 Highway 126
Blountville, TN
(423) 323-5555

Shoku Japanese Steakhouse Inc.
1921 Highway 394, Suite I
Blountville, TN
(423) 354-0444

Simply Delicious
2600 Volunteer Parkway
Bristol, TN
(423) 764-3354

Sportsman's Inn
1403 Bluff City Highway
Bristol, TN
(423) 968-7252

Subco East
2409 Volunteer Parkway
Bristol, TN
(423) 764-8382

Subway Sandwiches & Salads
2137 Volunteer Parkway
Bristol, TN
(423) 652-2234

3 Lady Seafood Restaurant
3110 Highway 126
Blountville, TN
(423) 323-2571

The Vineyard
603 Gate City Highway
Bristol, VA
(276) 466-4244

Wendy's
1367 Volunteer Parkway
Bristol, TN
(423) 968-5512

Local Attractions

One of the most awesome things to do while in Bristol for the August race is the annual NASCAR Hauler Parade which takes place on the Thursday night of the August race weekend. Thousands of race fans line up on the ten mile trek from Bristol Mall to Bristol Motor Speedway to see the slick haulers that carry the machines the NASCAR drivers race on the NASCAR circuit. This is truly a spectacle and one you do not want to miss. The parade usually kicks off around 9 p.m. and ends with an impressive fireworks display. If you are looking for a more up-close-and-personal view of the haulers, many of the rigs are on display in the Bristol Mall parking lot earlier in the day. Always check the team's website the week prior to find out time and location of appearances.

Abingdon Vineyard and Winery
20308 Alvarado Road
Abingdon, VA
(276) 623-1255

Appalachian Caverns
420 Cave Hill Road
Bristol, TN
(423) 323-2337

Appalachian GhostWalks and Ghost Tours
Highway TN-394 S.
Blountville, TN
(423) 743-9255

Belmont Lanes
100 Belmont Drive
Bristol, TN
(423) 764-5135

Bristol Caverns
1157 Bristol Caverns Highway
Bristol, TN
(423) 878-2011

Cedars Golf Course
115 Cedar Creek Road
Bristol, TN
(423) 989-0054

Clear Creek Golf Club
732 Harleywood Road
Bristol, VA
(276) 466-4833

Cooper's Gem Mine
1136 Big Hollow Road
Blountville, TN
(423) 323-5680

Corner Pocket Billiards
1742 Edgemont Avenue
Bristol, TN
(423) 764-8888

Country Club of Bristol
6045 Old Jonesboro Road
Bristol, TN
(423) 652-1700

The Gold Mine
2101 Fort Henry Drive
Kingsport, TN
(423) 247-5321

Hands On! Museum
315 E. Main Street
Johnson City, TN
(423) 434-4263

Lazer Venture
321 Broad Street
Kingsport, TN
(423) 246-6927

Rocky Mount Museum
200 Hyder Hill Road
Piney Flats, TN
(423) 538-7396

Sam's Go Kart & Game Room
991 Highway 126
Bristol, TN
(423) 968-7303

Troutfishers Guide Service
301 Royal Drive
Bristol, TN
(423) 360-1468

Warriors Path Riding Stables
1882 Fall Creek Road
Kingsport, TN
(423) 323-8543

William King Regional Arts Center
415 Academy Drive
Abingdon, VA
(276) 628-5005

Shopping

KEY
🚗 Automotive $ Discount
➕ Pharmacy   👕 Mall
☆ Specialty   👕 Department Store

☆ **Antiques Unlimited**
620 State Street
Bristol, TN
(423) 764-4211

$ **Bargain Shop Variety Mall**
2602 Highway 107
Chuckey, TN
(423) 257-8009

☆ **BeautiControl Cosmetics**
307 Bonham Road
Bristol, VA
(276) 669-3035

👕 **Belk**
500 Gate City Highway
Bristol, VA
(276) 669-5112

$ **Big Lots**
1103 Volunteer Parkway
Bristol, TN
(423) 652-7858

👕 **Boone Mall**
1180 Blowing Rock Road
Boone, NC
(828) 264-7286

👕 **Bristol Mall**
500 Gate City Highway
Bristol, VA
(276) 466-8331

$ **Burke's Outlet**
117 Hudson Drive
Elizabethton, TN
(423) 542-4571

$ **Dollar General**
3183 Highway 126
Blountville, TN
(423) 323-9007

$ Factory Stores of America
354 Shadowtown Road
Blountville, TN
(423) 354-0129

$ Family Dollar Store
1921 Highway 394
Blountville, TN
(423) 323-8224

$ Fred's Store
1375 Volunteer Parkway
Bristol, TN
(423) 274-0627

$ Goody's Family Clothing
33 Midway Street
Bristol, VA
(276) 669-8374

☂ JC Penney
510 Gate City Highway, Space 360
Bristol, VA
(276) 669-3184

🛒 Johnson City Mall
2011 N. Roan Street
Johnson City, TN
(423) 282-5312

$ Kmart
2854 W. State Street
Bristol, TN
(423) 968-7178

☆ New York & Company
2011 N. Roan Street
Johnson City, TN
(423) 282-4912

$ Peebles
730 W. Elk Avenue
Elizabethton, TN
(423) 543-3528

$ Sam's Club
1020 Sam Walton Drive
Kingsport, TN
(423) 323-1120

☂ Sears
500 Gate City Highway
Bristol, TN
(276) 645-3609

☆ Talbots
2511 N. Roan Street
Johnson City, TN
(423) 282-9342

$ Target
2116 N. Roan Street
Johnson City, TN
(423) 854-8899

$ T. J. Maxx
2116 N. Roan Street, # 2B
Johnson City, TN
(423) 854-9459

Traders Village Mall
2745 E. Stone Drive
Kingsport, TN
(423) 288-8204

$ Wal-Mart Supercenter
220 Century Boulevard
Bristol, TN
(423) 968-2777

Churches/ Worship Centers

Addilynn Memorial United Methodist
3225 Avoca Road
Bristol, TN
(423) 764-1747

Assemblies of God—Westhighland
2222 Volunteer Parkway
Bristol, TN
(423) 764-2222

Avoca Christian Church
2417 Volunteer Parkway
Bristol, TN
(423) 844-1080

Bellemont Presbyterian Church
2601 Volunteer Parkway
Bristol, TN
(423) 968-3722

Common Ground
2844 Highway 11 E.
Bristol, TN
(423) 764-5333

Elizabeth Chapel United Methodist
1041 Elizabeth Chapel Road
Bluff City, TN
(423) 538-6311

Faith Lutheran Church
2909 Weaver Pike
Bristol, TN
(423) 878-4831

Holy Trinity Greek Orthodox
150 Elizabeth Ann Circle
Bluff City, TN
(423) 538-0701

New Life Baptist Church
3620 Highway 390
Bluff City, TN
(423) 538-9017

New Life Tabernacle Church
618 Highway 126
Bristol, TN
(423) 989-0922

Seventh-Day Adventist Church
571 Highway 126
Bristol, TN
(423) 764-4232

St. Anne's Catholic Church
350 Euclid Avenue
Bristol, VA
276-669-8200

St. Columbia's Episcopal Church
607 Greenfield Place
Bristol, TN
(423) 764-2251

Volunteer Baptist Church
2695 Volunteer Parkway
Bristol, TN
(423) 764-5618

Walnut Hill Presbyterian Church
224 Midway Drive
Bristol, TN
(423) 764-8729

INSIDER TIP—

Weekend church services are
available trackside and on BMS
property. Because the worship
times vary from race to race and
are scattered around the track
property, check Bristol Motor
Speedway's website or call
(423) 989-6960 for times and
locations.

Medical Centers

Johnston Memorial Hospital
351 Court Street NE
Abingdon, VA
(276) 676-7000

Sycamore Shoals Hospital
1501 W. Elk Avenue
Elizabethton, TN
(423) 542-1300

Wellmont Bristol Regional Medical Center
1 Medical Park Boulevard
Bristol, TN
(423) 844-1121

Pet Medical Center

Banfield the Pet Hospital
3211 Peoples Street
Johnson City, TN
(423) 283-9077

CHICAGOLAND SPEEDWAY

Start | Finish Line

Pit Road

Garage Area

Infield

Track Information

Inaugural Year: 2001
Owner: Raceway Associates
City: Joliet, Illinois
Size: 1.5 miles
Banking: 18 degrees in turns, 11 degrees in tri-oval
Grandstand Capacity: 75,000

ADDRESS
Chicagoland Speedway
500 Speedway Boulevard
Joliet, IL 60433
(815) 727-7223
www.chicagolandspeedway.com

TICKET INFORMATION
Phone: (888) 629-7223
www.chicagolandspeedway.com

About the Track

The 1.5-mile track is what many call a cookie-cutter track, meaning it was cut out of the same mold as most of the other 1.5-mile tracks. The track continues to "season," making way for better racing action than what was believed to be the case in the track's early years. Chicagoland is one of thirteen intermediate tracks on the circuit, though not all intermediate tracks are of the cookie-cutter type.

Track History

Chicagoland Speedway is another baby in the bunch of NASCAR Sprint Cup Series tracks. The $130 million building project broke ground in September 1999. The track itself is actually located in Joliet, Illinois, which is southwest of Chicago, hence the name Chicagoland instead of Chicago Speedway. Track officials made the decision in 2007 to add lights to the facility, making Chicagoland one of only ten tracks on the Sprint Cup schedule with permanent lights.

Track Records

Most Wins: Kevin Harvick (2)
Most Top Five Finishes: Jeff
  Gordon (4)
Most Lead Changes: 20—on
  7/11/2004
Fewest Lead Changes: 13—on
  7/13/2003
Most Cautions: 10—most recently
  7/11/2005 (total of 2 times)
Fewest Cautions: 7—most recently
  on 7/13/2003 (total of 2 times)
Race Record: Kevin Harvick—
  136.832 mph (2 hours,

55 minutes, 37 seconds)
(7/14/2002)
Qualifying Record: Jimmie
Johnson—188.147 mph
(28.701 seconds) (7/8/2005)

Fast Facts

• The first NASCAR Sprint Cup Series race was run at Chicagoland Speedway on July 15, 2001, and was won by Kevin Harvick.

• Tony Stewart is the oldest driver to have won at Chicagoland Speedway—winning in July 2007, he was thirty-six years old (plus one month and twenty-five days).

• Chicagoland Speedway sits on 930 acres of land, which is large enough to accommodate forty-two United Centers (home of the Chicago Bulls and Blackhawks).

• The Chicagoland Speedway in Joliet, Illinois, is the only current NASCAR track where Arkansan Mark Martin has not finished in the top five.

• In 2006, Will Ferrell and the cast of *Talladega Nights* held a press conference at Chicagoland Speedway to promote the release of the blockbuster movie.

Parking

Chicagoland Speedway has five hundred acres of free parking for fans attending the race. All parking is on a first-come, first-served basis. Contact the track's main office at 815-727-7223 or check their website at www.chicagolandspeedway.com for up-to-date parking information.

Track Rules

According to the track's official website,www.chicagolandspeedway.com, the track's rules are as follows:

ITEMS ALLOWED IN THE GRANDSTANDS

✓ one unopened factory-sealed plastic bottle of water
✓ cell phones
✓ scanners and headsets
✓ cameras
✓ binoculars
✓ seat cushions
✓ pagers
✓ fanny packs
✓ purses
✓ backpacks
✓ camera bags
✓ small bags (not to exceed 14")

ITEMS *NOT* ALLOWED IN THE GRANDSTANDS

✗ coolers of any size
✗ food and beverages
✗ illegal drugs
✗ umbrellas
✗ glass containers
✗ pets (unless registered as an aid dog)
✗ fireworks
✗ sharp objects
✗ firearms
✗ weapons of any kind
✗ bicycles
✗ Rollerblades
✗ wagons
✗ scooters
✗ skateboards
✗ strollers
✗ folding chairs
✗ laser pointers
✗ large flags or poles of any type

Special Needs and Services

Chicagoland Speedway provides seating and parking for those needing special services or accessibility. One companion is allowed to accompany those with special needs. Contact Guest Services prior to arrival at 815-722-5500 for more information. Always ask for your parking to be near your seats.

Track Tours

Individual and group tours are given at Chicagoland Speedway from Monday through Friday between the hours of 9 a.m. and 4 p.m. All tours are scheduled in advance. For specific tour information call the track at 815-722-5500.

Souvenirs

Official track and driver-specific souvenirs can be purchased in Souvenir Alley, which is located in the Midway Promenade area, directly behind the Main Grandstand tower in between Expo Village and Hospitality Village.

About the Area

Chicagoland Speedway is located just southwest of Chicago, which has some of the best tourists attractions and shopping on the NASCAR Sprint Cup Tour (see local attractions section). While in town, make your way to the ESPN Zone and watch the highlights from the qualifying for the Sprint Cup race from Chicagoland. If you want to bypass the windy city altogether, hanging out in and around Joliet is a great way to unwind and relax. Race weather conditions can be pretty darn hot and steamy—don't let the fact that this track is in the Midwest fool you. However, moving the race to nighttime means relatively cooler and more comfortable temps.

CHAMBER OF COMMERCE

Joliet Region Chamber of
    Commerce & Industry
63 N. Chicago Street
Joliet, IL 60432
(815) 727-5371
www.jolietchamber.com

Transportation

AIRPORTS

Chicago Midway Airport (MDW)
5700 S. Cicero Avenue
Chicago, IL
(773) 838-0600
(Chicago Midway is approximately
    thirty-one miles to the track.)

**Chicago O'Hare International
    Airport (ORD)**
10000 W. O'Hare
Chicago, IL
(773) 686-2200
(Chicago O'Hare is thirty-four miles
    from the track.)

AIRLINES

AirTran (800) 247-8726
America West (800) 235-9292
American (800) 433-7300
Continental (800) 525-0280
Delta (800) 221-1212

Northwest (800) 225-2525
Southwest (800) 435-9792
United (800) 241-6522
US Airways (800) 943-5436
Virgin Atlantic (800) 862-8621

RENTAL CARS
Alamo (800) 327-9633
Avis (800) 331-1212
Budget (800) 527-0700
Enterprise (800) 736-8222
Hertz (800) 654-3131
National (800) 227-7368
Thrifty (800) 367-2277

Hotels

KEY
🐾 Pet Friendly   ≈ Pool
✕ Restaurant

≈ Best Western Inn
4380 Enterprise Drive
Joliet, IL
(815) 730-7500

🐾 Budget Inn
1806 McDonough Street
Joliet, IL
(815) 730-8800

🐾, ≈ Comfort Inn
135 S. Larkin Avenue
Joliet, IL
(815) 744-1770

🐾, ≈ Comfort Inn
3235 Norman Avenue
Joliet, IL
(815) 436-5141

Crest Hill Inn
2109 Plainfield Road
Crest Hill, IL
(815) 725-1632

Crown Inn
2219 1/2 W. Jefferson Street
Joliet, IL
(815) 744-1220

≈ Fairfield Inn Joliet North
3239 Norman Avenue
Joliet, IL
(815) 436-6577

≈ Hampton Inn—I-80
1521 Riverboat Center Drive
Joliet, IL
(815) 725-2424

≈ Hampton Inn-I-55
3555 Mall Loop Drive
Joliet, IL
(815) 439-9500

✕ Harrah's Joliet Casino & Hotel
151 N. Joliet Street
Joliet, IL
(815) 740-7800

🛏, ≈, ✕ **Holiday Inn Express**
411 S. Larkin Avenue
Joliet, IL
(815) 729-2000

🛏, ≈ **Holiday Inn Express—I-55 N**
3231 Norman Avenue
Joliet, IL
(815) 439-4200

≈ **Joliet Fairfield Inn South**
1501 Riverboat Center Drive
Joliet, IL
(815) 741-1261

🛏 **Joliet Inn**
19747 NE Frontage Road
Shorewood, IL
(815) 725-2180

🛏, ≈ **Manor Hotel**
23926 W. Eames Street
Channahon, IL
(815) 467-5385

🛏 **Motel 6**
1850 McDonough Street
Joliet, IL
(815) 729-2800

🛏, ≈ **Motel 6**
3551 Mall Loop Drive
Joliet, IL
(815) 439-1332

Plaza Hotel
26 W. Clinton Street
Joliet, IL
(815) 726-6195

≈ **Ramada Inn South**
1520 Commerce Lane
Joliet, IL
(815) 730-1111

🛏 **Red Roof Inn-Joliet**
1750 McDonough Street
Joliet, IL
(815) 741-2304

Super 8 Motel—I-80
1730 McDonough Street
Joliet, IL
(815) 725-8855

Super 8 Motel—I-55 N
3401 Mall Loop Drive
Joliet, IL
(815) 439-3838

≈ **Wingate Inn**
101 McDonald Avenue
Joliet, IL
(815) 741-2100

Camping

ON-SITE AND TRACK-OWNED CAMPING

Chicagoland Speedway offers a limited number of on-site and track-owned camping options due to the sellout factor of the campgrounds. The infield and Speedway Ridge areas are sold out years in advance. Currently, the track is not adding names to the wait list due to the number of persons already on the list. Call the track's main office number at 815-727-7223 for the latest camping or wait list information.

Lake Side Camping This grass area is on a first-come, first-served basis. The area offers electric hookups. Water and sewage is an additional fee.

Infield Reserved Sold out

Speedway Ridge Sold out

OFF-SITE CAMPING

Channahon State Park
25302 W. Story Street
Channahon, IL
(815) 467-4271

Empress RV Resort
2300 Empress Drive
Joliet, IL
(815) 744-9400

Hidden Lakes
749 S. State Route 53
Wilmington, IL
(815) 458-6511

Leisure Lake Membership Resort
21900 SW Frontage Road
Joliet, IL
(815) 741-9405

Martin Campground Inc.
2303 New Lenox Road
Joliet, IL
(815) 726-3173

Restaurants

KEY
🍔 Fast Food   🪑 Sit Down
🛍 Take out   🍷 Reservations

Must Eats

🪑 **Harrah's Joliet Casino**
151 N. Joliet Street
Joliet, IL
(815) 740-7800

This is one of the popular casinos around the track, but the best part of Harrah's is not the gambling . . . it's the seafood buffet. You will need a wheelbarrow to get you out.

The Kerry Piper
7900 Joliet Road
Willowbrook, IL
(630) 325-3732
If you love a little Irish flavor, make sure you pop in for some good Irish fair and the Irish music to go along. You can sit inside or out in the night air.

Al's Steak House
1990 W. Jefferson Street
Joliet, IL
(815) 725-2388

Applebee's
2795 Plainfield Road
Joliet, IL
(815) 254-9070

Baby Back Blues BBQ
23145 Lincoln Highway
Plainfield, IL
(815) 254-6939

Bob Evans
1776 McDonough Road
Joliet, IL
(815) 725-0160

Branmor's American Grill
300 Veteran's Parkway
Bolingbrook, IL
(630) 226-9926

Chicago Street Bar & Grill
75 N. Chicago Street
Joliet, IL
(815) 727-7171

Chili's Grill & Bar
1275 W. Broughton Road
Joliet, IL
(815) 378-5461

Cracker Barrel
1511 Riverboat Center Drive
Joliet, IL
(815) 744-0985

Diamands's Family Restaurant
3000 Plainfield Road
Joliet, IL
(815) 436-1070

Empress Restaurants
2300 Empress Drive
Joliet, IL
(815) 744-9400

Gallagher's Pub
160 E. North Street
Manhattan, IL
(815) 478-9803

Harrah's Restaurants
151 N. Joliet Street
Joliet, IL
(815) 740-7800

Harrison's Brewing Company
15845 LaGrange Road
Orland Park, IL
(708) 226-0100

Lone Star Steakhouse
2705 Plainfield Road
Joliet, IL
(815) 436-7600

Old Country Buffet
2811 Plainfield Road
Joliet, IL
(815) 254-0045

Old Fashioned Pancake House
2022 W. Jefferson Street
Joliet, IL
(815) 741-4666

Pizza Hut
1156 W. Jefferson Street
Joliet, IL
(815) 729-9300

Pizza Hut
2901 N. Plainfield Road
Joliet, IL
(815) 436-4166

Pizza Hut
19945 La Grange Road
Frankfort, IL
(815) 806-1110

Reel 'Em Inn Seafood Restaurant
704 N. Division
Plainfield, IL
(815) 254-5900

Texas Roadhouse
3151 Tonti Drive
Joliet, IL
(815) 577-9003

TGI Friday's
3340 Mall Loop Drive
Joliet, IL
(815) 254-1882

Local Attractions

WORTH THE TRIP

One of my favorite attractions near Chicagoland is the **Navy Pier,** which is located on Lake Michigan. There are boat tours running both day and night that are so much fun. Close by is the **Shedd Aquarium** and the **Sears Tower Skydeck.**

Adler Planetarium
1300 S. Lake Shore Drive
Chicago, IL
(312) 922-7827

Art Institute of Chicago
111 S. Michigan Avenue
Chicago, IL
(312) 443-3600

Challenge Park Extreme
2903 Schweitzer Road
Joliet, IL
(815) 726-2800

Chicago Children's Museum
700 E. Grand Avenue
Chicago, IL
(312) 527-1000

Chicago Cubs
1060 W. Addison
Chicago, IL
(773) 404-CUBS

Chicago White Sox
333 W. 35th Street
Chicago, IL
(312) 674-1000

Cinemark Movies 8
3101 Hennepin Drive
Joliet, IL
(815) 436-1455

Harrah's Joliet Casino
151 N. Joliet Street
Joliet, IL
(800) HAR-RAHS

Hartman Recreation Center
511 Collins Street
Joliet, IL
(815) 741-7279

Haunted Trails Family Amusement
1425 N. Broadway Street
Joliet, IL
(815) 722-7800

Inwood Golf Course
3000 W. Jefferson Street
Joliet, IL
(815) 741-7265

**Inwood Recreation Center Ice
    Arena**
3000 W. Jefferson Street
Joliet, IL
(815) 741-7275

**Museum of Broadcast
    Communications**
78 E. Washington Street
Chicago, IL
(312) 629-6000

Museum of Contemporary Art
220 E. Chicago Avenue
Chicago, IL
(312) 280-2660

Museum of Science and Industry
5700 S. Lake Shore Drive
Chicago, IL
(773) 684-1414

Navy Pier
600 E. Grand Avenue
Chicago, IL
(312) 595-7437

Peggy Notebaert Nature Museum
2430 N. Cannon Drive
Chicago, IL
(773) 549-0606

**Round Barn Farm & Recreation
Center**
24115 U.S. Highway 52
Manhattan, IL
(815) 478-3215

The Sears Tower Skydeck
233 S. Wacker Drive, Suite 3530
Chicago, IL
(312) 875-9696

Shedd Aquarium
1200 S. Lake Shore Drive
Chicago, IL
(312) 692-4352

**Smith Museum of Stained Glass
Windows**
800 E. Grand Avenue
Chicago, IL
(312) 595-7437

Terra Museum of American Art
664 N. Michigan Avenue
Chicago, IL
(312) 664-3939

Wedgewood Golf Course
Route 59 and Caton Farm Road
Joliet, IL
(815) 741-7270

Shopping

KEY
🚗 Automotive $ Discount
✚ Pharmacy   🏬 Mall
☆ Specialty   🎁 Department Store

$ Big Lots
1608 N. Larkin Avenue
Crest Hill, IL
(815) 744-0370

**🏬 Brentwood Cove Shopping
Center**
2207 S. Route 59
Plainfield, IL
(815) 436-3250

☆ Charlotte Russe
3340 Mall Loop Drive, Suite 1249
Joliet, IL
(815) 254-2474

$ Dollar General
2101 Plainfield Road
Crest Hill, IL
(815) 773-0970

☆ Eddie Bauer
2801 Plainfield Road
Joliet, IL
(815) 254-3777

$ Family Dollar Store
116 E. Jackson Street
Joliet, IL
(815) 722-2203

▶̇ Hillcrest Shopping Center
1701 N. Larkin Avenue
Crest Hill, IL
(815) 741-0196

$ Kmart
1500 W. Lincoln Highway
New Lenox, IL
(815) 485-4486

▶̇ Louis Joliet Shopping Town
3312 Mall Loop Drive
Joliet, IL
(815) 436-4784

▶̇ Park Place Plaza
18 Coventry Chase
Joliet, IL
(815) 729-1383

☆ Pier 1 Imports
3064 Plainfield Road
Joliet, IL
(815) 436-1287

$ Sam's Club
321 S. Larkin Avenue
Joliet, IL
(815) 744-2525

$ Target
2701 Plainfield Road
Joliet, IL
(815) 439-1029

$ T. J. Maxx
1701 N. Larkin Avenue
Crest Hill, IL
(815) 741-8240

▶̇ Village Square Plaza
868 N. State Street, Suite 1
Lockport, IL
(815) 838-9339

⊙ Walgreens
1514 Essington Road
Joliet, IL
(815) 744-5353

$ Wal-Mart
305 S. Larkin Avenue
Joliet, IL
(815) 744-7575

Churches/ Worship Centers

All Saints Greek Orthodox Church
102 N. Broadway Street
Joliet, IL
(815) 722-1727

Bethlehem Lutheran Church
412 E. Benton Street
Joliet, IL
(815) 726-4461

Church of God
613 Second Avenue
Joliet, IL
(815) 774-9254

First Church of the Nazarene
1009 S. Briggs Street
Joliet, IL
(815) 726-5426

First Presbyterian Church
805 Western Avenue
Joliet, IL
(815) 727-9259

Immanuel Free-Will Baptist
328 Wilhelm Court
Joliet, IL
(815) 726-8415

Ingalls Park United Methodist
105 Davison Street
Joliet, IL
(815) 722-2383

Sacred Heart Catholic Church
329 S. Ottawa Street
Joliet, IL
(815) 774-9204

St. Edward's Episcopal Church
206 N. Midland Avenue
Joliet, IL
(815) 725-6800

Trinity United Methodist Church
301 Fairbanks Avenue
Joliet, IL
(815) 723-1387

Medical Centers

Provena St. Joseph Medical Center
333 Madison Street
Joliet, IL
(815) 725-7133

Silver Cross Hospital
1200 Maple Road
Joliet, IL
(815) 740-1100

Pet Medical Centers

Banfield the Pet Hospital
2775 Plainfield Road
Joliet, IL
(815) 609-7091

VCA Joliet Animal Hospital
220 N. Hammes Avenue
Joliet, IL
(815) 729-0770

DARLINGTON RACEWAY

Pit Road

Infield

Garage Area

Pit Road

Start | Finish Line

Track Information

Inaugural Year: 1950
Owner: International Speedway
   Corporation (ISC)
City: Darlington, South Carolina
Size: 1.366 miles
Banking: 25 degrees in turns 1 and
   2, 23 degrees in turns 3 and 4
Grandstand Capacity: 60,000

ADDRESS
Darlington Raceway
1301 Harry Byrd Highway
Darlington, SC 29532

(866) 459-7223
www.darlingtonraceway.com

TICKET INFORMATION
Phone: (866) 459-7223
www.darlingtonraceway.com

About the Track

Darlington Raceway is the oldest
track on the NASCAR Sprint Cup
circuit. Buried deep in the low country of South Carolina, the track is as

rich in racing history as any track to ever exist. In 2004, ISC took one of the track's Sprint Cup events away, leaving the dated track with one event a year. While Darlington consistently sells out its lone event, the track is still rumored to be on the endangered list as the newer tracks in larger markets continue to threaten those of yesteryear.

Track History

Harold Brasington, a retired dirt track racer-turned-construction worker, bought seventy acres of farmland after taking notice of the crowds attending the 1948 Indy 500. Darlington got its weird egg shape due to a promise Sherman Ramsey made to the former owner of the land to not disturb a minnow pond on the property. The only way Ramsey could keep his promise was to create one corner tighter than the others, making Darlington a tough track for many drivers to maneuver. After a year of construction, Brasington struck a deal with his friend Bill France Sr. to run a 500-mile event, which turned out to be the very first Southern 500. The nickname, Lady in Black, refers to the black marks left on the white painted walls by competitors brushing the walls in the turns. The track is also referred to as the "track too tough to tame."

Track Records

Most Wins: David Pearson (10)
Most Top Five Finishes: Richard Petty (25)
Most Lead Changes: 41—on 9/6/1982
Fewest Lead Changes: 4—on 9/7/1960
Most Cautions: 15—on 3/26/1995
Fewest Cautions: 0—on 9/2/1963
Race Record: Dale Earnhardt Sr.—139.958 mph (3 hours, 34 minutes, 55 seconds) (3/28/1993)
Qualifying Record: Ward Burton—173.797 mph (28.295 seconds) (3/22/1996)

Fast Facts

- The first NASCAR Sprint Cup race was run at Darlington Raceway on September 4, 1950, and was won by Johnny Mantz.
- Harry Gant is the oldest driver to have won at Darlington—winning in September 1991, he was fifty-one years old (plus seven months and twenty-two days).
- Ricky Craven beat Kurt Busch to the finish line on March 16, 2003, by 0.002—making this the closest margin of victory ever in the history of Darlington Raceway.

- The late Dale Earnhardt referred to Darlington Raceway as his "first love."

Parking

General parking at Darlington Raceway is free for fans attending the race. All parking is first come, first served. Darlington Raceway does not allow overnight parking in the general parking areas. Contact the track's main office number at 866-459-7223 or go to their website at www.darlingtonraceway.com for up-to-date information on parking.

Track Rules

According to the track's official website at www.darlingtonraceway.com, the track's rules are as follows:

ITEMS ALLOWED IN THE GRANDSTANDS

- ✓ one clear plastic bag (no larger than 18″ × 18″ × 4″, no ice)
- ✓ one soft-sided bag (no larger than 6″ × 6″ × 12″)
- ✓ scanner
- ✓ fanny packs
- ✓ diaper bags
- ✓ binoculars
- ✓ cell phones
- ✓ cameras
- ✓ seat cushions

ITEMS *NOT* ALLOWED IN THE GRANDSTANDS

- ✗ firearms
- ✗ knives or pocketknives
- ✗ fireworks
- ✗ hard-sided coolers
- ✗ thermos bottles
- ✗ insulated cups of any size
- ✗ strollers
- ✗ umbrellas
- ✗ golf carts

Special Needs and Services

Darlington Raceway offers seating and parking for those needing special assistance or accessibility. One companion is allowed to accompany those with special needs. Call the track's main office number prior to arrival at 866-459-7223 for assistance. Always ask for parking near your seats.

INSIDER TIP—An ATM machine is located near Gate 16 in front of the Frontstretch Ticket Office.

Track Tours

Darlington Raceway gives daily track tours to groups and individuals every hour starting at 10 a.m. The last tour of the day leaves the museum at 4 p.m. The tours start at the Darlington Raceway Stock Car Museum, adjacent to the gift shop on Highway 151, where the tickets can also be purchased. The tour includes stops at the Sprint Cup garage area, the start-finish line, and the Gatorade Victory Lane.

Souvenirs

Official Darlington Raceway souvenirs can be purchased in the track gift shop located on Highway 151, adjacent to the track museum. Driver-specific trailers can be found on Souvenir Alley, which is located behind Tyler Tower near the main entrance to the grandstands. The track gift shop has extended hours during race weekend.

About the Area

Darlington (and nearby Florence), South Carolina, is diehard race country. Both towns are small in size but come to life when the race rolls into town. The townspeople are as friendly as it comes, much like one might expect from any small town in the USA. The climate in May is warm but very tolerable, unlike the hot and humid summer months. The low country is very special to me for many reasons: one is, I grew up in the heart of South Carolina; the other is my late husband Davey and I spent our honeymoon at this racetrack. Having been raised a few hours north of the track, I could not think of any better place to spend my honeymoon with my new hubby than good ole Darlington.

CHAMBER OF COMMERCE

Greater Darlington Chamber of
  Commerce
400 Pearl Street
Darlington, SC 29532
(843) 393-2641
www.darlingtonchamber.net

Transportation

AIRPORT

Florence Regional Airport (FLO)
2100 Terminal Drive
Florence, SC
(843) 669-5001
(Approximately twelve miles from
  the track.)

AIRLINES

Delta/ASA (800) 221-1212
US Airways (800) 428-4322

RENTAL CARS

Alamo (800) 462-5266

Avis (843) 230-4898

Budget (800) 527-0700 or
    (843) 667-1260

Enterprise (843) 669-4861 or
    (800) 261-7331

Hertz (843) 662-7930 or
    (800) 654-3131

National (800) 227-7368

Hotels

KEY

☞ Pet Friendly   ≈ Pool

✗ Restaurant

Best Value Inn

705 Washington Street

Darlington, SC

(843) 393-8990

☞, ≈ **Best Western Inn**

1808 W. Lucas Street

Florence, SC

(843) 678-9292

☞ **Colonial Inn**

415 S. Irby Street

Florence, SC

(843) 662-1486

☞, ≈ **Comfort Inn**

1916 W. Lucas Street

Florence, SC

(843) 665-4558

≈ **Comfort Inn**

903 S. Fifth Street

Hartsville, SC

(843) 383-0110

≈ **Country Inn & Suites Florence**

1739 Mandeville Road

Florence, SC

(843) 317-6616

≈, ✗ **Courtyard**

2680 Hospitality Boulevard

Florence, SC

(843) 662-7066

☞, ≈ **Days Inn—I-95 N**

2111 W. Lucas Street

Florence, SC

(843) 665-4444

☞, ≈, ✗ **Days Inn—I-95 S**

3783 W. Palmetto Street

Florence, SC

(843) 665-8550

☞, ≈ **Econo Lodge**

1811 W. Lucas Street

Florence, SC

(843) 665-8558

≈ **Fairfield Inn**

140 Dunbarton Drive

Florence, SC

(843) 669-1666

🛏, ≈ **Guest House International Inn & Suites**
2003 1/2 W. Lucas Street
Florence, SC
(843) 669-1921

≈ **Hampton Inn**
3000 W. Radio Drive
Florence, SC
(843) 629-9900

≈, ✗ **Hilton Garden Inn**
2671 Hospitality Boulevard
Florence, SC
(843) 432-3001

🛏, ≈, ✗ **Holiday Inn**
1819 W. Lucas Street
Florence, SC
(843) 665-4555

≈ **Holiday Inn Express & Suites**
3440 W. Radio Drive
Florence, SC
(843) 432-1500

≈ **Landmark Inn**
1301 S. Fourth Street
Hartsville, SC
(843) 332-2611

≈ **Marriott**
2670 Hospitality Boulevard
Florence, SC
(843) 317-9025

🛏 **Microtel Inn & Suites**
1912 Enterprise Drive
Florence, SC
(843) 629-1751

🛏, ≈ **Motel 6**
1834 W. Lucas Street
Florence, SC
(843) 667-6100

🛏, ≈ **Quality Inn & Suites Civic Center**
150 Dunbarton Drive
Florence, SC
(843) 664-2400

🛏, ≈, ✗ **Ramada Inn**
2038 W. Lucas Street
Florence, SC
(843) 669-4241

🛏 **Red Roof Inn**
2690 David H McLeod Boulevard
Florence, SC
(843) 629-9784

🛏, ≈, ✗ **Rodeway Inn Florence**
3024 TV Road
Florence, SC
(843) 669-1715

≈ **Sleep Inn**
1833 Florence Park Drive
Florence, SC
(843) 662-8558

≈ **Springhill Suites by Marriott**
2670 Hospitality Boulevard
Florence, SC
(843) 317-9050

⇄, ✕ **Suburban Extended Stay Hotel**
1914 W. Lucas Street
Florence, SC
(843) 665-2575

⇄, ≈ **Super 8 Motel**
1832 1/2 W. Lucas Street
Florence, SC
(843) 661-7267

⇄, ≈, ✕ **Thunderbird Motel**
2004 W. Lucas Street
Florence, SC
(843) 669-1611

⇄, ≈ **Travelodge**
3783 W. Palmetto Street
Florence, SC
(843) 673-0070

⇄, ≈, ✕ **Tree Top Inn**
3932 W. Palmetto Street
Florence, SC
(843) 662-7712

≈ **Wingate Inn**
2123 W. Lucas Street
Florence, SC
(843) 629-1111

⇄, ≈, ✕ **Young's Plantation Inn**
3311 Meadors Road
Florence, SC
(843) 669-4171

Camping

ON-SITE AND TRACK-OWNED CAMPING

Darlington Raceway is about as popular a camping spot as any track on the circuit. Darlington has several different options for camping. Many of these areas are sold out months in advance. Call the track at 866-459-7223 for fees and waiting list info.

Azalia and Palmetta Infield This infield area is for tents and pop-ups only. Dry camping!

Camp Darlington This fenced overnight parking area is for pop-ups and tents, located behind the Pearson Tower.

Magnolia Place This infield area is for tents and pop-ups only. Dry camping!

Petty/Pearson RV This area is for RVs only. All RVs must be self-contained.

Reserved Infield This VIP camping area is located in the infield and offers electrical hookups.

OFF-SITE CAMPING

Easterling Landing Campground
1540 Easterling Landing Road
Hartsville, SC
(843) 332-9810

The Farm Campground
604 Hill Crest Lane
McBee, SC
(843) 339-1338

Swamp Fox Camping
1600 Gateway Road
Florence, SC
(843) 665-9430

Restaurants

KEY
🍔 Fast Food   🪑 Sit Down
🥡 Takeout   ☎ Reservations

Must Eats

Raceway Grill
1207 Harry Bird Highway
Darlington, SC
(843) 393-9212
A favorite of NASCAR drivers and crew members for years, this café is a must for old-school racing fans.

Thunderbird Motor Inn
2004 W. Lucas Street
Florence, SC
(843) 669-1611
This hotel/restaurant is about as old-school as it comes. Race teams have been staying here for years. The food is good, and if you are into the bar scene, the hotel lounge is your place.

🪑 **Applebee's**
203 S. Fifth Street
Hartsville, SC
(843) 339-2611

🍔 **Arby's**
2034 W. Lucas Street
Florence, SC
(843) 679-2875

B&B Restaurant
1536 S. Main Street
Darlington, SC
(843) 393-9534

Bay Island Seafood
1316 S. Main Street
Darlington, SC
(843) 393-5986

Beacon Restaurant
1731 N. Fifth Street
Hartsville, SC
(843) 332-2022

Betty's Country Kitchen
110 S. Main Street
Darlington, SC
(843) 393-6184

BJS Restaurant
114 Ward Street
Darlington, SC
(843) 395-4014

Boss Hogs Smokehouse
1268 Harry Byrd Highway
Darlington, SC
(843) 393-9999

The Brown Bag
114 Cashua Street
Darlington, SC
(843) 393-0536

Burger King
225 Lamar Highway
Darlington, SC
(843) 393-1217

Cafe Bleu
6 Public Square
Darlington, SC
(843) 395-1171

Captain of the Seven Seas
1765 Harry Byrd Highway
Darlington, SC
(843) 393-6166

Carolina Lunch/Dairy Bar
318 Pearl Street
Darlington, SC
(843) 393-4531

Country Barn Restaurant
2233 W. Harry Byrd Highway
Darlington, SC
(843) 395-2257

Domino's Pizza
510 Pearl Street
Darlington, SC
(843) 395-1414

Ervin's Restaurant
502 S. Main Street
Darlington, SC
(843) 393-5136

♫ Golden Run Restaurant
608 Pearl Street
Darlington, SC
(843) 393-3927

♫ Goldrush Bar & Grill
2009 N. Governor Williams
  Highway
Darlington, SC
(843) 395-9980

♫ Great China Restaurant
120 Express Lane
Darlington, SC
(843) 393-8878

♫ House of Barbecue & Grill
3403 Lamar Highway
Darlington, SC
(843) 395-2445

♫ Huddle House
1503 S. Main Street
Darlington, SC
(843) 393-0202

♫ Jewel's Deluxe Restaurant
32 Public Square
Darlington, SC
(843) 393-5511

♫ Jin Jin
115 Pearl Street
Darlington, SC
(843) 393-2355

♫ J. Michael's Restaurant
636 Poole Street
Hartsville, SC
(843) 383-4272

♫ Joe's Grill
360 Russell Street
Darlington, SC
(843) 393-9140

🍔 Kentucky Fried Chicken
979 S. Governor Williams Highway
Darlington, SC
(843) 393-2584

🍟 Leo's Chicken Wings
1040 Pearl Street
Darlington, SC
(843) 398-1900

♫ Lindburgh's Bar-B-Que
1215 S. Main Street
Darlington, SC
(843) 393-6335

🍔 McDonald's
1501 S. Main Street
Darlington, SC
(843) 393-9733

♫ Momma's Sweetreats Cafe
2513 W. Lucas Street
Florence, SC
(843) 679-3989

Nick's BBQ House
310 S. Main Street
Darlington, SC
(843) 393-6684

Palmetto Subs
506 Pearl Street
Darlington, SC
(843) 393-7083

Pizza Hut
1502 S. Main Street
Darlington, SC
(843) 393-5201

Po-Boys Fish & Oysters
207 Siskron Street
Darlington, SC
(843) 393-6436

Raceway Grill
1207 Harry Byrd Highway
Darlington, SC
(843) 393-7339

Rancho Grande
1809 S. Fifth Street
Hartsville, SC
(843) 383-0561

Shoney's
2101 W. Lucas Street
Florence, SC
(843) 679-5935

Shug's Smokehouse Grill
2404 Kelleytown Road
Hartsville, SC
(843) 383-3747

Sonic
328 N. Fifth Street
Hartsville, SC
(843) 332-9158

Subway Sandwiches & Salads
1001 Pearl Street
Darlington, SC
(843) 393-6529

Takis Restaurant
609 Pearl Street
Darlington, SC
(843) 393-8979

Tony's Fireside Grill
626 S. Fifth Street
Hartsville, SC
(843) 332-1221

Villa Hermosa
1022 Pearl Street
Darlington, SC
(843) 393-6000

Wendy's
989 S. Governor Williams Highway
Darlington, SC
(843) 395-0042

Zaxby's
1236 S. Fourth Street
Hartsville, SC
(843) 339-2600

Local Attractions

For any race fan visiting Darlington Raceway, you must stop in the **Raceway Museum,** located on the track grounds. Truly understanding the history of this track is what makes Darlington so special. She has seen the best of the racers come through her gates . . . if only a track could talk. Walking through the museum is like taking a step back in time; a true treat and a history lesson all wrapped up in one.

Beaver Creek Golf Club
1133 E. Mciver Road
Darlington, SC
(843) 393-5441

Crossings Golf Course
3540 Shadow Creek Drive
Florence, SC
(843) 665-8040

Darlington Raceway Museum
1301 Harry Byrd Highway
Darlington, SC
(843) 395-8821

Florence Museum
558 Spruce Street
Florence, SC
(843) 662-3351

Hartsville Museum
222 N. Fifth Street
Hartsville, SC
(843) 383-3005

Jacob Kelley House Museum
2585 Kelleytown Road
Hartsville, SC
(843) 339-9511

Kalmia Gardens
1624 W. Columbia Avenue
Hartsville, SC
(843) 383-8145

Lee All Star Lanes
118 N. Cashua Drive
Florence, SC
(843) 669-5151

McLeod Farms Antique Museum
29247 Highway 151
McBee, SC
(843) 335-7409

Mr. Mark's Fun Park
1331 N. Cashua Drive
Florence, SC
(843) 669-7373

Skateland
25 Belt Line Boulevard
Florence, SC
(843) 669-7655

Southgate Bowling Center
1902 S. Irby Street
Florence, SC
(843) 661-5050

Swamp Fox Cinema
3400 Radio Road
Florence, SC
(843) 669-5466

Shopping

KEY
🚗 Automotive $ Discount
⊕ Pharmacy   👕🏬 Mall
☆ Specialty   👕 Department Store

👕 **Belk**
2701 David H McLeod Boulevard
Florence, SC
(843) 662-3201

$ **Dollar General**
504 Pearl Street
Darlington, SC
(843) 393-3840

$ **Family Dollar Store**
516 Lamar Highway
Darlington, SC
(843) 393-6651

$ **Fred's Store**
1920 W. Evans Street
Florence, SC
(843) 669-9280

$ **Goody's Family Clothing**
2801 David H McLeod Boulevard
Florence, SC
(843) 661-6559

$ **Kmart**
2011 Hoffmeyer Road
Florence, SC
(843) 669-5655

👕🏬 **Magnolia Mall**
2701 David H McLeod Boulevard
Florence, SC
(843) 669-0725

👕 **Peebles**
827 S. Fifth Street
Hartsville, SC
(843) 332-6252

☆ **Pier 1 Imports**
2601 David H McLeod Boulevard
Florence, SC
(843) 665-7897

$ **Ross Dress For Less**
1945 W. Palmetto Street
Florence, SC
(843) 317-9855

$ **Sam's Club**
200 N. Beltline Drive
Florence, SC
(843) 662-2769

⛺ **Sears**
2701 David H McLeod Boulevard,
   Unit C
Florence, SC
(843) 664-5828

⛺ **Stein Mart**
1945 W. Palmetto Street, Unit 150
Florence, SC
(843) 667-1443

☆ **Talbots**
2150 W. Evans Street, Suite 620
Florence, SC
(843) 292-9370

$ **Target**
2791 David H McLeod Boulevard
Florence, SC
(843) 667-6731

$ **T. J. Maxx**
1945 W. Palmetto Street
Florence, SC
(843) 679-3737

$ **Wal-Mart**
2530 David H McLeod Boulevard
Florence, SC
(843) 664-2020

$ **Wal-Mart Supercenter**
1150 S. Fourth Street
Hartsville, SC
(843) 383-4891

Churches/ Worship Centers

Calvary Baptist Church
505 W. Smith Avenue
Darlington, SC
(843) 393-1002

Christ Apostolic Church
109 Langston Road
Darlington, SC
(843) 393-0908

Church of God of Prophecy
920 W. Smith Avenue
Darlington, SC
(843) 393-1525

Cross & Crown Lutheran Church
3123 W. Palmetto Street
Florence, SC
(843) 669-2355

Darlington Church of God
701 N. Governor Williams Highway
Darlington, SC
(843) 393-7010

Darlington Presbyterian Church
311 Pearl Street
Darlington, SC
(843) 393-4851

Epworth United Methodist Church
706 Pearl Street
Darlington, SC
(843) 393-8692

First Church of God
620 N. Main Street
Darlington, SC
(843) 393-7942

First Pentecostal Holiness Church
598 W. Broad Street
Darlington, SC
(843) 393-8272

New Covenant Assembly
708 Indian Branch Road
Darlington, SC
(843) 395-9214

St. Anthony Catholic Church
2536 Hoffmeyer Road
Florence, SC
(843) 662-5674

Medical Centers

Carolina's Hospital
1590 Freedom Boulevard
Florence, SC
(843) 674-5000

McLeod Regional Medical Center
555 E. Cheves Street
Florence, SC
(843) 777-2000

Regency Hospital
121 E. Cedar Street
Florence, SC
(843) 661-3499

Pet Medical Centers

Florence Animal Hospital
1080 Old Ebenezer Road
Florence, SC
(843) 662-7074

Westside Veterinary Clinic
2230 W. Jody Road
Florence, SC
(843) 673-9233

DAYTONA INTERNATIONAL SPEEDWAY

Lake Lloyd

Infield

Garage Area

Pit Road

Road Course
(Not used for the
Sprint Cup Series)

Start | Finish Line

Track Information

Inaugural Year: 1959
Owner: ISC
City: Daytona Beach, Florida
Size: 2.5 miles
Banking: 31 degrees in turns,
    18 degrees in tri-oval
Grandstand Capacity: 168,000

ADDRESS
Daytona International Speedway
1801 W. International Speedway
    Boulevard
Daytona Beach, FL 32114
(386) 254-2700

(800) PIT-STOP
www.daytonainternationalspeedway
    .com

TICKET INFORMATION
Phone: (800) PIT-STOP
www.daytonainternationalspeedway
    .com

About the Track

The beaches of Daytona are where
NASCAR all started. Racers would
come from far and wide to compete

on the sands of Daytona Beach. It wasn't until the late 1950s that the cars finally hit the high banks of Daytona International Speedway. Daytona is always a wild race to watch because you never know what will happen. It is one of only two tracks (the other being Talladega) where NASCAR mandates the cars to use restrictor plates, which restricts airflow from the carburetor to the engine in order to slow down the cars. The Daytona 500 is one of the most (if not the most) prestigious races on the circuit.

Track History

In August 1954, Bill France Sr., a banker turned race car driver, convinced the Daytona area city officials to sign a contract allowing him to create what we know today as the Daytona International Speedway. Groundbreaking for the 2.5-mile facility took place November 25, 1957. Some two years later, the $3 million project was complete, although many questioned if the track would be completed on time. In an effort to gain additional building dollars needed to support the project, France took off to the Coca-Cola headquarters in Atlanta. After Coke turned France down, he went directly to their biggest competitor, the Pepsi company, who wrote France a check

on the spot. These much needed funds put the track project back on schedule and ultimately assured the track met its deadline.

Track Records

Most Wins: Richard Petty (10)
Most Top Five Finishes: Richard Petty (28)
Most Lead Changes: 60—on 2/17/1974
Fewest Lead Changes: 0—on 2/12/1960
Most Cautions: 12—on 7/1/1989
Fewest Cautions: 0—most recently on 2/11/1971 (total of 12 times)
Race Record: Buddy Baker— 177.602 mph (2 hours, 48 minutes, 55 seconds) (2/17/1980)
Qualifying Record: Bill Elliott—210.364 mph (42.783 seconds) (2/9/1987)

Fast Facts

- Bobby Allison is the oldest driver to have won at Daytona—winning in February 1988, he was fifty years old (plus two months and eleven days).
- The first NASCAR Sprint Cup race was run at Daytona International Speedway on February 22, 1959, and won by Lee Petty.

- The largest field to ever start a race at Daytona was sixty-eight cars back in 1960.
- The lowest starting position of a winner was thirty-third—Bobby Allison won from that slot in 1978.
- The Daytona 500 is referred to as the Great American Race.
- Scenes from *Days of Thunder* were filmed at Daytona International Speedway.
- The late, great Dale Earnhardt Sr. lost his life during the 2001 Daytona 500.
- Lake Lloyd, a popular fishing spot for drivers, is located inside the infield of the track.

Parking

Daytona International Speedway offers free parking in numerous areas, both on-site and off. All parking is first come, first served. For an up-to-date listing of park and ride options and the free shuttle service, go to www.daytonainternationalspeedway .com or call the track at 1-800-PIT-STOP.

Track Rules

According to the track's official website at www.daytonainternational speedway.com, the track's rules are as follows:

ITEMS ALLOWED IN THE GRANDSTANDS

- ✓ one soft-sided bag or cooler (no larger than 6″ × 6″ × 12″)
- ✓ one clear plastic bag (no larger than 18″ × 18″ × 4″, no ice)
- ✓ binoculars
- ✓ scanners
- ✓ headsets
- ✓ cameras (worn separately over the neck or on a belt)
- ✓ seat cushions

ITEMS *NOT* ALLOWED IN THE GRANDSTANDS

- ✗ firearms
- ✗ fireworks
- ✗ hard-sided coolers
- ✗ thermoses or insulated cups of any size
- ✗ flagpoles of any kind
- ✗ strollers
- ✗ glass containers
- ✗ umbrellas
- ✗ scooters
- ✗ bicycles
- ✗ skateboards
- ✗ golf carts
- ✗ pets (except animals trained to assist the disabled)

Special Needs and Services

Daytona offers seating and parking for those needing special assistance or accessibility. One companion is allowed to accompany those with special needs. Call the speedway office prior to arrival at 386-254-2700 or go to the track's website at www.daytonainternationalspeedway.com for the latest information on special needs. Always ask for parking near your seats.

Track Tours

Group and individual track tour packages can be obtained through the main ticket office or at Daytona 500 Experience, which is located at the main entrance of the track. The tour includes the infield, Victory Lane, the suites, and a lap around the track. It is advised to book tours in advance by calling 1-800-PIT-STOP. The number of race weekend tours are minimal due to on-track activities.

Souvenirs

Official Daytona souvenirs are available year-round inside the Daytona 500 Experience exhibit gift shop which is located on West International Speedway Boulevard, directly in front of the track. Driver-specific items can be found on Souvenir Alley, located on the corner of International Speedway Boulevard and Midway Boulevard. During event weekends, souvenir and concession stands are located throughout the facility.

About the Area

Daytona is one of my favorite spots on the circuit due to the beach and the racing atmosphere of the city. Racing and NASCAR are royalty in these parts and for good reason: it is the corporate headquarters of NASCAR. Many NASCAR bigwigs live in and around the Daytona area. The weather for race weekends in Daytona varies considerably since one event is in February, when the weather can be thirty-five degrees outside or a comfortable eighty degrees, and the other is in early July, which is *hot, hot, hot.* The July race is run at night under the lights, which does help with the hot and humid summer temps. Rain showers are always close by so bring along your rain gear. (Just remember, no umbrellas are allowed in the grandstands, so think raincoats, ponchos, and hats.)

CHAMBER OF COMMERCE
Daytona Beach/Halifax Area
126 E. Orange Avenue
Daytona Beach, FL 32115
(386) 255-0981
www.daytonachamber.com

Transportation

AIRPORT

Daytona Beach International
 Airport (DAB)
700 Catalina Drive
Daytona Beach, FL
(386) 248-8030
(Approximately one mile from the
 track.)

AIRLINES

AirTran Airways (800) 247-8726
Continental (800) 523-FARE
Delta (800) 221-1212
US Airways (800) 428-4322

RENTAL CARS

Alamo (800) 327-9622
Avis (800) 831-2847
Budget (800) 527-0700
Dollar (800) 860-4000
Enterprise (800) 736-8222
Hertz (800) 654-3131
National (800) 227-7368
Thrifty (800) 847-4389

Hotels

KEY
🐾 Pet Friendly   ≈ Pool
✗ Restaurant

Alpine Court Motel
518 S. Atlantic Avenue
Daytona Beach, FL
(386) 255-8558

🐾, ≈ **America's Best Value Inn**
905 S. Atlantic Avenue
Daytona Beach, FL
(386) 255-5432

≈ **Atlantic Economy Inn**
808 S. Atlantic Avenue
Daytona Beach, FL
(386) 252-4083

🐾 **Budget Host Inn**
1305 S. Ridgewood Avenue
Daytona Beach, FL
(386) 252-1142

Budget Inn of Daytona Beach
640 S. Ridgewood Avenue
Daytona Beach, FL
(386) 252-4647

Comfort Suites
90 Professional Boulevard
Daytona Beach, FL
(386) 947-9995

Coquina Inn Bed & Breakfast
544 S. Palmetto Avenue
Daytona Beach, FL
(386) 254-4969

≈ **Courtyard Daytona Beach**
1605 Richard Petty Boulevard
Daytona Beach, FL
(386) 255-3388

⌂, ≈, ✕ **Days Inn Speedway**
2900 W. International Speedway
   Boulevard
Daytona Beach, FL
(386) 255-0541

≈ **Days Inn**
544 S. Ridgewood Avenue
Daytona Beach, FL
(386) 255-4500

Daytona Resort & Club
1200 Ruger Place
Daytona Beach, FL
(386) 253-0601

⌂ **Deluxe Motel**
502 Ridgewood Avenue
Daytona Beach, FL
(386) 252-4750

≈, ✕ **Fountain Beach Resort**
313 S. Atlantic Avenue
Daytona Beach, FL
(386) 255-7491

Fountain Inn & Suites
749 Ridgewood Avenue
Holly Hill, FL
(386) 255-6511

≈ **Hampton Inn Speedway**
1715 W. International Speedway
Daytona Beach, FL
(386) 257-4030

Hawaii Motel
1361 S. Ridgewood Avenue
Daytona Beach, FL
(386) 255-2838

≈, ✕ **Hilton Garden Inn**
189 Midway Avenue
Daytona Beach, FL
(386) 944-4000

≈ **Holiday Inn Express**
2620 W. International Speedway
   Boulevard
Daytona Beach, FL
(386) 258-6333

⌂, ≈ **Homewood Suites**
165 Bill France Boulevard
Daytona Beach, FL
(386) 258-2828

Host Inn
315 Bellevue Avenue
Daytona Beach, FL
(386) 257-5900

Indian Palms Motel
828 Ridgewood Avenue
Daytona Beach, FL
(386) 253-2490

⌂, ≈ **La Quinta Inn**
2725 W. International Speedway
Daytona Beach, FL
(386) 255-7412

Palmetto House
336 S. Palmetto Avenue
Daytona Beach, FL
(386) 253-4895

Parkway Motel
1369 S. Ridgewood Avenue
Daytona Beach, FL
(386) 252-6413

Quality Inn
801 Ridgewood Avenue
Holly Hill, FL
(386) 254-7977

Raintree Motel & Apartments
530 S. Ridgewood Avenue
Daytona Beach, FL
(386) 252-3698

☺, ≈, ✕ Ramada Inn Speedway
1798 W. International Speedway
   Boulevard
Daytona Beach, FL
(386) 255-2422

Ranch Motel
1028 Ridgewood Avenue
Daytona Beach, FL
(386) 258-0249

Red Carpet Inn
1855 S. Ridgewood Avenue
South Daytona, FL
(386) 767-6681

Regency Inn
619 N. Ridgewood Avenue
Daytona Beach, FL
(386) 253-5936

Relax Inn
1225 S. Ridgewood Avenue
Daytona Beach, FL
(386) 253-5941

☺, ≈ Residence Inn
1725 Richard Petty Boulevard
Daytona Beach, FL
(386) 252-3949

Ridgewood Inn
128 Ridgewood Avenue
Daytona Beach, FL
(386) 252-6088

Royal Inn
810 S. Ridgewood Avenue
Daytona Beach, FL
(386) 255-7536

≈ Scottish Inn
1515 S. Ridgewood Avenue
Daytona Beach, FL
(386) 258-5742

Skyway Motel
906 S. Atlantic Avenue
Daytona Beach, FL
(386) 252-7377

Suburban Lodge
220 Bill France Boulevard
Daytona Beach, FL
(386) 274-4337

Sunshine Inn of Daytona Beach
1234 S. Ridgewood Avenue
Daytona Beach, FL
(386) 258-6997

♿, ≈ **Super 8 Motel—Speedway Area**
2992 W. International Speedway Boulevard
Daytona Beach, FL
(386) 253-0643

≈ **Super 8 Motel—Downtown/ U.S. Highway 1**
1242 S. Ridgewood Avenue
Daytona Beach, FL
(386) 255-5540

Travel Inn
850 S. Ridgewood Avenue
Daytona Beach, FL
(386) 253-6865

Travelodge
2250 W. International Speedway Boulevard
Daytona Beach, FL
(386) 255-3661

≈, ✖ **Travelodge Ocean Jewels Resort**
935 S. Atlantic Avenue
Daytona Beach, FL
(386) 252-2581

Tropic Air Motel
1000 S. Atlantic Avenue
Daytona Beach, FL
(386) 258-5083

Tropical Gables
1245 Ridgewood Avenue
Holly Hill, FL
(386) 676-0302

Camping

ON-SITE AND TRACK-OWNED CAMPING

Both reserved and unreserved camping sites are available at Daytona International Speedway. Many of the reserved areas are sold out on a yearly basis. The track will take your contact information and add you to their mailing list. You can do this by visiting the main ticket office or by calling the track at 1-800-PIT-STOP. Daytona also has a camping guide available online at www.daytonainternational speedway.com. This guide is updated from race to race and is very helpful for the fans interested in camping at Daytona.

Green Reserved This reserved, controlled access infield area is for self-contained camping and is located in turn 4.

Lake Lloyd This premium reserved area is for fans wanting the VIP camping treatment. The partially paved area located by Lake Lloyd in the infield of the track offers water, electric hookups, and cable TV, and has twenty-four-hour patrol service.

Orange Reserved This infield area is located in turns 3 and 4. This area is for cars, trucks, and tents only.

Red Reserved This reserved infield area is located right in the middle of the infield and is for self-contained units only.

Yellow Reserved This reserved infield area is located in turns 1 and 2. All units must be self-contained.

West Horseshoe Reserved This reserved infield area is located near the road course. All units must be self-contained.

West Lot Parking This overnight parking area is located on the outside of the track. All units must be self-contained.

OFF-SITE CAMPING

Daytona Beach Campground
4601 Clyde Morris Boulevard
Port Orange, FL
(386) 761-2663

KOA Campground
3003 W. International Speedway
  Boulevard
Daytona Beach, FL
(386) 257-6137

Restaurants

KEY
🍔 Fast Food   🪑 Sit Down
🥡 Takeout   ☎ Reservations

Must Eats

Ocean Deck
127 S. Ocean Avenue
Daytona Beach, FL
(386) 253-5224
  This beachfront team hangout has great seafood and lively nightlife. There is not a better place on the beach to slip in during the day for some oysters on the half shell.

Porto Fino
3124 S. Atlantic Avenue
Daytona Beach Shores, FL
(386) 767-9484

If you love Italian cuisine, owner George will make sure you get your food and your racing fix. Drivers have been eating here for years—just ask George, he will tell you. This is a favorite Allison family hangout. The eggplant parmesan is to die for.

🍴 **Ashoka Indian Cuisine**
1448 W. International Speedway
  Boulevard
Daytona Beach, FL
(386) 253-7662

🍴 **Bob Evans**
2000 W. International Speedway
  Boulevard
Daytona Beach, FL
(386) 258-8939

🍔 **Burger King**
1436 W. International Speedway
  Boulevard
Daytona Beach, FL
(386) 253-5709

🍴 **Cajun Cafe of Volusia Mall, Inc.**
1700 W. International Speedway
  Boulevard

Daytona Beach, FL
(386) 248-0063

🍴 **Cancun Lagoon Bar & Grill**
1735 International Speedway
  Boulevard
Daytona Beach, FL
(386) 255-6500

🍴 **Carrabba's Italian Grill**
2200 W. International Speedway
  Boulevard
Daytona Beach, FL
(386) 255-3344

🍟 **Checkers Drive-In Restaurant**
2210 W. International Speedway
  Boulevard
Daytona Beach, FL
(386) 252-2036

🍔 **Chick-fil-A**
1700 W. International Speedway
  Boulevard
Daytona Beach, FL
(386) 258-5883

🍴 **China Buffet**
1312 W. International Speedway
  Boulevard
Daytona Beach, FL
(386) 238-3399

🍟 **China Max**
1700 W. International Speedway
  Boulevard

Daytona Beach, FL
(386) 239-0051

Cracker Barrel
2325 W. International Speedway
  Boulevard
Daytona Beach, FL
(386) 248-0034

Denny's
1446 W. International Speedway
  Boulevard
Daytona Beach, FL
(386) 258-5460

Friendly's Ice Cream Shop
1810 W. International Speedway
  Boulevard
Daytona Beach, FL
(386) 238-0657

Heavenly Ham
345 Bill France Boulevard
Daytona Beach, FL
(386) 238-0026

Honey Baked Ham
1808 W. International Speedway
  Boulevard
Daytona Beach, FL
(386) 252-6444

Hooters
2100 W. International Speedway
  Boulevard
Daytona Beach, FL
(386) 238-0650

Jack's Steakery & Grill
1700 W. International Speedway
  Boulevard, Suite 142
Daytona Beach, FL
(386) 257-7755

Kentucky Fried Chicken
2310 W. International Speedway
  Boulevard
Daytona Beach, FL
(386) 258-5033

McDonald's
1700 W. International Speedway
  Boulevard
Daytona Beach, FL
(386) 258-1535

Mr. Dunderbak's
1700 W. International Speedway
  Boulevard
Daytona Beach, FL
(386) 258-1600

Mr. Goodcents Subs & Pasta
1808 W. International Speedway
  Boulevard, Suite 501
Daytona Beach, FL
(386) 238-2368

Olive Garden Italian Restaurant
1725 W. International Speedway
  Boulevard
Daytona Beach, FL
(386) 252-0639

🐔 **Outback Steakhouse**
1490 W. International Speedway
    Boulevard
Daytona Beach, FL
(386) 253-6283

🐔 **Piccadilly Cafeteria**
1700 W. International Speedway
    Boulevard
Daytona Beach, FL
(386) 258-5373

🍴 **Quiznos Sub**
1392 W. International Speedway
    Boulevard
Daytona Beach, FL
(386) 238-1811

🐔 **Ruby Tuesday**
1808 W. International Speedway
    Boulevard
Daytona Beach, FL
(386) 254-8828

🐔 **Sbarro**
1700 W. International Speedway
    Boulevard
Daytona Beach, FL
(386) 248-0062

🐔 **Sonny's Real Pit Bar-B-Q**
1500 W. International Speedway
    Boulevard
Daytona Beach, FL
(386) 248-3111

🐔 **Sorrento Deli Restaurant**
1344 W. International Speedway
    Boulevard
Daytona Beach, FL
(386) 255-1817

🍔 **Taco Bell**
2140 W. International Speedway
    Boulevard
Daytona Beach, FL
(386) 254-8226

🐔 **Uno Chicago Grill**
1798 W. International Speedway
    Boulevard
Daytona Beach, FL
(386) 252-8600

🍔 **Wendy's**
1441 International Highway
Daytona Beach, FL
(386) 258-8700

🐔 **Yuki Hana**
1448 W. International Speedway
    Boulevard
Daytona Beach, FL
(386) 238-8288

Local Attractions

WORTH THE TRIP

Planning at least an extra day of travel for **Walt Disney World** is a must when catching the races at Daytona. It is just too tempting to be only an hour's drive from Mickey without actually going. An easy plan is to go to Disney on Wednesday of race week, which leaves the rest of the weekend for racing. I would not recommend trying to do Disney in conjunction with the July Daytona race as the crowds at the park are too extreme (as is the heat). February is the perfect time for Disney and racing as it is one of the slowest times to go to Disney World and the other Orlando attractions. Trust me when I say you will see lots of race gear throughout Disney as many fans have caught on to this idea. Your second stop should be to the **Daytona 500 Experience** located on the grounds of the track. This museum/exhibit is a must stop for every race fan. It is both fun and informative. There are many race exhibits scattered around Daytona during race weeks. Always check with the chamber of commerce about sites and locations.

Atlantic Race Park
2122 S. Atlantic Avenue
Daytona Beach Shores, FL
(386) 226-8777

Birthplace of Speed Park
Atlantic Avenue and Granada
   Boulevard (SR 40),
   beach approach
Ormond Beach, FL
(386) 676-3216

Bongo Billy's Banana Boat Rides
Free pick up from your hotel to
   beach location
Daytona Beach, FL
(386) 235-2598

Daytona Beach Golf Club
600 Wilder Boulevard
Daytona Beach, FL
(386) 671-3500

Daytona Beach Jet Boats
4009 Halifax Drive
Port Orange, FL
(386) 631-5554

Daytona Beach Parasail, Inc.
On the beach
Daytona Beach, FL
(386) 547-6067

**Daytona Beach ThunderBirds
   Indoor Football Ocean Center**
101 N. Atlantic Avenue
Daytona Beach, FL
(386) 254-4545

Daytona Cruisers, Inc.
720 E. International Speedway
   Boulevard
Daytona Beach, FL
(386) 255-4469

Daytona 500 Experience
1801 W. International Speedway
   Boulevard

Daytona Beach, FL
(386) 947-6800

Ducer Cruzer Bike & SK8
137 Sunrise Boulevard
Daytona Beach Shores, FL
(386) 383-7433

Finest Kind II
133 Inlet Harbor Road
Ponce Inlet, FL
(877) 615-6606

Fun in the Sun Rentals
On the beach
Daytona Beach, FL
(386) 547-2449

Go-Kart City & Mystic Harbor Miniature Golf
4114 S. Nova Road
Port Orange, FL
(386) 761-2882

Halifax Harbor Marina
450 Basin Street
Daytona Beach, FL
(800) 343-2899

Haunts of the World's Most Famous Beach Ghost Tours
1202 Deneece Terrace
Holly Hill, FL
(386) 253-6034

Hooker Sport Fishing Charters
3948 S. Peninsula Drive
Daytona Beach, FL
(386) 760-8909

Indigo Lakes Golf Club
312 Indigo Drive
Daytona Beach, FL
(386) 254-3607

Manatee Scenic Cruises
133 Inlet Harbor Road
Ponce Inlet, FL
(800) 881-2628

Midwest Motorcycle Rental
2020 S. Atlantic Avenue
Daytona Beach Shores, FL
(888) 237-5853

River Queen II
450 Basin Street
Daytona Beach, FL
(866) 999-7560

SeaWorld Orlando
7007 Sea World Drive
Orlando, FL
800-327-2424

Sea-Ya Charters & Guide Service
2801 Sauls Street
South Daytona, FL
(386) 547-3680

Speed Park Motorsports
201 Fentress Boulevard
Daytona Beach, FL
(386) 253-3278

Sugar Mill Botanical Gardens
950 Old Sugar Mill Road
Port Orange, FL
(386) 767-1735

Universal Studios
1000 Universal Studios Plaza
Orlando, FL
(407) 363-8000

Walt Disney World
1675 N. Lake Buena Vista Drive
Orlando, FL
(407) 824-4321

Shopping

KEY
🚗 Automotive $ Discount
✚ Pharmacy 🏬 Mall
☆ Specialty 🏠 Department Store

☆ Aeropostale
1700 W. International Speedway
  Boulevard
Daytona Beach, FL
(386) 257-5028

$ Bealls Outlet
2455 W. International Speedway
  Boulevard

Daytona Beach, FL
(386) 252-4952

$ Big Lots
882 N. Nova Road
Daytona Beach, FL
(386) 258-8108

☆ Citi Trends
878 N. Nova Road
Daytona Beach, FL
(386) 252-2491

☆ Claire's
1700 W. International Speedway
  Boulevard
Daytona Beach, FL
(386) 253-8912

🏠 Dillard's
1700 W. International Speedway
  Boulevard
Daytona Beach, FL
(386) 255-8161

$ Dollar General
894 N. Nova Road
Daytona Beach, FL
(386) 253-4028

$ Dollar Tree
2455 W. International Speedway
  Boulevard, Suite 602
Daytona Beach, FL
(386) 238-0455

$ Family Dollar Store
208 N. Nova Road
Daytona Beach, FL
(386) 226-9972

⛺ JC Penney
1700 W. International Speedway
    Boulevard
Daytona Beach, FL
(386) 255-0971

$ Kmart
1300 W. International Speedway
    Boulevard
Daytona Beach, FL
(386) 252-9691

⛺ Macy's
1700 W. International Speedway
    Boulevard
Daytona Beach, FL
(386) 254-3300

$ Marshalls
1808 W. International Speedway
    Boulevard
Daytona Beach, FL
(386) 258-8855

☆ Old Navy
2500 W. International Speedway
    Boulevard
Daytona Beach, FL
(386) 257-0661

☆ Pier 1 Imports
2451 W. International Speedway
    Boulevard
Daytona Beach, FL
(386) 257-1200

$ Ross Dress For Less
2455 W. International Speedway
    Boulevard
Daytona Beach, FL
(386) 253-4308

$ Sam's Club
1175 Beville Road
Daytona Beach, FL
(386) 760-3330

⛺ Sears
1700 W. International Speedway
    Boulevard
Daytona Beach, FL
(386) 254-5228

☆ Stein Mart
2500 W. International Speedway
    Boulevard
Daytona Beach, FL
(386) 257-3363

$ Target
2380 W. International Speedway
    Boulevard
Daytona Beach, FL
(386) 257-4778

$ T.J. Maxx
2455 W. International Speedway
  Boulevard, Suite 800
Daytona Beach, FL
(386) 681-1076

Volusia Mall
1700 W. International Speedway
  Boulevard
Daytona Beach, FL
386-253-6783

$ Wal-Mart Supercenter
1101 Beville Road
Daytona Beach, FL
(386) 322-1124

Churches/
Worship Centers

Christ Community Church
329 N. Williamson Boulevard
Daytona Beach, FL
(386) 238-1956

Christ United Methodist Church
962 Derbyshire Road
Holly Hill, FL
(386) 255-4295

Church of Christ Westside
960 Dr Mary McLeod Bethune
  Boulevard
Daytona Beach, FL
(386) 255-8901

**Church of Jesus Christ of Latter-
  Day Saints**
1125 Sixth Street
Daytona Beach, FL
(386) 257-9223

First Baptist Church
118 N. Palmetto Avenue
Daytona Beach, FL
(386) 253-5691

First Presbyterian Church
620 S. Grandview Avenue
Daytona Beach, FL
(386) 253-4581

Holy Cross Lutheran Church
724 Big Tree Road
South Daytona, FL
(386) 767-6542

Pentecostal Apostolic Church
610 Cherry Street
Daytona Beach, FL
(386) 253-4951

Pentecost Church of God
458 Arthur Avenue
Daytona Beach, FL
(386) 253-0320

Seventh-Day Adventist Church
401 N. Williamson Boulevard
Daytona Beach, FL
(386) 255-5144

St. James Missionary Baptist
732 Tennessee Street
Daytona Beach, FL
(386) 248-0841

St. John CME Church
419 School Street
Daytona Beach, FL
(386) 257-2585

St. Mary's Episcopal Church
216 Orange Avenue
Daytona Beach, FL
(386) 255-3669

St. Paul's Catholic Church
317 Mullally Street
Daytona Beach, FL
(386) 252-5422

**Stewart Memorial United
  Methodist Church**
300 N. Dr. Martin Luther King Jr.
  Boulevard
Daytona Beach, FL
(386) 255-7222

Medical Center

Halifax Medical Center
303 N. Clyde Morris Boulevard
Daytona Beach, FL
(386) 254-4000

Pet Medical Centers

Banfield the Pet Hospital
1900 W. International Speedway
  Boulevard
Daytona Beach, FL
(386) 257-7787

Beville Animal Hospital
945 Beville Road
South Daytona, FL
(386) 788-3769

Driftwood Animal Hospital
932 Mason Avenue
Daytona Beach, FL
(386) 255-1407

Rawls Veterinary Hospital
127 E. Mason Avenue
Daytona Beach, FL
(386) 253-2525

DOVER
INTERNATIONAL SPEEDWAY

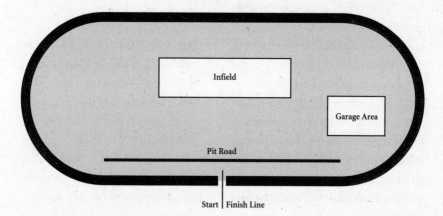

Track Information

Inaugural Year: 1969
Owner: Dover Motorsports, Inc.
City: Dover, Delaware
Size: 1 mile
Banking: 24 degrees
Grandstand Capacity: 140,000

ADDRESS

Dover International Speedway
1131 N. Dupont Highway
Dover, DE 19901
(800) 441-7223
www.doverspeedway.com

TICKET INFORMATION

Phone: (800) 441-RACE
www.doverspeedway.com

About the Track

Dover is about as predictable as it comes for races. The drivers always put on a great show for the 140,000 fans. Fans that come to Dover know they will see a good race. It is one of only three tracks on the circuit with a concrete surface. The drivers and fans love coming to Dover not only for the racing but also for the casinos and the host of great restaurants.

Track History

Dover Downs was originally built in 1969, three years after the groundbreaking. Dover was built to run horse racing and motorsports, giving the Delaware track a unique niche in racing venues. This continued until 2002 when the slot machines and harness racing were moved to the newly constructed Dover Downs Hotel and Casino. The original asphalt surface was replaced in 1995 with concrete, making Dover the first concrete-paved superspeedway on the NASCAR circuit. In 2008, Dover celebrated its fortieth anniversary.

Track Records

Most Wins: Richard Petty and Bobby Allison (7)
Most Top Five Finishes: Dale Earnhardt Sr. and Mark Martin (19)
Most Lead Changes: 29—most recently on 5/18/1986 (total of 2 times)
Fewest Lead Changes: 3—on 10/17/1971
Most Cautions: 16—on 9/19/1993
Fewest Cautions: 0—on 6/6/1971

Race Record: Mark Martin— 132.719 mph (3 hours, 0 minutes, 50 seconds) (9/21/1997)
Qualifying Record: Jeremy Mayfield—161.522 mph (22.288 seconds) (6/4/2004)

Fast Facts

- Harry Gant is the oldest driver to have won at Dover International Speedway—winning in May 1992, he was fifty-two years old (plus four months and twenty-one days).
- The first NASCAR Sprint Cup race was run at Dover International Speedway on July 6, 1969, and was won by Richard Petty.
- The races at Dover used to be five hundred miles long, but after the NASCAR rule that only tracks over one mile in length could run five hundred-mile races, Dover switched to the four hundred-mile format.
- Ricky Rudd won his first career speedway victory in the Delaware 500 at Dover Downs on September 14, 1986. Rudd beat runner-up Neil Bonnett by 5.08 seconds.
- The one-mile track is referred to as the Monster Mile.
- The track mascot, the concrete monster, stands forty-six feet tall and can be found in Victory Plaza.

- The race winner is expected to sign the seat number that matches their car number on the Monster Bridge, which is located near turn 3 of the track.

Parking

Dover International Speedway provides both free and fee-related parking. For up-to-date information on parking and fees contact the track's main office number at 1-800-441-7223 or go to www.doverspeedway .com. A limited amount of infield parking is available on a first-come, first-served basis.

Track Rules

According to the track's official web site at www.doverspeedway.com, the track's rules are as follows:

ITEMS ALLOWED IN THE GRANDSTANDS

- ✓ one hard-sided or soft-sided insulated cooler (no larger than 14″ × 14″ × 14″, no ice)
- ✓ scanner bag, fanny pack, purse, binocular bag, or camera bag (worn separately)
- ✓ one clear plastic bag (no larger than 18″ × 18″ × 4″, no ice)
- ✓ seat cushions
- ✓ scanners
- ✓ cameras
- ✓ binoculars

ITEMS NOT ALLOWED IN GRANDSTANDS

- ✗ glass
- ✗ alchohol
- ✗ umbrellas
- ✗ strollers
- ✗ knives
- ✗ fireworks
- ✗ scooters
- ✗ golf carts
- ✗ skateboards
- ✗ illegal drugs
- ✗ pets (unless special services animal)

Special Needs and Services

Dover provides special services and accessibility to those in need. The track allows a companion to accompany those with disabilities. Contact the track's main office prior to your arrival at 1-800-441-7223 for up-to-date information on seating and parking. Make sure you call prior to arrival and always ask for parking near your seats.

Track Tours

Dover does not provide track tours to the general public. Private tours are given on a case-by-case situation. Anyone interested in an organized tour can contact the track at 1-800-441-7223.

Souvenirs

There are Dover International Speedway souvenir trailers located around the track and along the Midway. Driver-specific souvenir trailers are located on Souvenir Alley, along the Midway on the south side of the track and along the northeast side of the track.

About the Area

The Dover area is known for its great food, horse racing, casinos, and motorsports. Dover is also the home of the Dover Air Force Base, located only two miles from Dover International. Dover AFB includes the largest mortuary in the Department of Defense. Their main purpose is to process military personnel killed in war and peacetime. The mortuary has processed countless bodies through the years. Some of the most notable would be the victims of the 1978 Jonestown Massacre, the remains of the 1986 Space Shuttle *Challenger*,

the crew of the 2003 Space Shuttle *Columbia*, and the remains of the 9/11 attacks, including the terrorists. The average temperature for the May race is seventy-nine degrees while the September race is a bit warmer at an average of eighty-four degrees.

CHAMBER OF COMMERCE
Central Delaware Chamber of
  Commerce
435 N. Dupont Highway
Dover, DE 19901
(302) 678-0892
www.cdcc.net

Transportation

AIRPORT
Philadelphia International Airport
  (PHL)
8800 Essington Avenue
Philadelphia, PA
(215) 937-6937
(Approximately fifty miles from the
  track.)

AIRLINES
AirTran Airways (800) AIR-TRAN
America West (800) 428-4322
American (800) 433-7300
Continental (800) 525-0280
Delta (800) 221-1212
Frontier (800) 432-1359
Midwest (800) 452-2022
Northwest (800) 225-2525
Southwest (800) 435-9792

United (800) 241-6522
US Airways (800) 428-4322

RENTAL CARS
Alamo (800) 327-9633
Avis (800) 331-1212
Budget (800) 527-0700
Dollar (800) 800-4000
Enterprise (800) 736-8222
Hertz (800) 654-3131
National (800) 227-7368

Hotels

KEY
↪ Pet Friendly   ≈ Pool
✗ Restaurant

≈ **Best Western Galaxy Inn**
1700 E. Lebanon Road
Dover, DE
(302) 735-4700

↪, ≈ **Comfort Inn**
U.S. 13 and Lockerman Street
Dover, DE
(302) 674-3301

≈ **Comfort Suites**
1654 N. Dupont Highway
Dover, DE
(302) 736-1204

Days Inn
272 N. Dupont Highway
Dover, DE
(302) 674-8002

≈, ✗ **Dover Downs Hotel and Conference Center**
1131 N. Dupont Highway
Dover, DE
(302) 857-2140

Dover Inn
428 N. Dupont Highway
Dover, DE
(302) 674-4011

↪ **Economy Inn**
4133 S. Dupont Boulevard
Smyrna, DE
(302) 653-9154

≈ **Fairfield Inn**
655 N. Dupont Highway
Dover, DE
(302) 677-0900

First State Inn
1760 N. Dupont Highway
Dover, DE
(302) 734-4042

≈ **Hampton Inn Dover**
1568 N. Dupont Highway
Dover, DE
(302) 736-3500

≈ **Holiday Inn Express**
1780 N. Dupont Highway
Dover, DE
(302) 678-0600

⌂, ≈ **Howard Johnson Express**
561 N. Dupont Highway
Dover, DE
(302) 678-8900

⌂ **Kent Budget Motel**
383 N. Dupont Highway
Dover, DE
(302) 674-2211

Microtel Inn and Suites
1703 E. Lebanon Road
Dover, DE
(302) 674-3800

⌂ **Red Roof Inn**
652 N. Dupont Highway
Dover, DE
(302) 730-8009

Relax Inn
640 S. Dupont Highway
Dover, DE
(302) 734-8120

Shamrock Motel
2171 S. Dupont Highway
Dover, DE
(302) 697-7505

⌂, ≈, ✗ **Sheraton**
1570 N. Dupont Highway
Dover, DE
(302) 678-8500

Twilight Haven Motel
1648 S. Dupont Boulevard
Smyrna, DE
(302) 653-9906

Camping

ON-SITE AND TRACK-OWNED CAMPING

Dover has limited camping options on-site. RVs are not allowed in the infield and tents are not allowed on the Dover property. For up-to-date information regarding on-site camping options at Dover International call the ticket office at 1-800-441-7223 or visit the track's website at www.doverspeedway.com

Lot 2 This reserved lot is used for three-day ticket holders. The spaces are filled with guests who meet the three-day ticket requirement.

Lots 6, 7 This RV camping area is for disabled guests. This area is filled on a first-come, first-served basis.

Lot 8 This area is a reserved camping location. All spots are filled on a first-come, first-served basis prior to race weekend.

Lots 9, 10 RVs are loaded in on a first-come, first-served basis. Hook-ups and showers are not available in any lots on speedway property.

OFF-SITE CAMPING

Duck Neck Campground
500 Double Creek Point Road
Chestertown, MD
(410) 778-3070

G & R Recreation Campground
4075 Gun and Rod Club Road
Houston, DE
(302) 398-8108

Holiday Park Campground
14620 Drapers Mill Road
Greensboro, MD
(410) 482-6797

Killens Pond State Park
5025 Killens Pond Road
Felton, DE
(302) 284-4526

Pine Haven Campground
22517 Corey Drive
Lincoln, DE
(302) 422-7117

Restaurants

KEY
🍔 Fast Food   🪑 Sit Down
🛍 Takeout   🍴 Reservations

Must Eats

Geno's Steaks
1219 S. Ninth Street
Philadelphia, PA
(215) 389-0659

Pat's King of Steaks
1237 E. Passyunk Avenue
Philadelphia, PA
(215) 468-1546

Geno's has the best Philly cheesesteak you will ever find, until you go right across the street to their friendly competitor, Pat's King of Steaks. Both restaurants are in Philly, which is an hour's drive, but worth the trip. Check out the pictures on the walls, you might be surprised (or not) at who has eaten in these dynamic must eats.

🪑 **Applebee's**
909 N. Dupont Highway
Dover, DE
(302) 741-2292

🍔 **Arby's**
705 N. Dupont Highway
Dover, DE
(302) 678-8099

🪑 **Bella-Villa Pizza Pasta**
1053 N. Dupont Highway
Dover, DE
(302) 674-4531

🍟 **Boardwalk Fries**
1365 N. Dupont Highway, Suite 3064
Dover, DE
(302) 734-2335

🪑 **Bob Evans**
1650 N. Dupont Highway
Dover, DE
(302) 678-5042

🍔 **Boston Market**
1151 N. Dupont Highway
Dover, DE
(302) 734-8431

🍔 **Chick-fil-A**
1365 N. Dupont Highway, Suite 3068
Dover, DE
(302) 736-5226

🪑 **China King Restaurant**
760 Walker Road
Dover, DE
(302) 730-1510

🪑 **Chinatown Buffet**
1071 N. Dupont Highway
Dover, DE
(302) 678-8868

🪑 **Chuck E. Cheese's**
1275 N. Dupont Highway
Dover, DE
(302) 736-9881

🪑 **Cobblestone Cafe**
408 State Street
Dover, DE
(302) 735-7874

🪑 **Country Eatery**
950 N. State Street
Dover, DE
(302) 674-8310

🍔 **Dairy Queen**
1365 N. Dupont Highway
Dover, DE
(302) 674-1801

🪑 **Denny's**
1141 N. Dupont Highway
Dover, DE
(302) 734-2913

🍔 **Domino's Pizza**
789 Walker Road
Dover, DE
(302) 674-1111

🍔 **Flamers Burgers & Chicken**
1365 N. Dupont Highway, Suite 3056
Dover, DE
(302) 734-0100

Golden Corral Buffet & Grill
391 N. Dupont Highway
Dover, DE
(302) 741-2120

Hibachi Japanese Steak House
691 N. Dupont Highway
Dover, DE
(302) 734-5900

Ichiban Japanese Restaurant
737 N. Dupont Highway
Dover, DE
(302) 677-0067

**Kirby & Holloway Family
  Restaurant**
656 N. Dupont Highway
Dover, DE
(302) 734-7133

La Tolteca Restaurant
859 N. Dupont Highway
Dover, DE
(302) 734-3444

Little Caesars Pizza
515 N. Dupont Highway
Dover, DE
(302) 678-1241

Lone Star Steakhouse & Saloon
365 N. Dupont Highway
Dover, DE
(302) 736-5836

Luigi's Pizza & Italian Restaurant
1047 Walker Road
Dover, DE
(302) 735-7611

McDonald's
879 N. Dupont Highway
Dover, DE
(302) 674-8573

Papa John's Pizza
1243 N. Dupont Highway
Dover, DE
(302) 734-2990

Pizza Hut
779 N. Dupont Highway
Dover, DE
(302) 736-0256

Popeye's Chicken & Biscuits
677 N. Dupont Highway
Dover, DE
(302) 678-9440

Quiznos Sub
1245 N. Dupont Highway
Dover, DE
(302) 674-5880

Red Lobster
271 N. Dupont Highway
Dover, DE
(302) 734-9122

℄ Romano's Restaurant
768 Walker Road
Dover, DE
(302) 736-1199

♠ Ruby Tuesday
1365 N. Dupont Highway
Dover, DE
(302) 734-5818

♦ Saladworks
1365 N. Dupont Highway
Dover, DE
(302) 744-9331

♠ Sakura Japan
1365 N. Dupont Highway, Suite
    3072
Dover, DE
(302) 744-9445

♠ Sbarro
1365 N. Dupont Highway
Dover, DE
(302) 672-9309

♠ Schucker's Pier 13 Restaurant
889 N. Dupont Highway
Dover, DE
(302) 674-1190

♠ Shanghai Garden
561 N. Dupont Highway
Dover, DE
(302) 678-5606

♦ Subway Sandwiches & Salads
1365 N. Dupont Highway
Dover, DE
(302) 734-7080

♠ Tango's Bistro
1570 N. Dupont Highway
Dover, DE
(302) 678-0100

♠ Taste of India
348 N. Dupont Highway
Dover, DE
(302) 677-0121

♦ Uno Pizzeria
1225 N. Dupont Highway
Dover, DE
(302) 674-5055

♦ Viet Kieu Restaurant
510 Jefferic Boulevard
Dover, DE
(302) 744-9300

Local Attractions

WORTH THE TRIP

While in Dover, you have to add some extra time to your trip to include the **Dover Downs Hotel and Casino.** I'm personally not into gambling, but if you are, then this is your place. Slot machines and even horse racing is what you will find at this four-star hotel. For the nongamblers, the casino complex also has a spa, shopping, and lots of great food. This is one of the most popular driver and team hangouts. Don't be surprised to see your favorite driver taking his chance with lady luck.

Shopping

KEY
🚗 Automotive $ Discount
⊕ Pharmacy   🛍 Mall
☆ Specialty   🏬 Department Store

Biggs Museum of American Art
406 Federal Street
Dover, DE
(302) 674-2111

$ Big Lots
1005 N. State Street
Dover, DE
(302) 735-7670

Club Kids
1720 S. Governors Avenue
Dover, DE
(302) 677-1720

🏬 Boscov's Department Store
1365 N. Dupont Highway, Suite 3000
Dover, DE
(302) 734-9210

Delaware Agricultural Museum
866 N. Dupont Highway
Dover, DE
(302) 734-1618

$ Dollar General
1365 N. Dupont Highway
Dover, DE
(302) 678-0311

DNR Paintball
3833 N Dupont Highway
Dover, DE
(302) 730-8664

🛍 Dover Mall
1365 N. Dupont Highway, Suite 5061
Dover, DE
(302) 734-0415

Dover Downs Hotel and Casino
1131 N. Dupont Highway
Dover, DE
(800) 711-5882

$ Family Dollar Store
1007 N. State Street
Dover, DE
(302) 736-9731

Jolly Time Family Fun Center
Dover Air Park
83 Glenn Street
Dover, DE
(302) 734-3623

☂ **JC Penney**
1365 N. Dupont Highway, Suite
   5000
Dover, DE
(302) 674-4200

$ **Kmart**
515 N. Dupont Highway
Dover, DE
(302) 678-8020

☂ **Kohl's Department Store**
299 N. Dupont Highway
Dover, DE
(302) 735-7610

☂ **Macy's**
1365 N. Dupont Highway
Dover, DE
(302) 736-0974

☆ **Once Upon A Child**
1249 N. Dupont Highway
Dover, DE
(302) 698-4110

$ **Roses Store**
84 E. Glenwood Avenue
Smyrna, DE
(302) 653-0834

$ **Sam's Club**
1572 N. Dupont Highway
Dover, DE
(302) 678-4220

☂ **Sears**
1000 Dover Mall
Dover, DE
(302) 342-0124

☆ **Talbots**
1404 Forrest Avenue
Dover, DE
(302) 677-1899

$ **Target**
148 John Hunn Brown Road
Dover, DE
(302) 741-0466

$ **T.J. Maxx**
1091 N. Dupont Highway
Dover, DE
(302) 736-3886

$ **Value City Department Store**
650 S. Bay Road Suite 15
Dover, DE
(302) 735-8500

$ **Wal-Mart**
1574 N. Dupont Highway
Dover, DE
(302) 674-2159

$ **Wal-Mart Supercenter**
263 Walmart Drive
Camden Wyoming, DE
(302) 698-9170

Churches/
Worship Centers

Bethuel Seventh-Day Adventist
25 N. Queen Street
Dover, DE
(302) 678-2499

Calvary Baptist Church
410 Fulton Street
Dover, DE
(302) 736-6554

Christ Episcopal Church
501 S. State Street
Dover, DE
(302) 734-5731

Church of the Living God
506 Mary Street
Dover, DE
(302) 734-4443

**Edgehill Community Church of
   God**
702 Maple Parkway
Dover, DE
(302) 674-5886

First Baptist Church of Dover
301 Walker Road
Dover, DE
(302) 674-1980

First United Pentecostal Church
4462 W. Denneys Road
Dover, DE
(302) 678-3837

Grace Presbyterian Church
350 McKee Road
Dover, DE
(302) 734-8150

Holy Cross Catholic Church
631 S. State Street
Dover, DE
(302) 674-5780

Hope United Methodist Church
12 W. Division Street
Dover, DE
(302) 739-9882

Immanuel Apostolic Church
1406 Forrest Avenue
Dover, DE
(302) 678-2007

Liberty Church
1150 W. State College Road
Dover, DE
(302) 734-3820

Presbyterian Church of Dover
54 S. State Street
Dover, DE
(302) 734-3313

St. Andrew's Lutheran Church
425 N. Dupont Highway
Dover, DE
(302) 736-1617

Wesley United Methodist Church
209 S. State Street
Dover, DE
(302) 678-9966

Medical Centers

Bayhealth Medical Center
640 S. State Street
Dover, DE
(302) 674-4700

Kent General Hospital
640 S. State Street
Dover, DE
(302) 744-7400

Pet Medical Centers

Brenford Animal Hospital PA
4118 N. Dupont Highway
Dover, DE
(302) 678-9418

Delmarva Animal Emergency
Center
1482 E. Lebanon Road
Dover, DE
(302) 697-0850

HOMESTEAD-MIAMI SPEEDWAY

Start | Finish Line

Pit Road

Lake

Garage Area

Lake

Track Information

Inaugural Year: 1995
Owner: ISC
City: Homestead, Florida
Size: 1.5 miles
Banking: 18 to 20 degree variable around track
Grandstand Capacity: 65,000

ADDRESS
Homestead-Miami Speedway
One Speedway Boulevard
Homestead, FL 33035
(305) 230-7223
www.homesteadmiamispeedway
.com

TICKET INFORMATION
Phone: (866) 409-RACE
www.homesteadmiamispeedway
.com

About the Track

Homestead-Miami Speedway was constructed in south Florida in an effort to rebuild after the devastation left behind from Hurricane Andrew. The original track, which opened in 1995, was not quite what everyone had expected of the quad-oval surface. Racing was subpar at best. In 1997, an $8.2 million overhaul turned the track into a traditional continuous oval. In 2003, the track decided to add variable banking, which finally provided the great racing fans are coming back for each year. Homestead-Miami is also the host of the final NASCAR Sprint Cup event. The championship battle usually comes down to the closing laps of this race. This race sells out for that very reason.

Track History

Promotor Ralph Sanchez set out on a mission in August 1993 to build a $70 million speedway. The site for the 1.5-mile oval quickly caught the attention of International Speedway Corporation, who currently owns and operates the track. The track officially opened its doors in November 1995, playing host to a NASCAR Busch Series event. Later came the Cup series and soon after open wheels quickly discovered the beauty and competition of the south Florida track. Homestead-Miami Speedway hosts the final race of the season for the NASCAR Sprint Cup Series, NASCAR Nationwide Series, NASCAR Craftsman Truck Series, and the Indy Racing League.

Track Records

Most Wins: Greg Biffle (3)

Most Top Five Finishes: Mark Martin (4)

Most Lead Changes: 21—most recently on 11/20/2005 (total of 2 times)

Fewest Lead Changes: 12—on 11/17/2002

Most Cautions: 14—on 11/21/2002

Fewest Cautions: 1—on 11/14/1999

Race Record: Tony Stewart— 140.335 mph (2 hours, 51 minutes, 14 seconds) (11/14/1999)

Qualifying Record: Jamie McMurray—184.111 mph (29.816 seconds) (11/14/2003)

Fast Facts

- The first NASCAR Sprint Cup race was run at Homestead-Miami Speedway on November 14, 1999, and was won by Tony Stewart.
- Bill Elliott is the oldest driver to have won at Homestead-Miami Speedway—winning in November 2001, he was forty-six years old (plus one month and three days).
- The Homestead-Miami Speedway has 750 TV monitors on the premises.

- The Homestead-Miami Speedway is considered by many to be one of the most beautiful tracks on the circuit with aqua, purple, and silver among the track colors.
- Truck series driver John Nemechek, Grand Am racer Jeff Clinton, and Indy series regular Paul Dana all suffered fatal injuries at Homestead-Miami Speedway.

Parking

Parking on Homestead-Miami Speedway property is free of charge. The track does not allow overnight parking. All parking is on a first-come, first-served basis. For up-to-date information on parking call the track's main office number at 305-230-7223 or go to www.home steadmiamispeedway.com

Track Rules

According to the track's official website at www.homesteadmiamispeed way.com, the track's rules are as follows:

ITEMS ALLOWED IN THE GRANDSTANDS

- ✓ one soft-sided bag/cooler per person (no larger than 6″ × 6″ × 12″)
- ✓ one clear plastic bag per person (no larger than 18″ × 18″ × 4″, no ice)
- ✓ cameras and video cameras
- ✓ scanners
- ✓ cell phones
- ✓ seat cushions

ITEMS *NOT* ALLOWED IN THE GRANDSTANDS

- ✗ strollers
- ✗ chairs
- ✗ wagons
- ✗ bicycles
- ✗ Rollerblades
- ✗ skateboards
- ✗ pets (unless legally registered aid pets)
- ✗ umbrellas
- ✗ glass containers/bottles of any kind

Special Needs and Services

Handicapped parking is available on a first-come, first-served basis. All fans needing special assistance should purchase tickets prior to arrival. Always ask for parking near your seats. Homestead-Miami allows one companion to accompany the disabled. For ticket information call 305-230-7223 or consult www .homesteadmiamispeedway.com.

INSIDER TIP—If you want the cream of the crop seats at Homestead-Miami check out the Pit Road Box Seats. They are not cheap, but the box seat package is pretty awesome. For more info on these premium seats call the track at 305-230-5232.

Track Tours

Homestead-Miami Speedway does offer track tours to individuals and groups interested in getting an inside look at the track. The track tour includes pit road, Victory Lane, the garage area, and the suites. Tickets for the tour are available at the main ticket office or by calling 305-230-5232. It is wise to book your tour prior to your arrival.

Souvenirs

Official track souvenirs can be purchased in the gift shop, located in the lobby of the Administrative Building near the main entrance to the track. Driver-specific souvenirs are located in Souvenir Alley on the front exterior stretch of the track. On race weekends racing merchandise is also available throughout the facility.

INSIDER TIP— Temporary ATMs are located throughout the facility during race weekends.

About the Area

Fans from all over the United States love to flock to the Miami area in November for the finale weekend of NASCAR's top-three series, but that is not the only reason fans love this south Florida destination. The Miami area offers lots of warm sunshine, great eating, incredible shopping, a lively nightlife scene, awesome hotels, and the beautiful sands of the Atlantic Ocean. Oh, and have I mentioned racing? For many fans November brings cold temperatures back home so heading south for sun, fun, and fast cars is a no-brainer. If you have never visited this track, make a point to do it at least once. Loyal fans make their way back each November due to their newfound love for the track and the area.

CHAMBER OF COMMERCE
The Greater Homestead/Florida
  City Chamber of Commerce
43 N. Krome Avenue
Homestead, FL 33030
(305) 247-2332
www.chamberinaction.com

Transportation

AIRPORT

Miami International Airport (MIA)
4200 NW 21st Street
Miami, FL
(305) 876-7000
(Approximately twenty-five miles
    from the track.)

AIRLINES

American (800) 433-7300
Continental (800) 525-0280
Delta (800) 221-1212
Northwest (800) 225-2525
United (800) 241-6522
US Airways (800) 428-4322

RENTAL CARS

Alamo (800) 327-9633
Avis (800) 331-1212
Budget (800) 527-0700
Dollar (800) 800-4000
Enterprise (800) 325-8007
Hertz (800) 654-3131
National (800) 227-7368
Royal (800) 314-8616
Thrifty (800) 367-2277

Hotels

KEY
🐾 Pet Friendly ≈ Pool
✖ Restaurant

A-1 Budget Motel
30600 S. Dixie Highway
Homestead, FL
(305) 247-7032

Bel Air Motel
1202 N. Krome Avenue
Homestead, FL
(305) 248-2277

≈ Best Western
411 S. Krome Avenue
Florida City, FL
(305) 246-5100

Best Western Gateways
1 Strano Boulevard
Homestead, FL
(305) 247-0079

≈ Budget Host Inn
815 N. Krome Avenue
Florida City, FL
(305) 248-2741

Caribe Motel
841 N. Krome Avenue
Homestead, FL
(305) 247-2442

≈ Comfort Inn
333 SE First Avenue
Florida City, FL
(305) 248-4009

♿, ≈ **Coral Roc Motel**
1100 N. Krome Avenue
Florida City, FL
(305) 246-2888

♿ **Country Lodge**
651 N. Krome Avenue
Florida City, FL
(305) 245-2376

Deluxe Inn Motel
28475 S. Dixie Highway
Homestead, FL
(305) 248-5622

≈ **Econo Lodge**
553 NE First Avenue
Florida City, FL
(305) 248-9300

♿, ≈ **Everglades Motel**
605 S. Krome Avenue
Homestead, FL
(305) 247-4117

≈ **Fairway Inn**
100 U.S. Highway 1
Florida City, FL
(305) 248-4202

♿, ≈ **Floridian Inn of Homestead**
990 N. Homestead Boulevard
Homestead, FL
(305) 247-7020

≈ **Hampton Inn**
124 E. Palm Drive
Florida City, FL
(305) 247-8833

♿, ≈ **Holiday Inn Express**
35200 S. Dixie Highway
Homestead, FL
(305) 247-3414

♿ **Holiday Motel**
1405 N. Krome Avenue
Florida City, FL
(305) 248-8681

Kent Motel
22345 S. Dixie Highway
Miami, FL
(305) 258-2114

≈ **Knights Inn**
1223 NE First Avenue
Florida City, FL
(305) 247-6633

Park Motel
600 S. Krome Avenue
Homestead, FL
(305) 247-6731

♿ **Royal Tern Motel**
26476 S. Dixie Highway
Homestead, FL
(305) 258-3034

≈ **Travelodge**
409 SE First Avenue
Florida City, FL
(305) 248-9777

Camping

ON-SITE AND TRACK-OWNED CAMPING

Homestead-Miami Speedway allows only self-contained vehicles on the track proper. All sites will be assigned at arrival. Make note that all who choose to camp will have to purchase a minimum of two race tickets in order to be allowed to camp on track premises. For more info on camping at Homestead call the track at 305-230-7223 or check www .homesteadmiamispeedway.com.

Palm Drive This reserved area offers security, water and dump station, and portal restrooms. Septic is additional.

OFF-SITE CAMPING

Camper Site & RV Park
601 NW Third Avenue
Florida City, FL
(305) 248-7889

Everglades National Park
40001 State Road 9336
Homestead, FL
(305) 242-7700

Homestead Trailer Park
31 SE Second Road
Homestead, FL
(305) 247-4021

Larry & Penny Thompson Park
12451 SW 184th Street
Miami, FL
(305) 232-1049

Miami Everglades Campground
20675 SW 162nd Avenue
Miami, FL
(305) 233-5300

Pine Isle Mobile Home Park
28600 SW 132nd Avenue
Homestead, FL
(305) 248-0783

Restaurants

KEY
🍔 Fast Food   🪑 Sit Down
🥡 Takeout   ☎ Reservations

Must Eats

The Fish House
102401 Overseas Highway
Key Largo, FL
(305) 451-4665

This is by far the best fish house on the NASCAR Sprint Cup circuit. The fish is as fresh as it comes. You would swear their chef runs out back to catch your fish once you order. It melts in your mouth!

Mutineer Restaurant
11 SE First Avenue
Florida City, FL
(305) 245-3377
You will think you are ship-wrecked when you walk into this family-style restaurant. The pirates serve up really great seafood in a fun shiplike atmosphere.

Big Daddy's Pizza
13376 SW 288th Street
Homestead, FL
(305) 247-1600

Broadway Street Deli
2022 NE Eighth Street
Homestead, FL
(305) 245-7266

Burger King
30390 S. Dixie Highway
Homestead, FL
(305) 247-7181

Canton Chinese Restaurant
1657 NE Eighth Street
Homestead, FL
(305) 248-9956

Chili's
2220 NE Eighth Street
Homestead, FL
(786) 243-8902

Domino's Pizza
1615 NE Eighth Street
Homestead, FL
(305) 246-3030

El Rancho Viejo
29363 SW 152nd Avenue
Homestead, FL
(305) 242-0599

Galindo's Cafe
1330 N. Flagler Avenue
Homestead, FL
(305) 242-4449

Happy House
28708 S. Dixie Highway
Homestead, FL
(305) 248-6639

Ka Chin Chinese Restaurant
45 N. Homestead Boulevard
Homestead, FL
(305) 246-0108

Kentucky Fried Chicken
30010 S. Dixie Highway
Homestead, FL
(305) 247-1590

☎ Key West Grill
250 E. Palm Drive
Florida City, FL
(305) 247-1551

🍴 La Isla Borinquen Cafe
1541 SE 12th Avenue
Homestead, FL
(305) 248-7177

🍴 Latin Garden Cafe & Market
2086 NE Eighth Street
Homestead, FL
(305) 246-1464

🍴 Latin House Cafe
1871 NE Eighth Street
Homestead, FL
(786) 243-8818

🍴 La Union Restaurant
1530 NE Eighth Street
Homestead, FL
(305) 242-1376

🍕 Little Caesars Pizza
29625 S. Dixie Highway
Homestead, FL
(305) 245-6006

☎ Mario's Latin Cafe
1020 N. Homestead Boulevard
Homestead, Fl
(305) 247-2470

🍔 McDonald's
30335 S. Dixie Highway
Homestead, FL
(305) 247-6484

🍴 Nikko Japanese Restaurant
827 N. Homestead Boulevard
Homestead, FL
(305) 242-8772

🍕 Papa John's Pizza
829 N. Homestead Boulevard
Homestead, FL
(305) 247-6757

🍴 Peking House Restaurant
899 N. Homestead Boulevard
Homestead, FL
(305) 248-2270

☎ Pericos
1661 NE Eighth Street
Homestead, FL
(305) 245-0001

🍕 Pizza Hut
28640 S. Dixie Highway
Homestead, FL
(305) 247-6100

🍴 Pollo Tropical
915 N. Homestead Boulevard
Homestead, FL
(305) 245-0410

Quiznos Sub
698 N. Homestead Boulevard,
  Unit 101
Homestead, FL
(305) 247-6772

Roman Noble Pizza
13695 SW 288th Street
Homestead, FL
(305) 247-3663

Ruberto's Pizza & Deli
12783 SW 280th Street
Homestead, FL
(305) 258-1460

Ruby Tuesday
801 NE Eighth Street
Homestead, FL
(305) 245-2292

Subway Sandwiches & Salads
3090 NE 41st Terrace
Homestead, FL
(305) 247-1905

Taco Bell
987 N. Homestead Boulevard
Homestead, FL
(305) 242-1159

Wendy's
30130 S. Dixie Highway
Homestead, FL
(305) 248-6996

Local Attractions

WORTH THE TRIP

There are many fun things to do while visiting the Homestead-Miami area, but don't forget the beautiful south Florida beaches. While most places in the United States are battling frigid temperatures in November, south Florida almost always delivers perfect temps and weather conditions for a relaxing day of sand, sun, and ocean waves.

Biscayne National Park
9700 SW 328th Street
Homestead, FL
(305) 230-1144

Everglades Safari Park
26700 SW Eighth Street
Miami, FL
(305) 226-6923

Gold Coast Railroad Museum
12450 SW 152nd Street
Miami, FL
(305) 253-4675

Homestead Bayfront Park
9698 SW 328th Street
Homestead, FL
(305) 230-3034

Miami Art Central
5960 SW 57th Avenue
Miami, FL
(305) 455-3333

Modello Park
28450 SW 152nd Avenue
Homestead, FL
(305) 247-1553

Palmetto Golf Course
9300 SW 152nd Street
Palmetto Bay, FL
(305) 235-1069

Parrot Jungle
14475 SW 264th Street
Homestead, FL
(305) 258-6453

Pioneer Museum
826 N. Krome Avenue
Florida City, FL
(305) 246-9531

Skylift Holding LLC
1109 Ponce De Leon Boulevard
Coral Gables, FL
(305) 444-0422

Wings over Miami Museum
14710 SW 128th Street
Miami, FL
(305) 233-5197

World Chess Hall of Fame
13755 SW 119th Avenue
Miami, FL
(786) 242-4255

Shopping

KEY
🚗 Automotive $ Discount
⊕ Pharmacy   🏬 Mall
☆ Specialty   ⛫ Department Store

🏬 **Avocado Shopping Center**
29601 SW 162nd Avenue
Homestead, FL
(786) 243-9204

$ **Bealls Outlet**
250 E. Palm Drive, Suite 135
Florida City, FL
(786) 243-0174

$ **Big Lots**
120 NE Eighth Street
Homestead, FL
(786) 243-3992

$ **BJ's Wholesale Club**
10425 Marlin Road
Cutler Bay, FL
(305) 254-8444

🏬 **Cutler Ridge Mall**
20505 S. Dixie Highway
Cutler Bay, FL
(305) 235-8562

🛍 **Cauley Square Shops**
22400 Old Dixie Highway
Miami, FL
(305) 258-3543

$ **Dollar Savings**
27321 S. Dixie Highway
Homestead, FL
(305) 242-2030

$ **Dollar Tree**
907 N. Homestead Boulevard
Homestead, FL
(305) 245-1110

$ **Family Dollar Store**
30378 Old Dixie Highway
Homestead, FL
(305) 248-4309

👕 **JC Penney**
20505 S. Dixie Highway
Cutler Bay, FL
(305) 252-9836

$ **Kmart**
20505 S. Dixie Highway
Cutler Bay, FL
(305) 254-0455

👕 **Macy's**
20507 S. Dixie Highway
Cutler Bay, FL
(305) 252-5311

$ **Marshalls**
1099 N. Homestead Boulevard
Homestead, FL
(305) 248-2144

🛍 **Naranja Shopping Center**
25001 SW 127th Avenue
Homestead, FL
(305) 258-1996

$ **Prime Outlets at Florida City**
250 E. Palm Drive
Florida City, FL
(305) 248-4727

$ **Ross Dress For Less**
20505 S. Dixie Highway
Cutler Bay, FL
(305) 252-0957

👕 **Sears**
20701 SW 112th Avenue
Cutler Bay, FL
(305) 378-5195

🛍 **Southland Mall**
20505 S. Dixie Highway
Cutler Bay, FL
(305) 235-8880

$ **Target**
20500 SW 112th Avenue
Cutler Bay, FL
(305) 235-0839

$ Wal-Mart Supercenter
33501 S. Dixie Highway
Homestead, FL
(305) 242-4447

Churches/
Worship Centers

Apostolic Assembly
16100 SW 296th Street
Homestead, FL
(305) 242-9707

Christian Family Worship Center
27500 Old Dixie Highway
Homestead, FL
(305) 248-9598

Church of Jesus Christ of Latter-
   Day Saints
29600 SW 167th Avenue
Homestead, FL
(305) 246-2986

Eastside Baptist Church
1541 SE 12th Avenue
Homestead, FL
(786) 243-3399

First Christian Church
1001 NE 15th Street
Homestead, FL
(305) 247-3849

First Church of Christ Science
225 SE Fourth Street
Homestead, FL
(305) 247-6322

First United Methodist Church
622 N. Krome Avenue
Homestead, FL
(305) 248-4770

Gateway Church of Christ
1800 E. Mowry Drive
Homestead, FL
(305) 245-7171

Homestead Assembly Christian
1100 Old Dixie Highway
Homestead, FL
(305) 247-0340

Homestead Mennonite Church
30695 SW 162nd Avenue
Homestead, FL
(305) 248-1659

Life Pointe Church
1100 Old Dixie Highway
Homestead, FL
(305) 247-0889

New Hope Assembly of God
29351 SW 169th Avenue
Homestead, FL
(305) 248-1536

St. John's Episcopal Church
145 NE Tenth Street
Homestead, FL
(305) 247-5343

**St. Martin De Porres Catholic
Church**
14881 SW 288th Street
Homestead, FL
(305) 248-5355

Seventh-Day Adventist Church
1117 NE First Terrace
Homestead, FL
(305) 248-3443

Shalom Foursquare Gospel Center
28610 SW 152nd Avenue
Homestead, FL
(305) 247-1222

South Dade Baptist Church
17105 SW 296th Street
Homestead, FL
(305) 247-3516

Medical Centers

Baptist Hospital of Miami
8950 N. Kendall Drive
Miami, FL
(786) 573-6000

Homestead Hospital
160 NW 13th Street
Homestead, FL
(786) 243-8000

**Jackson South Community
Hospital**
9333 SW 152nd Street
Palmetto Bay, FL
(305) 256-5309

Pet Medical Centers

Gilley Animal Clinic
27008 S. Dixie Highway
Homestead, FL
(305) 247-1777

Homestead Animal Hospital
1250 N. Flagler Avenue
Homestead, FL
(305) 247-3845

Veterinary Specialists
91 NE Sixth Street
Homestead, FL
(305) 246-1701

INDIANAPOLIS MOTOR SPEEDWAY

Track Information

Inaugural Year: 1994
Owner: The Hulman-George Family
City: Indianapolis, Indiana
Size: 2.5 miles
Banking: 9 degrees
Grandstand Capacity: 250,000

ADDRESS
Indianapolis Motor Speedway
4790 W. 16th Street
Indianapolis, IN 46222
(317) 492-6784

www.indianapolismotorspeedway
.com

TICKET INFORMATION
Phone: (800) 822-4639
www.indianapolismotorspeedway
.com

About the Track

Indy is the oldest nondirt track in the United States. The original surface was made of 3.2 million bricks and was built in 1909. The track today does not have a brick racing surface but it is still referred to as the "Brickyard." Even though the track is the oldest, it took until 1994 to get into NASCAR's top series. Many fans will tell you that racing stock cars is not the best on the flat 2.5-mile track, but the competitors don't seem to mind. Winning at the Brickyard is one of the most coveted trophies. When a driver wins at Indy, he and his team kiss a three-foot line of bricks (made from the original bricks) strategically positioned at the start-finish line.

Track History

The groundbreaking and construction of the $3 million original track surface project only took five months. The first event took place on August 14, 1909, but it was not cars that were the first to race on the newly constructed track; it was motorcycles. The first car racing took place soon after on August 19, 1909. Due to the instability of the original track surface of crushed stone and tar, the races were halted after accidents on the track led to five fatalities in three days. It was at this time the brick surface was laid to ensure safer racing for competitors. Carl G. Fisher, a former racer and an auto parts and highway pioneer, led the way to bring in the 3.2 million bricks to cover the ragged racing sur-

face. The speedway reopened in 1910 with a car count of sixty-six cars and thankfully no fatalities. The bricks had done their job. The first Indy 500 took place in May 1911 with an estimated crowd of eighty thousand people, all of whom paid a dollar entrance fee. In 1961, the final remaining area of brick racing surface was covered with asphalt, which is what the surface is made of today.

Track Records

Most Wins: Jeff Gordon (4)
Most Top Five Finishes: Jeff Gordon (7)
Most Lead Changes: 21—8/6/1994
Fewest Lead Changes: 9—most recently on 8/8/2004 (total of 2 times)
Most Cautions: 13—on 8/8/2004
Fewest Cautions: 1—on 8/5/1995
Race Record: Bobby Labonte— 155.912 mph (2 hours, 33 minutes, 56 seconds) (8/5/2000)
Qualifying Record: Casey Mears—186.293 mph (48.311 seconds) (8/7/2004)

Fast Facts

- The first NASCAR Sprint Cup race was run at Indianapolis Motor Speedway (IMS) on August 6, 1994, and was won by Jeff Gordon.
- Bill Elliott is the oldest driver to have won at Indianapolis Motor Speedway—winning in August 2002, he was forty-six years old (plus nine months and twenty-seven days).
- Of the original paving bricks first placed on the track, only the famous "yard of bricks" is still exposed at the start-finish line as a nostalgic reminder of the past.
- The most cars to complete the full distance of the Allstate 400 is thirty-five (in 2006). The fewest number of cars to complete the full distance of the Allstate 400 is fourteen (in 2000).
- In September 1991, A. J. Foyt filmed a commercial for Sears Craftsman tools at the Indianapolis Motor Speedway. While they were filming in the garage area, Foyt and speedway president Tony George decided to take Foyt's NASCAR Winston Cup car for a few laps around the track. This made Foyt the first driver to drive a NASCAR stock car around the Indianapolis Motor Speedway. Tony George ended up taking a few laps around the track himself that same day.
- In 1996, when Dale Jarrett won at Indy, he began the tradition of the winning driver and crew kissing the bricks at the start-finish line of IMS. This "new" tradition has now even moved over to the Indianapolis 500.
- The Indianapolis Motor Speedway is often referred to as the Brickyard and considered by many to be the "racing capital of the world." Others refer to the Indy 500 as the "greatest spectacle in racing."
- In 1975, the Indianapolis Motor Speedway was placed on the register of historic places and was designated a National Historic Landmark in 1987, making Indy the only motorsports facility to hold this honor.
- Indy played host of the opening ceremonies for the 1987 Pan American Games.
- The track was closed during World War I for the use of a military hub for repairs.
- From 1931 to 1935 there were fifteen fatalities on the track.

Parking

The Indianapolis Motor Speedway has ample parking for race fans, some of which is free while other areas have a fee attached. The track does not allow overnight parking for motorcycles or cars. All parking is on a first-come, first-served basis. For up-to-date information on parking at Indy, call the track at 317-492-6700 or go to www.indianapolis motorspeedway.com.

Track Rules

According to the track's official website at www.indianapolismotor speedway.com, the track's rules are as follows:

ITEMS ALLOWED IN THE GRANDSTANDS
- ✓ small backpacks
- ✓ hard- or soft-sided coolers (no larger than 14″ × 14″ × 14″)
- ✓ purses, backpacks, and other bags (not to exceed 14″ × 14″ × 14″)
- ✓ food and beverages (no glass containers)
- ✓ binoculars
- ✓ scanners
- ✓ cameras
- ✓ umbrellas

ITEMS *NOT* ALLOWED IN THE GRANDSTANDS
- ✗ glass containers
- ✗ weapons
- ✗ firearms
- ✗ fireworks and flares
- ✗ animals or pets (other than Seeing Eye dogs)
- ✗ strollers
- ✗ folding chairs or lawn chairs
- ✗ Rollerblades
- ✗ skateboards
- ✗ skates
- ✗ scooters
- ✗ bicycles, golf carts, or mopeds

Special Needs and Services

Indianapolis Motor Speedway does provide seating and parking for guests who have special needs or are in need of special services. For up-to-date information concerning special needs and services call the track prior to your arrival at 317-492-6700 and request a special services representative. Always ask to have your parking near your seats. Indy does allow one companion to accompany the special needs guest.

Track Tours

The track does give scheduled track tours upon request. The tour includes the garage area, pit road, infield, and the famous three-foot strip of bricks located at the start-finish line. Call the track at 317-492-6700 to arrange a tour. All tours must be scheduled and confirmed prior to arrival. Individual and group tours are allowed.

Souvenirs

Sovenirs for the Indianapolis Motor Speedway can be purchased at its online store at www.indianapolismotor speedway.com. The track always has numerous stand-alone souvenir stands scattered around the track on race weekend. The driver-specific merchandise trailers are available on Souvenir Alley located near the main front entrance of the track.

About the Area

Indianapolis is known for its motorsports roots and you can see it everywhere you look. This is definitely racing country, not to be confused with stock car country. In fact, it is the open wheel cars that really rule the roost in this midwestern town. The Cup boys have rolled in to town once a year since 1994, but it is the open wheels who have reigned over this turf for years on end. Many Cup racers like Tony Stewart, Robby Gordon, and Jeff Gordon have called this area home at some point in their lives.

Tony Stewart recently moved back to the Midwest to be close to where he grew up, which is only a hop, skip, and a jump from the Brickyard. Racing just about anywhere in late July is hot and humid, and this race is no exception. If you are planning a trip to the Allstate 400 at the Brickyard, expect extremely warm temperatures. Bring the sunscreen, shades, and a hat.

CHAMBER OF COMMERCE

Greater Indianapolis Chamber of
  Commerce
Chase Tower
111 Monument Circle, Suite 1950
Indianapolis, IN 46204
(317) 464-2200
www.indychamber.com

Transportation

AIRPORT

Indianapolis International Airport
  (IND)
2500 S. High School Road
Indianapolis, IN
(317) 487-5151
(Approximately four miles from the
  track.)

AIRLINES

Air Tran (800) 247-8726
American Airlines/American Eagle
  (800) 433-7300

Continental/Continental Express
   (800) 523-3273
Delta/Delta Connection
   (800) 221-1212
Frontier (800) 432-1359
Midwest Connect (800) 452-2022
Northwest Airlines/KLM Royal
   Dutch Airlines (800) 225-2525
Southwest Airlines (800) 435-9792
United/United Express
   (800) 864-8331
US Airways/US Airways Express/
   America West (800) 428-4322

RENTAL CARS
Alamo (800) 327-9633
Avis (800) 230-4898
Budget (800) 527-0700
Dollar (800) 800-3665
Enterprise (800) 736-8222
Hertz (800) 654-3131
National (800) 227-7368
Thrifty (800) 847-4389

Hotels

KEY
🐾 Pet Friendly
≈ Pool   ✕ Restaurant

🐾, ✕ **Adam's Mark Hotels &
   Resorts**
2544 Executive Drive
Indianapolis, IN
(317) 248-2481

American Inn West
5630 Crawfordsville Road
Indianapolis, IN
(317) 248-1471

🐾 **Best Western Airport Suites**
55 S. High School Road
Indianapolis, IN
(317) 246-1505

🐾, ✕ **Brickyard Crossing Resort**
4400 W. 16th Street
Indianapolis, IN
(317) 241-2500

🐾, ≈ **Budget Inn and Fantasy
   Suites**
2602 N. High School Road
Indianapolis, IN
(317) 291-8800

🐾, ≈ **Candlewood Suites**
5250 W. Bradbury Avenue
Indianapolis, IN
(317) 241-9595

🐾, ≈ **Clarion Hotel Waterfront
   Plaza**
2930 Waterfront Parkway W. Drive
Indianapolis, IN
(317) 299-8400

≈ **Comfort Inn**
5855 Rockville Road
Indianapolis, IN
(317) 487-9800

&, ✗ **Courtyard by Marriott—
Downtown**
501 W. Washington Street
Indianapolis, IN
(317) 635-4443

≈ **Days Inn—Speedway**
3740 N. High School Road
Indianapolis, IN
(317) 293-6550

& **Dollar Inn**
6331 Crawfordsville Road
Indianapolis, IN
(317) 248-8500

& **Dollar Inn Airport**
6231 W. Washington Street
Indianapolis, IN
(317) 486-1100

≈ **Fairfield Inn and Suites—
Airport**
5220 W. Southern Avenue
Indianapolis, IN
(317) 244-1600

≈ **Hyatt Suites**
5500 W. Bradbury Avenue
Indianapolis, IN
(317) 227-0950

&, ≈ **Jameson Inn**
3850 Eagle View Drive
Indianapolis, IN
(317) 299-6165

&, ≈ **La Quinta Inn—Airport**
5316 W. Southern Avenue
Indianapolis, IN
(317) 247-4281

& **Lees Inn Indianapolis**
5011 N. Lafayette Road
Indianapolis, IN
(317) 297-8880

Mayfair Motel
2040 Lafayette Road
Indianapolis, IN
(317) 634-5940

&, ≈ **Motel 6**
6330 Debonair Lane
Speedway, IN
(317) 293-3220

&, ≈ **Motel 6**
5241 W. Bradbury Avenue
Indianapolis, IN
(317) 248-1231

&, ≈, ✗ **Ramada Limited—West**
3851 Shore Drive
Indianapolis, IN
(317) 297-1848

& **Red Roof Inn—Indianapolis
Speedway**
6415 Debonair Lane
Indianapolis, IN
(317) 293-6881

⌒, ≈ **Residence Inn—Airport**
5224 W. Southern Avenue
Indianapolis, IN
(317) 244-1500

⌒, ≈ **Residence Inn—Downtown
    on the Canal**
350 W. New York Street
Indianapolis, IN
(317) 822-0840

Sleep Inn
5845 Rockville Road
Indianapolis, IN
(317) 247-4100

⌒ **Travelodge**
4630 Lafayette Road
Indianapolis, IN
(317) 293-9060

University Place Conference
850 W. Michigan Street
Indianapolis, IN
(317) 269-9000

⌒, ≈ **Wingate Inn Airport**
5797 Rockville Road
Indianapolis, IN
(317) 243-8310

Camping

ON-SITE AND TRACK-OWNED CAMPING

Indianapolis Motor Speedway offers a variety of camping options ranging in prices. For an up-to-date list of on-site camping options contact the track at 317-492-6700 or go to www.indianapolismotorspeedway .com. It is best to call prior to arrival for any updated info. Always request the list of rules for the specific area you choose to camp in, as many rules are lot specific.

Lots 1-A, 1-C, 2, and 3 This grass surface area is for tent and RV parking. This is a dry camping area with no amenities.

Lot 3-P This asphalt surface area is for RVs only. This is a dry camping area with no amenities.

Lot 4 This grass surface camping area is for RV and tent camping. No amenities.

Lot 4-P This "premium" camping area is on a crushed stone surface and is for RV camping only. No amenities.

Lot 6 This grass surface camping area is for RVs only. No amenities.

OFF-SITE CAMPING

Indiana State Fairgrounds
1202 E. 38th Street
Indianapolis, IN
(317) 927-7500

KOA Indianapolis Northeast
5896 W. 200 North
Greenfield, IN
(317) 894-1397

Lake Haven Retreat
1951 W. Edgewood Avenue
Indianapolis, IN
(317) 807-2267

Raceview Family Campground
9801 E. County Road 300 North
Indianapolis, IN
(317) 852-5115

3-Point Lake Campgrounds
902 E. Bunker Hill Road
Mooresville, IN
(317) 831-5120

Restaurants

KEY

🍔 Fast Food   🍗 Sit Down
🛍 Takeout   🍷 Reservations

Must Eats

Slippery Noodle
372 S. Meridian
Indianapolis, IN
(317) 631-6974
   The food is good but the music is better. Live blues each night in this intimate setting.

St. Elmo Steakhouse
127 S. Illinois Street
Indianapolis, IN
(317) 635-0636
   Reservations are a must on race weekend. The steaks are to die for and you might just see your favorite driver here. This is a must stop on the circuit for drivers and crews.

🍗 **Applebee's**
5664 Crawfordsville Road
Indianapolis, IN
(317) 247-8222

🍔 **Arby's**
5950 Crawfordsville Road
Indianapolis, IN
(317) 240-3605

🍗 **Brickyard Crossing Resort**
4400 W. 16th Street
Indianapolis, IN
(317) 241-2500

🍔 **Burger King**
3401 W. 16th Street
Indianapolis, IN
(317) 637-6665

🛍 **Butler's Pizza**
3347 W. Tenth Street
Indianapolis, IN
(317) 687-8658

🍱 **Canton Express Chinese Restaurant**
5945 Crawfordsville Road, Suite G
Indianapolis, IN
(317) 240-3309

🪑 **Cattie's Corner**
1002 Main Street
Indianapolis, IN
(317) 244-7329

🪑 **Charlie Brown's Pancake & Steak House**
1038 Main Street
Indianapolis, IN
(317) 243-2502

🍱 **China Wok**
5317 W. Tenth Street
Indianapolis, IN
(317) 248-9990

🍔 **Church's Chicken**
4850 W. 16th Street
Indianapolis, IN
(317) 248-9151

🍱 **Domino's Pizza**
4545 Rockville Road
Indianapolis, IN
(317) 240-3030

🍱 **Donatos Pizza**
5620 Crawfordsville Road, Suite AA
Indianapolis, IN
(317) 487-2880

🍱 **Einstein Bros. Bagels**
5999 Crawfordsville Road
Indianapolis, IN
(317) 481-9888

🪑 **Grindstone Charley's**
5822 Crawfordsville Road
Indianapolis, IN
(317) 481-1870

🪑 **Hook Fish & Chicken**
3106 W. 16th Street
Indianapolis, IN
(317) 423-0588

🍱 **Junkyard Dogs**
5240 W. 16th Street
Indianapolis, IN
(317) 481-0838

🪑 **King Ribs Bar-B-Q**
3145 W. 16th Street
Indianapolis, IN
(317) 488-0223

🪑 **Kin's Restaurant**
2802 Lafayette Road
Indianapolis, IN
(317) 283-8881

🍔 **Long John Silver's**
3350 W. 16th Street
Indianapolis, IN
(317) 632-2324

🪑 **Marble's Southern Cookery**
2310 Lafayette Road
Indianapolis, IN
(317) 687-0631

🍟 **Marco's Pizza**
5391 Rockville Road
Indianapolis, IN
(317) 472-3900

🪑 **Maria Lombardo Mexican Restaurant**
5250 W. Tenth Street
Indianapolis, IN
(317) 481-0818

🍔 **McDonald's**
3435 W. 16th Street
Indianapolis, IN
(317) 632-3863

🪑 **MCL Cafeteria**
6002 Crawfordsville Road
Indianapolis, IN
(317) 241-9497

🍟 **Merritts Pizza**
5250 W. 16th Street
Indianapolis, IN
(317) 246-7000

🪑 **Mug 'n' Bun Chicken & Pizza**
5211 W. 10th Street
Speedway, IN
(317) 247-9186

🪑 **Nick's Chili Parlor**
2621 Lafayette Road
Indianapolis, IN
(317) 924-5005

🍟 **Number One Chinese Restaurant**
5808 Crawfordsville Road
Indianapolis, IN
(317) 487-9888

🍟 **Papa Murphy's Take 'n' Bake**
5945 Crawfordsville Road
Indianapolis, IN
(317) 244-7272

🍟 **Pasquale's Pizza & Carry Out**
3623 W. 16th Street
Indianapolis, IN
(317) 632-4331

🍟 **Peking**
835 Beachway Drive
Indianapolis, IN
(317) 390-1882

🍟 **Penn Station East Coast Subs**
835 Beachway Drive, Suite 100
Indianapolis, IN
(317) 243-7366

🍟 **Pizza Hut**
5570 Crawfordsville Road
Speedway, IN
(317) 247-6649

Quiznos Sub
5841 Crawfordsville Road
Indianapolis, IN
(317) 481-8570

Rally's Hamburgers
3124 W. 16th Street
Indianapolis, IN
(317) 636-3814

Ruben's Cue
2440 Lafayette Road, Suite 3
Indianapolis, IN
(317) 423-7001

Sandango's
3336 W. Tenth Street
Indianapolis, IN
(317) 972-4470

Sino Buffet
5698 Crawfordsville Road
Indianapolis, IN
(317) 243-0088

Subway Sandwiches & Salads
5682 Crawfordsville Road
Indianapolis, IN
(317) 244-7827

Super China Buffet
5389 Rockville Road
Indianapolis, IN
(317) 243-9638

Super Jumbo Restaurant
2340 Lafayette Road
Indianapolis, IN
(317) 916-0379

Taco Bell
3502 W. 16th Street
Indianapolis, IN
(317) 631-4604

Tortilleria Angelita
5242 Rockville Road
Indianapolis, IN
(317) 248-9771

Wendy's
6025 W. Tenth Street
Indianapolis, IN
(317) 240-0857

White Castle
3367 W. Tenth Street
Indianapolis, IN
(317) 685-1697

Local Attractions

At the top of my list of things to do while catching a race at Indy is touring the **Indianapolis Motor Speedway Hall of Fame Museum.** The history of this track alone is worth the ticket price. Many of the exhibits are centered around open wheel racing, but you will get your fill of NASCAR's greatest moments at the track as well.

Brickyard Crossing Golf Course
4400 W. 16th Street
Indianapolis, IN
(317) 492-6572

**The Children's Museum of
   Indianapolis**
3000 N. Meridian Street
Indianapolis, IN
(317) 334-3322

Colonel Eli Lilly Civil War Museum
4790 W. 16th Street
Indianapolis, IN
(317) 232-7615

**Eiteljorg Museum of American
   Indians and Western Art**
500 W. Washington Street
Indianapolis, IN
(317) 636-9378

Hook's Discovery & Learning
3200 Cold Spring Road
Indianapolis, IN
(317) 951-2222

Indian War Memorial
431 N. Meridian Street
Indianapolis, IN
(317) 232-7615

Indiana State Museum
650 W. Washington Street
Indianapolis, IN
(317) 232-1637

**Indianapolis Motor Speedway Hall
   of Fame Museum**
4790 W. 16th Street
Indianapolis, IN
(317) 492-6747

Indianapolis Museum of Art
4000 Michigan Road
Indianapolis, IN
(317) 920-2659

Indianapolis Zoo
1200 W. Washington Street
Indianapolis, IN
(317) 630-2001

National Art Museum of Sport
850 W. Michigan Street
Indianapolis, IN
(317) 274-3627

White River State Park
801 W. Washington Street
Indianapolis, IN
(317) 233-2434

Shopping

KEY
🚗 Automotive $ Discount
⊕ Pharmacy   🛍 Mall
☆ Specialty   ⌂ Department Store

$ Big Lots
4711 W. 30th Street
Indianapolis, IN
(317) 299-6217

☆ **Body Gear**
2816 E. 38th Street
Indianapolis, IN
(317) 377-1760

$ **Family Dollar Store**
5397 Rockville Road
Indianapolis, IN
(317) 244-0812

☆ **Burlington Coat Factory**
3919 Lafayette Road
Indianapolis, IN
(317) 328-0376

☆ **Gap**
714 N. Senate Avenue
Indianapolis, IN
(317) 917-7919

🛍 **Circle Center Mall**
49 W. Maryland Street
Indianapolis, IN
(317) 681-8000

🛍 **Glendale Mall**
6101 N. Keystone Avenue
Indianapolis, IN
(317) 251-9281

$ **Dollar General**
2310 Cunningham Road
Indianapolis, IN
(317) 244-2160

$ **Kmart**
6780 W. Washington Street
Indianapolis, IN
(317) 247-4771

$ **Dollar Tree**
5926 Crawfordsville Road
Indianapolis, IN
(317) 487-2977

👕 **Kohl's Department Store**
5660 Crawfordsville Road
Indianapolis, IN
(317) 244-7666

☆ **Eddie Bauer**
49 W. Maryland Street, Suite F12
Indianapolis, IN
(317) 632-4441

🛍 **Lafayette Square**
3919 Lafayette Road
Indianapolis, IN
(317) 291-6390

$ **Factory Card Outlet**
10397 E. U.S. Highway 36
Avon, IN
(317) 209-1008

👕 **Macy's**
3919 Lafayette Road, Suite 756
Indianapolis, IN
(317) 293-8330

$ **Marshalls**
5120 W. 38th Street
Indianapolis, IN
(317) 297-1025

☆ **Rainbow**
2802 Lafayette Road, Suite 810
Indianapolis, IN
(317) 931-9326

⊓ **Nordstrom**
130 S. Meridian Street
Indianapolis, IN
(317) 636-2121

$ **Sam's Club**
5805 Rockville Road
Indianapolis, IN
(317) 248-3577

☆ **Once Upon a Child**
130 S. Girls School Road
Indianapolis, IN
(317) 273-8622

⊓ **Sears**
6022 Crawfordsville Road
Indianapolis, IN
(317) 248-2445

⊓ **Parisian**
1 W. Washington Street
Indianapolis, IN
(317) 971-6200

🏬 **Southern Plaza Shopping Center**
4200 S. East Street
Indianapolis, IN
(317) 791-0420

☆ **Park Avenue Fashion**
3723 Commercial Drive
Indianapolis, IN
(317) 388-0688

☆ **Talbots**
49 W. Maryland Street, Suite 209
Indianapolis, IN
(317) 636-6044

☆ **Pier 1 Imports**
4150 Lafayette Road, Suite A
Indianapolis, IN
(317) 293-5777

$ **Target**
6925 W. 38th Street
Indianapolis, IN
(317) 329-1034

☆ **Plato's Closet**
8238 Rockville Road
Indianapolis, IN
(317) 271-1234

$ **T. J. Maxx**
50 N. Illinois Street
Indianapolis, IN
(317) 972-0273

$ Value City Department Store
5110 W. Pike Plaza Road
Indianapolis, IN
(317) 297-6625

$ Wal-Mart Supercenter
9500 E. U.S. Highway 36
Avon, IN
(317) 209-0857

Churches/
Worship Centers

Church of Christ—Speedway
4956 W. Tenth Street
Indianapolis, IN
(317) 243-8040

Community Fellowship Church
2150 Lafayette Road
Indianapolis, IN
(317) 637-2000

El Shaddia Apostolic Assembly
940 N. Tibbs Avenue
Indianapolis, IN
(317) 822-3516

Fairfax Christian Church
602 N. Berwick Avenue
Indianapolis, IN
(317) 632-2914

First Assembly of God
435 N. Lynhurst Drive
Indianapolis, IN
(317) 241-8884

Freedom Missionary Baptist Church
350 N. Fuller Drive
Indianapolis, IN
(317) 243-2764

Heavenly Life Church
4150 W. Michigan Street
Indianapolis, IN
(317) 484-2381

Holy Trinity Catholic Church
2618 W. Saint Clair Street
Indianapolis, IN
(317) 631-2939

St. Andrew Presbyterian Church
3535 Kessler Boulevard North Drive
Indianapolis, IN
(317) 925-2815

St. Andrew's Lutheran Church
6118 Crawfordsville Road
Indianapolis, IN
(317) 243-6684

St. Christopher Catholic Church
5301 W. 16th Street
Indianapolis, IN
(317) 241-6314

St. John's Episcopal Church
5625 W. 30th Street
Indianapolis, IN
(317) 293-0372

St. Luke's United Church of Christ
5360 W. 16th Street
Indianapolis, IN
(317) 241-5647

Speedway Christian Church
5110 W. 14th Street
Indianapolis, IN
(317) 244-7656

Speedway Church of Nazarene
5020 Crawfordsville Road
Speedway, IN
(317) 244-0142

**Speedway United Methodist
  Church**
5065 W. 16th Street
Indianapolis, IN
(317) 241-1563

Truth Apostolic Church
2051 N. Luett Avenue
Indianapolis, IN
(317) 263-6003

Wesleyan Holiness Church
3817 Rockville Road
Indianapolis, IN
(317) 241-3175

Medical Centers

Indiana University Hospital
550 University Boulevard
Indianapolis, IN
(317) 274-5000

Larue D. Carter Memorial Hospital
2601 Cold Spring Road
Indianapolis, IN
(317) 941-4000

Methodist Hospital
1701 N. Senate Boulevard
Indianapolis, IN
(317) 962-2000

Riley Hospital for Children
702 Barnhill Drive
Indianapolis, IN
(317) 274-5000

St. Vincent Hospital
3400 Lafayette Road
Indianapolis, IN
(317) 338-2345

Westview Hospital
3630 Guion Road
Indianapolis, IN
(317) 920-8439

Wishard Memorial Hospital
2732 W. Michigan Street
Indianapolis, IN
(317) 554-4601

Pet Medical Centers

Airport Animal Emergency Center
5235 W. Washington Street
Indianapolis, IN
(317) 248-0832

Noah's All Pet Veterinary Hospital
3825 W. Washington Street
Indianapolis, IN
(317) 481-1738

INFINEON RACEWAY

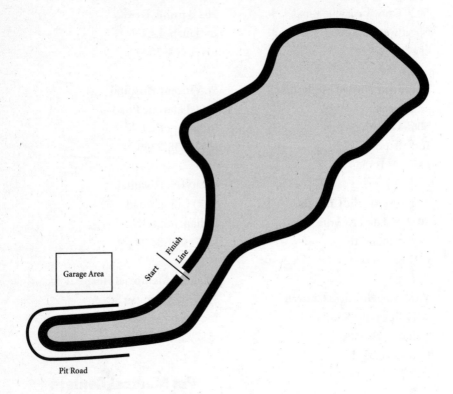

Track Information

Inaugural Year: 1989
Owner: SMI
City: Sonoma, California
Size: 1.99 miles
Banking: Varying
Grandstand Capacity: 30,000

ADDRESS
Infineon Raceway
29355 Arnold Drive
Sonoma, CA 95476
(800) 870-7223
www.infineonraceway.com

TICKET INFORMATION
Phone: (800) 870-7223
www.infineonraceway.com

About the Track

Infineon is one of only two road courses on the NASCAR Sprint Cup circuit. Its eleven right and left turns make it fun to watch for road-course fans. Many NASCAR fans argue that road-course racing does not have a place in the Cup schedule, but do not expect NASCAR to drop this race anytime soon. There seem to be just as many NASCAR fans that love the road courses and feel the switch up from the normal left turn/oval racing is good for the sport. While some drivers like Jeff Gordon, Robby Gordon, Kevin Harvick, and Tony Stewart seem to have figured out the winding trail, the majority of the drivers would rather never have to see a road course again. On the flip side, Infineon is a favorite of the drivers' wives and girlfriends as the shopping is great and the track is right in the middle of wine country.

Track History

Sears Point Raceway broke ground in 1967. In just over a year, the $70 million road-course project was complete. It would not be until 1989 that the NASCAR Sprint Cup Series would make its way to the hills of Sonoma. Up until this time, NASCAR chose to run their premier series at the nearby Riverside International Raceway. Riverside was flattened in 1988 to build a shopping mall, so NASCAR, looking for another road course in the general area, decided to give Sears Point the race. In 2002, SMI found a high-paying corporate sponsor to claim the naming rights to the California track. The track known as Sears Point instantly became Infineon Raceway, even though most drivers and fans still refer to the track as Sears Point.

Track Records

Most Wins: Jeff Gordon (5)
Most Top Five Finishes: Ricky Rudd (10)
Most Lead Changes: 10—most recently on 6/23/2002 (total of 4 times)
Fewest Lead Changes: 3—on 6/11/1989
Most Cautions: 9—on 6/10/1990
Fewest Cautions: 3—most recently on 6/23/2002 (total of 4 times)

Race Record: Ricky Rudd—81.007 mph (2 hours, 42 minutes, 8 seconds) (6/23/2002)

Qualifying Record: Jeff Gordon—94.325 mph (75.950 seconds) (6/26/2005)

Fast Facts

- The first NASCAR Sprint Cup race was run at Infineon Raceway on June 11, 1989, and was won by Ricky Rudd.
- Ricky Rudd is the oldest driver to have won at Infineon Raceway—winning in June 2002, he was forty-five years old (plus nine months and eleven days).
- Dale Earnhardt Sr. won his first and only NASCAR road-course race at Infineon Raceway in 1995.

Parking

Infineon provides free parking for fans attending the race. All parking is first come, first served. Overnight parking is not allowed in the general parking area. For up-to-date parking information call the track's main number at 1-800-870-7223 or visit www.infineonraceway.com.

Track Rules

According to the track's official website at www.infineonraceway.com, the track's rules are as follows:

ITEMS ALLOWED IN GRANDSTANDS

- ✓ bags and/or backpacks (no larger than 18″ × 18″ × 6″)
- ✓ coolers (no larger than 15″ × 15″ × 15″)
- ✓ plastic bottles
- ✓ seat cushions
- ✓ cameras
- ✓ binoculars
- ✓ scanners

ITEMS *NOT* ALLOWED IN THE GRANDSTANDS

- ✗ cans
- ✗ bottles/glass containers
- ✗ golf carts
- ✗ skateboards
- ✗ strollers
- ✗ bikes
- ✗ scooters
- ✗ fireworks
- ✗ firearms
- ✗ knives of any kind
- ✗ lawn chairs
- ✗ umbrellas

Special Needs and Services

Infineon provides seating and parking for fans needing special assistance or accessibility. Each guest with special needs is allowed one companion to accompany them. Call the track at 1-800-870-7223 prior to arrival. Always ask for your parking to be near your seats.

Track Tours

Group and individual track tours are conducted at Infineon by reservation only. The tour includes a trip to the infield, Victory Lane, and pit road. To make reservations call the track at 1-800-870-7223.

Souvenirs

Official track souvenirs can be purchased on race day in the numerous free standing booths scattered throughout the track grounds. Driver-specific souvenirs can be found on Souvenir Alley, located to the right of the main entrance to the track. You can also purchase track merchandise at the track's online store at www.infineonraceway.com.

About the Area

If you have never been to California wine country before, you are missing out. Sonoma is a quaint town surrounded by countless wineries. This has always been one of my favorite stops on the circuit, not only because I love good wine but because the area is so unique. All of the attractions of San Francisco are only a short drive away, not to mention the food is to die for. I am not a road-course fan per se, but I sure would love to visit this track twice a year. The weather is perfect in late June, making the stay even more enjoyable. If you are thinking of venturing out to a new track, pack the wine and cheese and go for it.

CHAMBER OF COMMERCE
Sonoma Valley Chamber of
  Commerce
651-A Broadway
Sonoma, CA 95476
(707) 996-1033
www.sonomachamber.com

INSIDER TIP—ATMs are located at the Raceway Café, at the main grandstand next to the winner's circle.

Transportation

AIRPORTS

Oakland International Airport (OAK)
1 Airport Drive
Oakland, CA
(510) 563-3300
(Oakland International Airport is approximately thirty-three miles from the track.)

San Francisco International Airport (SFO)
Highway 101
San Francisco, CA
(650) 821-8211
(San Francisco International Airport is approximately thirty-seven miles from the track.)

AIRLINES

American (800) 433-7300
ATA (800) 435-9282
Continental (800) 525-0280
Delta (800) 221-1212
JetBlue (800) 538-2583
Southwest (800) 435-9792
United (800) 241-6522
US Airways (800) 428-4322

RENTAL CARS

Avis (800) 331-1212
Budget (800) 527-0700
Dollar (800) 800-4000
Enterprise (800) 261-7331
Fox Rent A Car (800) 225-4369

Hertz (800) 654-3131
National (800) 227-7368
Thrifty (800) 847-4389

Hotels

KEY
⌂ Pet Friendly   ≈ Pool
✗ Restaurant

≈, ✗ Barcelo Hotel
1010 Northgate Drive
San Rafael, CA
(415) 479-8800

≈, ✗ Best Western Novato Oaks
215 Alameda Del Prado
Novato, CA
(415) 883-4400

⌂, ≈, ✗ Best Western Petaluma
200 S. McDowell Boulevard
Petaluma, CA
(707) 763-0994

⌂, ≈ Best Western Sonoma Valley
550 Second Street W.
Sonoma, CA
(707) 938-9200

≈, ✗ Butterfly Effect Motel
3700 Broadway Street
American Canyon, CA
(707) 674-2550

⌂, ≈, ✕ **Carneros Inn**
4048 Sonoma Highway
Napa, CA
(707) 299-4900

Cooperage Inn
301 First Street W.
Sonoma, CA
(707) 996-7054

≈ **Courtyard—Novato San
    Francisco Bay Area**
1400 N. Hamilton Parkway
Novato, CA
(415) 883-8950

≈, ✕ **Econo Lodge Inn and Suites**
275 Alameda Del Prado
Novato, CA
(415) 883-2406

≈, ✕ **El Dorado Hotel**
405 First Street W.
Sonoma, CA
(707) 996-3220

≈ **Fairfield Inn and Suites**
3800 Broadway Street
American Canyon, CA
(707) 643-3800

≈, ✕ **Fairmont Sonoma Mission
    Inn**
100 Boyes Boulevard
Sonoma, CA
(707) 938-9000

≈, ✕ **Four Points by Sheraton**
1010 Northgate Drive
San Rafael, CA
(415) 479-8800

⌂, ≈, ✕ **Inn Marin**
250 Entrada Drive
Novato, CA
(415) 883-5952

✕ **Ledson Hotel**
480 First Street E.
Sonoma, CA
(707) 996-9779

⌂, ≈, ✕ **Lodge at Sonoma**
1325 Broadway
Sonoma, CA
(707) 935-6600

≈, ✕ **MacArthur Place**
29 E. MacArthur Street
Sonoma, CA
(707) 938-2929

Metro Hotel
508 Petaluma Boulevard S.
Petaluma, CA
(707) 773-4900

⌂ **Motel 6**
1455 Marine World Parkway
Vallejo, CA
(707) 643-7611

✎, ≈, ✕ **Novato Days Inn**
8141 Redwood Boulevard
Novato, CA
(415) 897-7111

≈ **Regency Inn**
4326 Sonoma Boulevard
Vallejo, CA
(707) 643-4150

✎, ≈, ✕ **Sheraton—Petaluma**
745 Baywood Drive
Petaluma, CA
(707) 283-2888

Sonoma Chalet Bed & Breakfast
18935 Fifth Street W.
Sonoma, CA
(707) 938-3129

Sonoma Creek Inn
239 Boyes Boulevard
Sonoma, CA
(707) 939-9463

Thistle Dew Inn
171 W. Spain Street
Sonoma, CA
(707) 938-2909

Traveler's Inn
444 Tennessee Street
Vallejo, CA
(707) 644-4411

✎, ≈ **Travelodge**
7600 Redwood Boulevard
Novato, CA
(415) 892-7500

Trojan Horse Inn
19455 Sonoma Highway
Sonoma, CA
(707) 996-2430

Victorian Garden Inn
316 E. Napa Street
Sonoma, CA
(707) 996-5339

Camping

ON-SITE AND TRACK-OWNED CAMPING

Infineon Raceway offers a variety of camping options for race fans in four different camping areas. Call the track at 707-933-3943 for up-to-date information and camping fees. It is always a good idea to request a current list of rules for the specific area you choose to camp in, as it is not uncommon for each area to have its own set of rules.

Carousel Campground The Carousel Campground is Infineon Raceway's version of infield RV camping at its best! You are surrounded by racing in the Carousel Campground, although the views of the track from the campground are limited. This area is only for self-contained RVs.

Cougar Mountain Campground Cougar Mountain is located on the west side of the track. The shuttle runs to and from this site throughout race weekend. This area is first come, first served so get there early.

50 Acres Campground The fifty-acre campground is located across Highway 121 just behind turn 7 on the road course. This area is for tents, pop-ups, trucks, and RVs. Dry camping only.

Trackside RV Terrace The Trackside RV Terrace is located on the west side of the raceway overlooking turns 3 and 4 on the road course. This area is dry camping only.

Turn 8 Campground The newest camping option at Infineon is located on the main ring road. This is the best view available from a camping standpoint. Dry camping.

OFF-SITE CAMPING

KOA Campgrounds
840 Garfield Drive
Petaluma, CA
(707) 782-9156

Larkspur RV Park
11 Rich Street
Greenbrae, CA
(415) 461-8739

Rodeo Mobile Home & RV Park
1530 Armstrong Avenue
Novato, CA
(415) 897-1271

RV Park of San Rafael
742 Francisco Boulevard W.
San Rafael, CA
(415) 261-0111

Silver Penny RV Park
7060 Redwood Boulevard
Novato, CA
(415) 892-3701

Skyline Wilderness Park
2201 Imola Avenue
Napa, CA
(707) 252-0481

Tradewinds RV Park
239 Lincoln Road W.
Vallejo, CA
(707) 643-4000

Restaurants

KEY

🍔 Fast Food   🪑 Sit Down
🥡 Takeout   🍷 Reservations

Must Eats

Della Santina's Trattoria
133 E. Napa Street
Sonoma, CA
(707) 935-0576

You will feel like you stepped back in time when you walk in the door. Lamb is one of the many specialties on the menu. Traditional Sonoma/Napa Valley food. The wine list is exceptional!

Murphy's Irish Pub
464 First Street E.
Sonoma, CA
(707) 935-0660

Traditional Irish fare with dark beer on tap. You can dine in or out and hear live music. A real don't miss!

🥡 **Babe's Burgers & Franks**
2660 Fremont Drive
Sonoma, CA
(707) 938-9714

🪑 **Brown's Binyerd**
1009 First Street
Novato, CA
(415) 897-1925

🍔 **Burger King**
216 Vintage Way
Novato, CA
(415) 897-0233

🪑 **Cacti Restaurant**
1200 Grant Avenue
Novato, CA
(415) 898-2234

🪑, 🥡 **Cafe Cruiser**
8 Digital Drive, Suite 108
Novato, CA
(415) 382-0670

🥡 **Carl's Jr.**
35 Rowland Way
Novato, CA
(415) 898-6180

🪑 **Chevys Fresh Mex**
128 Vintage Way, Suite W
Novato, CA
(415) 898-7345

🪑 **China House**
1222 Grant Avenue
Novato, CA
(415) 897-9630

China Palace
7089 Redwood Boulevard
Novato, CA
(415) 892-6563

Corner Stone Market Cafe
23584 Highway 121
Sonoma, CA
(707) 935-1681

Cucina Viansa
21481 Eighth Street E.
Sonoma, CA
(707) 935-5656

Danny's Cafe
1433 Grant Avenue
Novato, CA
(415) 892-3404

Denny's
7330 Redwood Boulevard
Novato, CA
(415) 897-6086

Ever Rain Restaurant
312 Montego Key
Novato, CA
(415) 892-6563

Extreme Pizza
104 Vintage Way
Novato, CA
(415) 898-6575

Fuzhou Super Buffet
6090 Redwood Boulevard, Suite H
Novato, CA
(415) 899-1668

Garden Court Restaurant
8141 Redwood Boulevard
Novato, CA
(415) 892-8700

Golden Egg Omelet House
807 Grant Avenue
Novato, CA
(415) 897-7707

Grant Avenue Bar & Grill
807 Grant Avenue
Novato, CA
(415) 897-9157

Grazie
823 Grant Avenue
Novato, CA
(415) 878-0202

Happy Garden Restaurant
385 Bel Marin Keys Boulevard
Novato, CA
(415) 883-8017

Henry's Downtown
1433 Grant Avenue
Novato, CA
(415) 892-3404

High Tech Burrito
942 Diablo Avenue
Novato, CA
(415) 897-8083

Hilltop Cafe
850 Lamont Avenue
Novato, CA
(415) 892-2222

IHOP Restaurant
144 Vintage Way
Novato, CA
(415) 892-2232

**Italian Delite Submarine
  Sandwiches**
971 Front Street
Novato, CA
(415) 892-9221

Jennie Low's Chinese Cuisine
120 Vintage Way, Suite D9
Novato, CA
(415) 892-8838

Kentucky Fried Chicken
7145 Redwood Boulevard
Novato, CA
(415) 893-0465

Kitchen at 868 Grant
868 Grant Avenue
Novato, CA
(415) 892-6100

La Hacienda Taqueria
1401 Grant Avenue
Novato, CA
(415) 897-5514

Las Guitarras
1017 Reichert Avenue
Novato, CA
(415) 892-3171

Levy Restaurants
29355 Arnold Drive
Sonoma, CA
(707) 939-1454

Mario's Italian Subs
934 Diablo Avenue
Novato, CA
(415) 897-6720

Masa Sushi
813 Grant Avenue
Novato, CA
(415) 892-0081

Matsuyama
939 Front Street
Novato, CA
(415) 209-9823

May Lee's Chinese Restaurant
247 Shoreline Highway
Mill Valley, CA
(415) 383-8888

McDonald's
7340 Redwood Boulevard
Novato, CA
(415) 897-6101

Moylan's Brewery & Restaurant
15 Rowland Way
Novato, CA
(415) 898-4677

Pacifica Pizza
975 Diablo Avenue
Novato, CA
(415) 892-4333

Papa Murphy's Take 'n' Bake Pizza
922 Diablo Avenue
Novato, CA
(415) 892-6999

Papa's Taverna
5688 Lakeville Highway
Petaluma, CA
(707) 769-8545

Pasta Pomodoro
140 Vintage Way
Novato, CA
(415) 899-1861

Pueblo Taqueria Mi
905 Grant Avenue
Novato, CA
(415) 878-0122

Red Boy Pizza
940 Diablo Avenue
Novato, CA
(415) 897-1180

Schellville Grill
22900 Broadway
Sonoma, CA
(707) 996-5151

Soup Caffe
401 Bel Marin Keys Boulevard
Novato, CA
(415) 382-0232

Taco Bell
180 Rowland Way
Novato, CA
(415) 898-4003

Taqueria Real
354 Bel Marin Keys Boulevard
Novato, CA
(415) 382-0522

Taxi's Hamburgers
924 Diablo Avenue
Novato, CA
(415) 898-8294

Local Attractions

WORTH THE TRIP

This is a great race to add a few days in for sightseeing and local attractions. Due to the fact that you are right smack-dab in the middle of wine country, you have to tour a winery (or two), even if you do not drink wine. Every hotel (and the local chamber of commerce) will have a winery guide that will give you a list of the wineries and hours of tours. If the wineries do not interest you, in less than an hour you can be in San Francisco, which has more fun wrapped in one city than should be allowed. Make sure you visit **Alcatraz** while in San Fran.

Alcatraz Cruises
Pier 33 (located on The
   Embarcadero at Bay Street)
San Francisco, CA
(415) 981-7625

Bicycle Museum
1200 Milton Road
Napa, CA
(707) 224-1710

**Carolyn Parr Museum of National
   History**
3107 Browns Valley Road
Napa, CA
(707) 255-6465

Cornerstone Gardens
23570 Arnold Drive
Sonoma, CA
(707) 933-3010

Depot Park Museum
270 First Street W.
Sonoma, CA
(707) 938-1762

Di Rosa Preserve: Art & Nature
5200 Sonoma Highway
Napa, CA
(707) 226-5991

Eagle Vines Golf Club
580 S. Kelly Road
Napa, CA
(707) 257-4470

Mare Island Historic Park Tour
328 Seawind Drive
Vallejo, CA
(707) 557-1538

**Marin Museum of the American
   Indian**
2200 Novato Boulevard
Novato, CA
(415) 897-4064

Military Antiques & Museum
300 Petaluma Boulevard N.
Petaluma, CA
(707) 763-2220

Napa Firefighters Museum
1201 Main Street
Napa, CA
(707) 259-0609

Napa-Sonoma Marketplace
Visitors Center
101 Antonina Drive
American Canyon, CA
(707) 642-0686

Novato History Museum
815 De Long Avenue
Novato, CA
(415) 897-4320

Platypus Tours
1015 Shetler Avenue
Napa, CA
(707) 631-0757

Six Flags
2001 Marine World Parkway
Vallejo, CA
(707) 643-6722

Sonoma Golf Club
17700 Arnold Drive
Sonoma, CA
(707) 935-3608

Sonoma Valley Museum of Art
551 Broadway
Sonoma, CA
(707) 939-7862

Traintown Railroad Rides
20264 Broadway
Sonoma, CA
(707) 938-3912

Vallejo Naval & Historical Museum
734 Marin Street
Vallejo, CA
(707) 643-0077

Shopping

KEY
🚗 Automotive $ Discount
➕ Pharmacy   🏬 Mall
☆ Specialty   🏬 Department Store

Worth the Time

I love the downtown Sonoma area. The stores and cafés are all conveniently located on the town square, which makes you feel like you are in the deep South instead of smack-dab in the middle of California wine country. The stores are all boutique-style shops with many unique items. Tip to the wise: have the store ship your items home so you do not have to hassle with extra cargo on your return trip.

☆ **Banana Republic**
629 Factory Stores Drive
Napa, CA
(707) 257-6312

⌂ **Barneys New York**
821 Factory Stores Drive
Napa, CA
(707) 224-0200

$ **Ben Franklin**
136 Vintage Way
Novato, CA
(415) 897-2231

$ **Big Lots**
928 Diablo Avenue
Novato, CA
(415) 892-7598

☆ **Canyon Corners**
100 American Canyon Road
American Canyon, CA
(707) 255-8075

🏬 **Canyon Plaza**
3417 Broadway Street
American Canyon, CA
(707) 255-8075

$ **Costco**
300 Vintage Way
Novato, CA
(415) 899-1330

$ **DD's Discounts**
3355 Sonoma Boulevard
Vallejo, CA
(707) 553-1818

☆ **DKNY**
607 Factory Stores Drive
Napa, CA
(707) 226-3853

$ **Dollar Tree**
3475 Sonoma Boulevard
Vallejo, CA
(707) 645-9083

$ **Factory 2-U**
3435 Sonoma Boulevard
Vallejo, CA
(707) 644-9414

☆ **Guess**
2200 Petaluma Boulevard N.
Petaluma, CA
(707) 766-6028

$ **Kmart**
261 N. McDowell Boulevard
Petaluma, CA
(707) 778-6234

⌂ **Kohl's Department Store**
1190 Admiral Callaghan Lane
Vallejo, CA
(707) 649-9851

⌂ **Macy's**
100 Vintage Way
Novato, CA
(415) 892-3333

$ **Marshalls**
204 Vintage Way
Novato, CA
(415) 892-7322

⌂ **McCaulou's Department Stores**
201 W. Napa Street Suite 18
Sonoma, CA
(707) 996-4465

☆ **Mervyns**
701 Sereno Drive
Vallejo, CA
(707) 643-8811

🛒 **Nave Shopping Center**
50800 Nave Drive
Novato, CA
(415) 479-8788

🛒 **Pacheco Plaza Shopping Center**
366 Ignacio Boulevard
Novato, CA
(415) 883-4648

☆ **Pier 1 Imports**
108 Vintage Way
Novato, CA
(415) 897-4460

🛒 **Red Hill Shopping Center**
19 Pamaron Way
Novato, CA
(415) 382-1185

🛒 **Redwood Square Shopping Center**
480 Redwood Street
Vallejo, CA
(707) 552-5536

$ **Ross Dress For Less**
116 Vintage Way
Novato, CA
(415) 898-6466

⌂ **Saks Fifth Avenue**
2200 Petaluma Boulevard N., Suite 1300
Petaluma, CA
(707) 778-6011

☆ **Talbots**
1331 First Street
Napa, CA
(707) 255-5617

$ **Target**
200 Vintage Way
Novato, CA
(415) 892-3313

🛒 **Vintage Oaks at Novato**
208 Vintage Way, Suite 100
Novato, CA
(415) 897-9999

Walkenhorst's
1774 Industrial Way
Napa, CA
(707) 255-3017

$ **Wal-Mart**
5180 Sonoma Boulevard
Vallejo, CA
(707) 557-4393

Churches/ Worship Centers

All Saints Lutheran Church
2 San Marin Drive
Novato, CA
(415) 892-1669

Calvary Chapel
5470 Nave Drive
Novato, CA
(415) 382-2069

Christ Church North Bay
6965 Redwood Boulevard
Novato, CA
(415) 892-3303

Christian Science Church
1209 Grant Avenue
Novato, CA
(415) 897-1424

Church of Christ
833 Sweetser Avenue
Novato, CA
(415) 892-7365

Church of Jesus Christ of Latter Day Saints
787 Kendon Lane
Novato, CA
(415) 892-5650

Faith Presbyterian Church
276 E. Napa Street
Sonoma, CA
(707) 933-8794

First Baptist Church
542 First Street E.
Sonoma, CA
(707) 996-3443

Nativity of Christ Greek Church
1110 Highland Drive
Novato, CA
(415) 883-1998

New Life Assembly of God
23109 S. Central Avenue
Sonoma, CA
(707) 935-0777

New Life Christian Center
1370 S. Novato Boulevard
Novato, CA
(415) 892-0714

Open Door Christian Church
1915 Novato Boulevard
Novato, CA
(415) 897-5556

Seventh-Day Adventist Church
495 San Marin Drive
Novato, CA
(415) 897-2600

Sonoma United Methodist Church
109 Patten Street
Sonoma, CA
(707) 996-2151

**Sonoma Valley Community
    Church**
181 Chase Street
Sonoma, CA
(707) 938-8100

St. Anthony's Catholic Church
1000 Cambridge Street
Novato, CA
(415) 883-2177

Trinity Church—Orthodox
8 Doris Avenue
Novato, CA
(415) 897-3410

Trinity Episcopal Church
275 E. Spain Street
Sonoma, CA
(707) 938-4846

Victory Christian Center
220 San Luis Way
Novato, CA
(415) 897-0136

Medical Centers

Novato Community Hospital
180 Rowland Way
Novato, CA
(415) 209-1300

Sonoma Valley Hospital
347 Andrieux Street
Sonoma, CA
(707) 935-5000

Pet Medical Centers

Animal Kind
833 Vallejo Avenue
Novato, CA
(415) 897-9696

Country Vet
511 Atherton Avenue
Novato, CA
(415) 897-8380

Novato Veterinary Hospital
7454 Redwood Boulevard
Novato, CA
(415) 897-2173

Sonoma Veterinary Clinic
21003 Broadway
Sonoma, CA
(707) 938-4455

KANSAS SPEEDWAY

Infield

Garage Area

Pit Road

Start | Finish Line

Track Information

Inaugural Year: 2001
Owner: International Speedway
 Corporation (ISC)
City: Kansas City, Kansas
Size: 1.5 miles
Banking: 15 degrees
Grandstand Capacity: 80,187

ADDRESS
Kansas Speedway
400 Speedway Boulevard
Kansas City, KS 66111
(866) 460-7223
www.kansasspeedway.com

TICKET INFORMATION
Phone: 866-460-7223
www.kansasspeedway.com

About the Track

This Midwest track has only been a part of the NASCAR Sprint Cup circuit for a handful of years now, but it has already established a loyal fan base. As with most new tracks, the racing at Kansas gets better each year. Kansas is one of many intermediate tracks on the circuit, meaning the length of the track (1.5 miles) is the middle ground between short tracks like Bristol and superspeedways like Daytona. The intermediate tracks make up the largest group of tracks on the circuit.

Track History

ISC, led by Lesa Kennedy (daughter of Bill France Jr.) set out in October 1996 to find a location in the Midwest suitable to build a track worthy of hosting NASCAR's elite series and other racing series. In January 1996, ISC made its decision official to build in the Kansas City, Kansas, area. Grounbreaking took place for the 1.5-mile facility on May 25, 1999; almost two years later the construction was complete. The very first Cup series event was held in front of a sold-out crowd, and Jeff Gordon took the win for the inaugural event.

Track Records

Most Wins: Jeff Gordon (2)

Most Top Five Finishes: Jeff Gordon, Ryan Newman, Tony Stewart (3)

Most Lead Changes: 24—on 10/10/2004

Fewest Lead Changes: 13—on 9/29/2002

Most Cautions: 13—on 9/30/2001

Fewest Cautions: 7—on 10/9/2005

Race Record: Mark Martin— 137.774 mph (2 hours, 54 minutes, 25 seconds) (10/9/2005)

Qualifying Record: Matt Kenseth— 180.856 mph (29.858 seconds) (10/8/2005)

Fast Facts

- The first NASCAR Sprint Cup race was run at Kansas Speedway on September 30, 2001, and was won by Jeff Gordon.
- Mark Martin is the oldest driver to have won at the Kansas Speedway—winning in October 2005, he was forty-six years old (plus nine months).
- The most cars still running at a race's end at Kansas Speedway was thirty-eight. This has happened two different times, most recently in October 2006.
- The race logo painted in the infield grass of Kansas Speedway is equal to the size of a football field.
- Eleven million yards of dirt was used to construct the speedway, which is enough dirt to fill 1 million dump trucks.

Parking

Parking at Kansas Speedway is free to fans attending the race. For up-to-date parking call the track at

866-460-7223 or visit www.kansas speedway.com prior to arrival. All parking is on a first-come, first-served basis. Overnight parking is not allowed in the general parking areas.

Track Rules

According to the track's official website at www.kansasspeedway.com, the track's rules are as follows:

ITEMS ALLOWED IN GRANDSTANDS

- ✓ one soft-sided bag/cooler (no larger than 6″ × 6″ × 12″, may contain ice)
- ✓ one clear plastic bag (no larger than 18″ × 18″ × 4″, no ice)
- ✓ food and beverages
- ✓ binoculars
- ✓ scanners
- ✓ headsets
- ✓ cameras
- ✓ seat cushions

ITEMS *NOT* ALLOWED IN THE GRANDSTANDS

- ✗ glass containers
- ✗ folding chairs
- ✗ bicycles
- ✗ wagons
- ✗ scooters
- ✗ seat cushions with a hollow metal tube construction
- ✗ firearms
- ✗ fireworks
- ✗ hard-sided coolers
- ✗ thermoses
- ✗ insulated cups of any size
- ✗ strollers
- ✗ umbrellas
- ✗ skateboards
- ✗ Rollerblades
- ✗ posters/banners and flagpoles

Special Needs and Services

Kansas Speedway accommodates anyone needing special services, including wheelchair accessibility. One companion ticket can be purchased for each wheelchair ticket purchased. For more information contact the ticket office at 866-460-7223. There are limited seats available so call prior to arrival. Always ask for your parking to be near your seats.

INSIDER TIP—Kansas offers a limited number of tickets for prerace pit passes and the Fan Walk area. Both will get you up close to the behind-the-scenes action. Call the ticket office at 866-460-7223 for more info.

Track Tours

Group tours (ten-person minimum) are available at Kansas Speedway but are by appointment only. Kansas does not allow walk-up tour requests at any time. The one-hour tour includes pit road, Victory Lane, the view from one of the suites, and the history of the track. For more information on scheduling a group tour, contact the track at 866-460-7223.

Souvenirs

Official Kansas Speedway and driver-specific souvenirs can be purchased at Souvenir Alley in the Souvenir and Display Midway, located on either side of the main entrance of the track.

INSIDER TIP—ATMs are located in the Fan Walk area.

About the Area

The Kansas Speedway is located in a bistate metro area, which includes Kansas and Missouri. The track itself is only fifteen miles west of downtown Kansas City, Kansas, which lends itself to lots of things to do and see outside of the racing. Even though this location is new to the NASCAR Cup-level scene, the love for racing is obvious by the warm welcome race fans receive from the locals. Many drivers' wives love the shopping in this area, and the crews rave over the great food. The area continues to grow. In fact, the Hard Rock Hotel and Casino is currently under construction and when completed will overlook the speedway. Count on mild temperatures when catching a race at Kansas. Early October brings a true look of fall as the leaves are almost in full color for race weekend.

CHAMBER OF COMMERCE

Greater Kansas City Chamber of
   Commerce
911 Main Street
Kansas City, MO 64105
(816) 221-2424
www.kcchamber.com

Transportation

AIRPORT

Kansas City International Airport
   (MCI)
601 Brasilia Avenue
Kansas City, MO
(816) 243-5237
(Approximately fourteen miles from
   the track.)

AIRLINES

American (800) 433-7300
Continental (800) 525-0280
Delta (800) 221-1212
ExpressJet (888) 958-9538
Frontier (800) 432-1359
Great Lakes (307) 432-7000
Midwest (800) 452-2022
Northwest (800) 225-2525
Southwest (800) 435-9792
United (800) 241-6522
US Airways (800) 943-5436

RENTAL CARS

Alamo (800) 327-9633
Avis (800) 331-1212
Capps (816) 464-4812
Dollar (816) 270-1473
Enterprise (800) 736-8222
Hertz (800) 654-3131
Midwest (816) 464-4700
National (800) 227-7368
Payless (816) 464-2100
Thrifty (800) 367-2277

Hotels

KEY
🐾 Pet Friendly　　≈ Pool
✕ Restaurant

≈ American Motel

7949 Splitlog Avenue
Kansas City, KS
(913) 299-2999

Chateau Avalon

701 Village West Parkway
Kansas City, KS
(913) 596-6000

Clarks Motel

1807 Merriam Lane
Kansas City, KS
(913) 236-6626

≈ Comfort Inn

234 N. 78th Street
Kansas City, KS
(913) 299-5555

🐾, ≈ Comfort Inn

6401 Frontage Road
Merriam, KS
(913) 262-2622

🐾 Crest Motel

8600 State Avenue
Kansas City, KS
(913) 299-4269

🐾 Econo Lodge

504 N. Main Street
Lansing, KS
(913) 727-2777

🐾, ≈ Extended Stay America

8015 Lenexa Drive
Shawnee Mission, KS
(913) 894-5550

Gables Motel
6831 State Avenue
Kansas City, KS
(913) 299-8111

≈, ✕ **Great Wolf Lodge**
10401 Cabela Drive
Kansas City, KS
(913) 299-7001

≈ **Hampton Inn**
1400 Village West Parkway
Kansas City, KS
(913) 328-1400

≈ **Hampton Inn**
16555 Midland Drive
Shawnee, KS
(913) 248-1900

≈ **Hampton Inn**
7400 Frontage Road
Shawnee Mission, KS
(913) 722-0800

≈, ✕ **Hilton Garden Inn**
520 Minnesota Avenue
Kansas City, KS
(913) 342-7900

≈ **Holiday Inn Express—Kansas
City**
13031 Ridge Drive
Bonner Springs, KS
(913) 721-5300

≈ **Holiday Inn Express—Lansing**
120 Express Lane
Lansing, KS
(913) 250-1000

≈ **Holiday Inn Express—Village
West**
1931 Prairie Crossing Street
Kansas City, KS
(913) 328-1024

⇔ **Homestead Studio Suites Hotel**
6451 Frontage Road
Shawnee Mission, KS
(913) 236-6006

⇔, ≈ **Howard Johnson**
7508 Shawnee Mission Parkway
Shawnee Mission, KS
(913) 262-9600

⇔, ≈ **Microtel Inn & Suites**
7721 Elizabeth Avenue
Kansas City, KS
(913) 334-3028

Penrod Motel Resort
224 S. 86th Street
Kansas City, KS
(913) 788-9143

⇔, ≈ **Regency Inn**
4725 State Avenue
Kansas City, KS
(913) 287-5511

Camping

ON-SITE AND TRACK-OWNED CAMPING

Kansas Speedway offers three camping areas—the Blue Ox Motorhome Terrace, the Blue Ox Reserved Infield, and Kansas Campground—all three of which offer overnight camping. The majority of the on-site campgrounds have long waiting lists. Contact the track at 866-460-7223 for up-to-date camping rules, fees, wait list, and general information. It is best to request the rules for the specific area you choose to camp in, as each area tends to have its own set of rules.

Kansas Campground The Kansas Campground is located in the southeast corner of the speedway, behind the backstretch. This 561-space lot offers a shuttle service to and from the track. Motor homes and RVs must be self-contained in this area.

The Blue Ox Motorhome Terrace (Sold out) The Motorhome Terrace is the track's premier motor home area. The Terrace offers excellent views of the entire speedway from the exterior bluff around the track above turns 2, 3, and 4. All motor homes must be self-contained in this area. This area is currently on a wait list. There is a fee to be added to the wait list.

The Blue Ox Reserved Infield (Sold out) The Reserved Infield at Kansas Speedway literally puts you in the eye of the storm of the race action. There are two areas to choose from in the infield: the Front Runners Club, which are camping spots closest to the track, and the Speedway Club, which are nontrackside spots. All motor homes and RVs must be self-contained in this area. This area is currently on a wait list. There is a fee to be added to the wait list.

OFF-SITE CAMPING

Cottonwood Camping
115 S. 130th Street
Bonner Springs, KS
(913) 422-8038

Oak Lane Mobile Home Park
400 E. Eisenhower Road
Lansing, KS
(913) 727-3757

Suncatcher Lake
24836 Tonganoxie Road
Leavenworth, KS
(913) 351-0505

Walnut Grove RV Park
10218 Johnson Drive
Shawnee Mission, KS
(913) 262-3023

Restaurants

KEY
🍔 Fast Food   🪑 Sit Down
🛍️ Takeout   📞 Reservations

Must Eats

Dave and Buster's
1843 Village West Parkway
Kansas City, KS
(913) 981-6815
    This is the perfect pit stop for the kid in all of us. Video games galore and the American fare is good. This is a favorite of the crew guys while in Kansas.

Famous Dave's BBQ
1320 Village West Parkway
Kansas City, KS
(913) 334-8646
    Famous Dave's is good ole southern BBQ at its best.

🪑 **Alvarados Casa De Tacos**
8224 New Jersey Avenue
Kansas City, KS
(913) 334-8226

🪑 **Applebee's**
1700 Village West Parkway
Kansas City, KS
(913) 788-9421

🍔 **Arby's**
600 Tulip Drive
Bonner Springs, KS
(913) 441-7949

🪑 **Bob Evans**
1704 Village West Parkway
Kansas City, KS
(913) 299-1278

🪑 **Bo'dans**
8919 Leavenworth Road
Kansas City, KS
(913) 788-8484

🪑 **Charlie D's Catfish Cabin**
1000 N. 82nd Street
Kansas City, KS
(913) 334-3400

🪑 **Cheeseburger in Paradise**
1705 Village West Parkway
Kansas City, KS
(913) 334-4500

🪑 **Chipotle Mexican Grill**
1813 Village West Parkway
Kansas City, KS
(913) 299-9221

Culver's
1925 Prairie Crossing Street
Kansas City, KS
(913) 400-7300

Evergreen Chinese Restaurant
13034 Kansas Avenue
Bonner Springs, KS
(913) 441-6484

Frontier Steakhouse
9338 State Avenue
Kansas City, KS
(913) 788-9159

Granite City Food & Brewery
1701 Village West Parkway
Kansas City, KS
(913) 334-2255

Hooters
1712 Village West Parkway
Kansas City, KS
(913) 788-4668

IHOP Restaurant
1919 Prairie Crossing Street
Kansas City, KS
(913) 788-4468

Jay's Family Restaurant
13832 Parallel Avenue
Kansas City, KS
(913) 721-2171

Johnny Carino's Italian
1706 Village West Parkway
Kansas City, KS
(913) 299-8253

Kentucky Fried Chicken
14 N. 130th Street
Bonner Springs, KS
(913) 721-1311

Lone Star Steakhouse & Saloon
1501 Village West Parkway
Kansas City, KS
(913) 334-9995

Longhorn Steakhouse
1708 Village West Parkway
Kansas City, KS
(913) 788-4400

Mazzio's Pizza
13035 Canaan Drive
Bonner Springs, KS
(913) 721-1133

McDonald's
606 S. 130th Street
Bonner Springs, KS
(913) 422-7817

Mr. Goodcents Subs & Pastas
13021 Kansas Avenue
Bonner Springs, KS
(913) 441-4041

Nick-N-Willy's Pizza
1829 Village West Parkway
Kansas City, KS
(913) 328-1600

Outback Steakhouse
1851 Village West Parkway
Kansas City, KS
(913) 334-2147

Pizzaville
104 S. Fourth Street
Edwardsville, KS
(913) 441-5010

Planet Sub
1843 Village West Parkway
Kansas City, KS
(913) 788-9899

Quiznos Sub
1601 Village West Parkway
Kansas City, KS
(913) 334-2017

Saddle Ranch Chop House
1843 Village West Parkway
Kansas City, KS
(913) 299-1100

Side Pockets
620 S. 130th Street
Bonner Springs, KS
(913) 441-6700

Sonic Drive-In
1714 Village West Parkway
Kansas City, KS
(913) 299-2335

Stix Restaurant
1847 Village West Parkway
Kansas City, KS
(913) 299-3788

Subway Sandwiches & Salads
10902 Parallel Avenue
Kansas City, KS
(913) 299-9101

Taco Bell
14 N. 130th Street
Bonner Springs, KS
(913) 721-1311

Taco John's
13020 Kansas Avenue
Bonner Springs, KS
(913) 422-7304

Taco Via
10940 Parallel Avenue
Kansas City, KS
(913) 788-2261

Taste of China
570 S. Fourth Street
Edwardsville, KS
(913) 422-2565

🍴 **Ted's Montana Grill**
1713 Village West Parkway
Kansas City, KS
(913) 788-4567

🍴 **Twisters Grill & Bar**
13100 Kansas Avenue
Bonner Springs, KS
(913) 667-3700

🍴 **Waffle House**
4 S. 130th Street
Bonner Springs, KS
(913) 721-5200

🍔 **Wendy's**
10548 Parallel Avenue
Kansas City, KS
(913) 334-4957

🍴 **W J McBride's Irish Pub**
1340 Village West Parkway
Kansas City, KS
(913) 788-7771

🍴 **Wyandot Barbeque**
8441 State Avenue
Kansas City, KS
(913) 788-7554

Local Attractions

WORTH THE TRIP
If you are a Harley fan, you will want to visit the **Harley-Davidson Factory,** located in Kansas City, Missouri. The 358,000-square foot vehicle and power train plant was built in 1998. Tours of the factory are offered Monday through Friday from 9 a.m. to 1:30 p.m. Be aware the tickets are on a first-come, first-served basis so calling in advance is suggested. Note that kids under twelve are not allowed to tour the factory. This is a fun and informative tour even if you are not into Harleys.

Advantage Golf
12616 W. 62nd Terrace
Shawnee Mission, KS
(913) 248-1600

Agricultural Hall of Fame
630 Hall of Fame Drive
Bonner Springs, KS
(913) 721-1075

Airline History Museum
201 NW Lou Holland Drive
Kansas City, MO
(816) 421-3401

Bonner Springs Parks and Recreation
200 E. Third Street
Bonner Springs, KS
(913) 422-3404

Campanile Bell Tower
Memorial Drive
Lawrence, KS
(785) 864-3835

Carroll Mansion
1128 Fifth Avenue
Leavenworth, KS
(913) 682-7759

Children's Museum—Kansas City
4601 State Avenue
Kansas City, KS
(913) 287-8888

City of Fountains Foundation
104 W. Ninth Street, Suite 30
Kansas City, MO
(816) 842-2299

Harley-Davidson Factory
11401 W. Congress Avenue
Kansas City, MO
877-883-1450

Lions Park
300 W. Morse Avenue
Bonner Springs, KS
(913) 441-4461

Old Shawnee Town
11501 W. 57th Street
Shawnee, KS
(913) 248-2360

Ole Bill's Museum
801 N. State Route 291
Liberty, MO
(816) 781-1062

Wonderscope Children's Museum
5705 Flint Street
Shawnee, KS
(913) 268-4176

Wyandotte County Lake Park
3488 West Drive
Kansas City, KS
(913) 596-7077

Shopping

KEY
🚗 Automotive $ Discount
⊕ Pharmacy   🏬 Mall
☆ Specialty   👕 Department Store

$ Big Lots
7533 State Avenue
Kansas City, KS
(913) 299-0416

$ Costco
9350 Marshall Drive
Lenexa, KS
(913) 227-3700

$ Deals-Nothing Over A Dollar
15810 Shawnee Mission Parkway
Shawnee Mission, KS
(913) 248-8106

👕 Dillard's
4913 Johnson Drive
Mission, KS
(913) 262-3332

$ **Dollar General**
612 S. 130th Street
Bonner Springs, KS
(913) 441-9851

$ **Dollar Tree**
7650 State Avenue
Kansas City, KS
(913) 334-2598

$ **Family Dollar Store**
8119 State Avenue
Kansas City, KS
(913) 334-4313

$ **418 Penney**
7726 State Avenue
Kansas City, KS
(913) 788-3685

Indian Springs Shopping Center
4601 State Avenue
Kansas City, KS
(913) 287-9393

JC Penney
10904 Stadium Parkway
Kansas City, KS
(913) 334-0285

$ **Kmart**
7836 State Avenue
Kansas City, KS
(913) 299-6017

Kohl's Department Store
15500 Shawnee Mission Parkway
Shawnee, KS
(913) 248-0442

Legends at Village West
1843 Village West Parkway
Kansas City, KS
(913) 788-3700

Macy's
45 Osage Avenue
Kansas City, KS
(913) 321-7900

$ **Marshalls**
5840 Antioch Road
Shawnee Mission, KS
(913) 432-7765

Oak Park Mall
11461 W. 95th Street
Overland Park, KS
(913) 888-4400

☆ **Once Upon a Child**
12204 Shawnee Mission Parkway
Shawnee, KS
(913) 631-3700

☆ **Pier 1 Imports**
15300 Shawnee Mission Parkway
Shawnee, KS
(913) 962-1219

☆ **Plato's Closet**
12156 Shawnee Mission Parkway
Shawnee, KS
(913) 631-1000

$ **Sam's Club**
12200 W. 95th Street
Lenexa, KS
(913) 894-0084

🏍 **Scooters Legends Mall**
1843 Village West Parkway
Kansas City, KS
(913) 328-1454

$ **Stein Mart**
11800 W. 95th Street
Overland Park, KS
(913) 894-5632

☆ **Talbots**
Shops at Boardwalk
8650 N. Boardwalk
Kansas City, MO
(816) 505-0460

$ **Target**
15700 Shawnee Mission Parkway
Shawnee, KS
(913) 962-8222

🏍 **Ten Quivira Shopping Center**
11950 Shawnee Mission Parkway
Shawnee, KS
(913) 631-4547

$ **T.J. Maxx**
1821 Village West Parkway
Kansas City, KS
(913) 299-6245

$ **Wal-Mart Supercenter**
12801 Kansas Avenue
Bonner Springs, KS
(913) 441-6751

Churches/ Worship Centers

Bethel Presbyterian Church
2907 N. 81st Street
Kansas City, KS
(913) 299-2479

Bonner Springs Church of the Nazarene
742 N. Nettleton Avenue
Bonner Springs, KS
(913) 441-1458

Church of Jesus Christ of Latter-Day Saints
8616 Haskell Avenue
Kansas City, KS
(913) 299-1982

Cross Roads Church
13027 Kansas Avenue
Bonner Springs, KS
(913) 422-8733

Edwardsville Assembly Church
643 Edwardsville Drive
Kansas City, KS
(913) 441-4442

**Edwardsville United Methodist
   Church**
302 N. Fourth Street
Edwardsville, KS
(913) 422-5384

Emmaus Lutheran Church
12900 Kansas Avenue
Bonner Springs, KS
(913) 441-3243

Grace Christian Fellowship Church
9200 Parallel Parkway
Kansas City, KS
(913) 299-9799

Haven Baptist Church
10638 Parallel Parkway
Kansas City, KS
(913) 299-3706

Holy Angels Catholic Church
15438 Leavenworth Road
Basehor, KS
(913) 724-1665

Maywood Community Church
11201 Parallel Parkway
Kansas City, KS
(913) 721-2760

Piper Bible Church
12107 Leavenworth Road
Kansas City, KS
(913) 400-7191

**Serbian Orthodox Church of
   St. George**
3700 N. 123rd Street
Kansas City, KS
(913) 721-2047

St. Martin Fields Episcopal Church
1501 Edwardsville Drive
Edwardsville, KS
(913) 422-5879

St. Patrick's Church Rectory
1086 N. 94th Street
Kansas City, KS
(913) 788-2644

Victoria Tabernacle
2205 N. 102nd Street
Kansas City, KS
(913) 299-7888

Westside Church of Christ
8740 State Avenue
Kansas City, KS
(913) 788-3443

**Wyandotte United Methodist
   Church**
7901 Oakland Avenue
Kansas City, KS
(913) 788-5503

Medical Centers

Providence Medical Center
8929 Parallel Parkway
Kansas City, KS
(913) 596-4000

Providence Medical Center
51 N. 12th Street
Kansas City, KS
(913) 281-7777

Shawnee Mission Medical Center
9100 W. 74th Street
Shawnee Mission, KS
(913) 676-2000

**University of Kansas Medical
    Center**
3901 Rainbow Boulevard
Kansas City, KS
(913) 588-5000

Pet Medical Centers

Monticello Animal Hospital
22026 W. 66th Street
Shawnee, KS
(913) 422-0301

Piper Heritage Veterinary Clinic
3140 N. 99th Street
Kansas City, KS
(913) 299-0010

Welborn Pet Hospital
7860 Washington Avenue
Kansas City, KS
(913) 334-6770

LAS VEGAS MOTOR SPEEDWAY

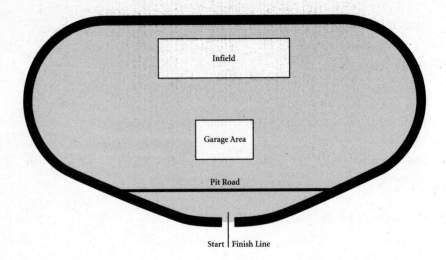

Track Information

Inaugural Year: 1998
Owner: SMI
City: Las Vegas, Nevada
Size: 1.5 miles
Banking: 12 degrees
Grandstand Capacity: 137,000

ADDRESS

Las Vegas Motor Speedway
7000 Las Vegas Boulevard N.
Las Vegas, NV 89115
(800) 644-4444
www.lvms.com

TICKET INFORMATION

Phone: (800) 644-4444
www.lvms.com

About the Track

The Las Vegas Motor Speedway (LVMS) has had its share of growing pains while in search of the perfect racing surface. Many drivers will tell you the track is pretty darn near perfection now but only after undergoing a major reconfiguration in 2006, which entailed increasing the level of banking. The track did this by progressively banking the entire 1.5-mile track surface. This drastic change proved to make a dramatic difference in the racing, making side-by-side racing much more doable than in races before the reconfiguration.

Track History

Construction of the massive Las Vegas Motor Speedway began in 1995. The $200 million construction project was overseen by Las Vegas businessman Richie Clyne, along with race veterans Mel Larson and Hugh McDonough. The Indy Racing League hit the track soon after its completion in 1996. It took NASCAR two years after the completion to bring the Cup series to the track, although the NASCAR Truck series raced at LVMS in 1996 and the Nationwide series in 1997. The track currently sits on 1,600 acres and houses many different types of tracks, including the Bullring, the dirt track, and a drag strip used for Friday night drag strip racing.

Track Records

Most Wins: Jeff Burton, Jimmie Johnson, and Matt Kenseth (2)
Most Top Five Finishes: Jeff Gordon, Mark Martin, and Tony Stewart (4)
Most Lead Changes: 25—most recently on 3/13/2005 (total of 2 times)
Fewest Lead Changes: 13—on 3/5/2000
Most Cautions: 10—on 3/13/2005
Fewest Cautions: 2—most recently on 3/5/2000 (total of 2 times)
Race Record: Mark Martin— 146.554 mph (2 hours, 43 minutes, 58 seconds) (3/1/1998)
Qualifying Record: Kasey Kahne— 174.904 mph (30.874 seconds) (3/5/2003)

Fast Facts

- The first NASCAR Sprint Cup race was run at Las Vegas Motor Speedway on March 1, 1998, and was won by Mark Martin.
- Sterling Marlin is the oldest driver to have won at Las Vegas Motor Speedway—winning in March 2002, he was forty-four years old (plus eight months and one day).
- LVMS is referred to by many as the "Diamond in the Desert." The track is also known as the "House of Roush" due to the fact that

car owner Jack Roush has had so much success at this track with his stable of drivers. Some simply call the track the Blue Oval since most races have been won in Fords.

- Pit Boss is the track's mascot.
- The track is used by the Las Vegas Metropolitan Police Department as their officer driver training facility.

Parking

LVMS offers free parking to all the race fans attending race weekend. Overnight parking is not allowed in the general parking areas. All parking is on a first-come, first-served basis. For more info on parking at LVMS, call the track at 1-800-644-4444 or go to www.lvms.com.

Track Rules

According to the track's official website at www.lvms.com, the track's rules are as follows:

ITEMS ALLOWED IN THE GRANDSTANDS

- ✓ seat cushions (not to exceed 18")
- ✓ cameras
- ✓ binoculars
- ✓ scanners
- ✓ bottled water
- ✓ fanny packs

ITEMS *NOT* ALLOWED IN GRANDSTANDS

- ✗ umbrellas
- ✗ coolers
- ✗ food
- ✗ beverages (bottled water allowed)
- ✗ illegal drugs
- ✗ fires
- ✗ grills
- ✗ fireworks
- ✗ weapons of any description
- ✗ folding chairs
- ✗ glass containers
- ✗ pets (except service animals assisting those with disabilities)
- ✗ scaffolds
- ✗ noisemakers or horns
- ✗ helium balloons
- ✗ beach balls

Note: *The LVMS grandstands are smoke free on NASCAR weekends. Smokers will be allowed to smoke on the concourse level.*

INSIDER TIP—Lost and found is located near the administration building. After an event all lost and found items are transferred to the LVMS security department.

Special Needs and Services

LVMS does offer seating and parking for fans needing special assistance and accessibility. Fans needing special assistance are allowed one companion to accompany them. Call the track at 1-800-644-4444 for up-to-date info and specifics. Make sure to ask for your parking to be near your seats.

Track Tours

Individual speedway tours operate Monday through Saturday from 9 a.m. to 4 p.m. and Sundays from 11 a.m. to 4 p.m. Tours leave at the top of each hour from the Speedway World gift shop, which is located at the main entrance of the track. Speedway tours include viewing all nine tracks at the Las Vegas Motor Speedway, a visit to a luxury suite, and access to the infield of the superspeedway. It is best to call the track at 1-800-644-4444 prior to your arrival and check for any changes to the tour schedule. Group tours are available only by reservation.

Souvenirs

Las Vegas Motor Speedway souvenirs are available in the Speedway World gift shop, located on the first floor of the track administration building or at the track's online store at www .lvms.com. Driver-specific souvenirs are available in Souvenir Alley, adjacent to the main entrance.

INSIDER TIP—ATMs are located beneath the grandstand seating area as well as on the first floor of the LVMS administration building. The LVMS infield ATM services location is in the Finish Line Grill.

About the Area

Vegas is a stop on the NASCAR tour like no other. What's not to love about a city that never sleeps? There is more to do in this city than a race fan could ever hope to accomplish in one weekend; more of a reason to come back year after year, which is what most race fans who attend an event at Vegas do. The race is a near sellout each year due largely in part to the racing and of course the host city. Race fans can expect pleasant temperatures in March for race weekend. The average temp for Vegas this time of year is seventy-eight degrees.

CHAMBER OF COMMERCE

Las Vegas Chamber of Commerce
3720 Howard Hughes Parkway
Las Vegas, Nevada 89169
(702) 735-1616
www.lvchamber.com

Transportation

AIRPORT

McCarran International Airport
  (LAS)
5757 Wayne Newton Boulevard
Las Vegas, NV
(702) 261-5211
(Approximately fifteen miles from
  the track.)

AIRLINES

American (800) 433-7300
Continental (800) 525-0280
Delta (800) 221-1212
Northwest (800) 225-2525
Southwest (800) 435-9792
Sun Country (800) 752-1218
United (800) 241-6522
US Airways (800) 428-4322

RENTAL CARS

Airport Rent-A-Car (702) 795-0800
Alamo (702) 388-2142
Allstate Car Rental (702) 736-6147
Assured Auto Rental (702) 597-9710
Avis (702) 261-5595
Budget (702) 736-1212
Car Temps USA (702) 263-8411

Dollar (702) 739-8408
Dream Car & Motorcycle Rentals
  (702) 731-6452
Enterprise (702) 795-8842
Fantasy Car Rental (702) 795-3636
Frugal Car Rental (702) 897-1954
Hertz (702) 736-4900
National (702) 261-5391
Priceless Car Rental (888) 866-7283
Rent A Vette (702) 736-2592
Royal Rent-A-Car (702) 683-6472
Savmor Rental Car (702) 737-2839
Thrifty (702) 896-7600
US Rent-A-Car (702) 798-6100
Value Rent-A-Car (702) 733-8886
X-Press Rent A Car (702) 795-4008

Hotels

KEY
🐾 Pet Friendly   ≈ Pool
✗ Restaurant

Barker Motel
2600 Las Vegas Boulevard N.
North Las Vegas, NV
(702) 642-1138

Branding Iron Motel
2519 Las Vegas Boulevard N.
North Las Vegas, NV
(702) 642-6618

≈, ✗ **Cannery Hotel & Casino**
2121 E. Craig Road
North Las Vegas, NV
(702) 507-5700

♿, ≈ **Comfort Inn North**
910 E. Cheyenne Avenue
North Las Vegas, NV
(702) 399-1500

♿, ≈ **Emerald Suites-Nellis**
4555 Las Vegas Boulevard N
Las Vegas, NV
(702) 946-9999

≈ **Holiday Inn Express**
4035 N. Nellis Boulevard
Las Vegas, NV
(702) 644-5700

≈ **Holiday Inn Express-N Las
 Vegas**
4540 Donovan Way
North Las Vegas, NV
(702) 649-3000

Knotty Pine Motel
1900 Las Vegas Boulevard N.
North Las Vegas, NV
(702) 642-8300

♿, ≈ **La Quinta Inn Las Vegas Nellis**
4288 N. Nellis Boulevard
Las Vegas, NV
(702) 632-0229

♿, ≈ **Nellis Lodge**
4244 Las Vegas Boulevard N.
Las Vegas, NV
(702) 643-9220

♿ **Peterson Motel & Apartments**
2112 N. Nellis Boulevard
Las Vegas, NV
(702) 452-8199

♿, ≈, ✕ **Ramada Inn Speedway
 Casino**
3227 Civic Center Drive
North Las Vegas, NV
(702) 399-3297

Starlite Motel
1873 Las Vegas Boulevard N.
North Las Vegas, NV
(702) 642-1750

♿, ≈ **Super 8 Motel**
4435 Las Vegas Boulevard N.
Las Vegas, NV
(702) 644-7878

Thrift Suites
4244 Las Vegas Boulevard N.
Las Vegas, NV
(702) 644-9595

Vegas Chalet Motel
2401 Las Vegas Boulevard N.
North Las Vegas, NV
(702) 642-2115

♿ **Vegas Verdee Motel**
1635 N. Main Street
North Las Vegas, NV
(702) 307-5755

Camping

ON-SITE AND TRACK-OWNED CAMPING

LVMS offers several different camping options to race fans. It is always best to contact the track by calling 1-800-644-4444 or to visit www.lvms .com for up-to-date camping information, including camping fees.

Boulevard RV The Boulevard lot is adjacent to the back straightaway. Tram service is available from this lot. Dry camping only in this lot.

Bullring RV The Bullring area is located in the pits of the Bullring short track. This area is dry camping only.

Checkered Flag RV The Checkered Flag area is the track's premier RV lot. Located behind turn 1, it is a short walk to the grandstand seating area. This area is dry camping only.

Hollywood RV The Hollywood RV area is located at Gate 1 near the Bullring and go-cart tracks. Tram service is available from this lot. This area is dry camping only.

Infield RV As the name suggests, this infield RV area is located in the infield of the track. This area is for dry camping only.

Motorhome Hill The Motorhome Hill area is located above the backstretch providing a view of the entire racetrack. This area offers full hookups.

Turn 3 RV The turn 3 lot is located behind turn 3. This area is dry camping only.

OFF-SITE CAMPING

American Campgrounds
3440 Las Vegas Boulevard N.
Las Vegas, NV
(702) 643-1222

Camp-Out Inc.
1007 E. Cheyenne Ave
North Las Vegas, NV
(702) 399-1027

Hitchin' Post RV Park
3640 Las Vegas Boulevard N.
Las Vegas, NV
(702) 644-1043

King's Row Trailer Park
3660 Boulder Highway
Las Vegas, NV
(702) 457-3606

Nevada Tent & Event
4550 Copper Sage Street, Suite A
Las Vegas, NV
(702) 436-8050

Restaurants

KEY

🍔 Fast Food   🪑 Sit Down
📦 Takeout   🕭 Reservations

Must Eats

**Harrah's Las Vegas Casino
Flavors Buffet**
3475 Las Vegas Boulevard S.
Las Vegas, NV
(702) 369-5000

There are many all-you-can-eat buffets in Vegas but none as good as Harrah's. This is one of the few buffets where you will find crab legs.

Red Rock Casino Resort and Spa
11011 W. Charleston Boulevard
Las Vegas, NV
(702) 797-7777

This is a little off the beaten path from the main strip in Vegas, but the food makes it worth the trip. The prices are even better. If you want good food at an affordable price . . . you have found it.

🍔 **Arby's**
725 N. Nellis Boulevard
Las Vegas, NV
(702) 452-8177

🪑 **Barcelona Restaurant**
4385 N. Nellis Boulevard
Las Vegas, NV
(702) 644-7901

🪑 **Big Dog's Bar & Grill**
1511 N. Nellis Boulevard
Las Vegas, NV
(702) 459-1099

🪑 **Blueberry Hill Family
Restaurant**
4435 Las Vegas Boulevard N.
Las Vegas, NV
(702) 643-9600

🪑 **Buffalo Wild Wings Grill & Bar**
150 Centennial Parkway, Suite 101
North Las Vegas, NV
(702) 649-3054

🍔 **Burger King**
4328 Stealth Avenue
Nellis Air Force Base, NV
(702) 644-3374

📦 **Burgers Joints**
4955 E. Craig Road
Las Vegas, NV
(702) 644-0789

📦 **Capriotti's Sandwich Shop**
7240 W. Azure Drive
North Las Vegas, NV
(702) 655-1234

Chilean & American Cafe
1210 Honey Lake Street
Las Vegas, NV
(702) 227-9220

China Kitchen
4985 E. Craig Road
Las Vegas, NV
(702) 651-8828

Church's Chicken
2839 Las Vegas Boulevard N.
North Las Vegas, NV
(702) 642-9100

Country Cafe
3603 Las Vegas Boulevard N.,
   Suite 118
Las Vegas, NV
(702) 644-4811

Del Taco
43830 N. Nellis Boulevard
Las Vegas, NV
(702) 644-6857

Denny's
3230 Losee Road
North Las Vegas, NV
(702) 649-7671

Domino's Pizza
3266 Las Vegas Boulevard N., Suite 8
Las Vegas, NV
(702) 644-3030

Dora Maria's Restaurant
4889 E. Craig Road
Las Vegas, NV
(702) 644-5209

Fast Lane Cafe
6825 Speedway Boulevard,
   Unit 101B
Las Vegas, NV
(702) 651-9977

**Golden Phoenix Chinese
   Cuisine**
2345 E. Centennial Parkway
North Las Vegas, NV
(702) 457-6688

Hamburger Hut N' Market
2512 E. Cheyenne Avenue
North Las Vegas, NV
(702) 657-9202

Hungry Horse Restaurant
1301 E. Colton Avenue
North Las Vegas, NV
(702) 633-7121

Hush Puppy
1820 N. Nellis Boulevard
Las Vegas, NV
(702) 438-0005

Italian Delights
4375 Las Vegas Boulevard N.,
   Suite 13
Las Vegas, NV
(702) 651-9555

🍔 **Jack in the Box**
4385 Las Vegas Boulevard N.
Las Vegas, NV
(702) 643-6569

🍴 **Juke Joint Bar & Grill**
4230 E. Craig Road
North Las Vegas, NV
(702) 307-2082

🍔 **Kentucky Fried Chicken**
1990 N. Nellis Boulevard
Las Vegas, NV
(702) 452-0482

🍴 **KJ's Buffalo Grill**
1645 N. Lamb Boulevard
Las Vegas, NV
(702) 444-8234

🍴 **Levy Restaurants**
7000 Las Vegas Boulevard N.
Las Vegas, NV
(702) 632-8300

🥪 **Manhattan Pizza II**
4955 E. Craig Road
Las Vegas, NV
(702) 643-6664

🍔 **McDonald's**
4350 N. Nellis Boulevard
Las Vegas, NV
(702) 632-8916

🥪 **Memphis Championship
Barbeque**
4379 Las Vegas Boulevard N.
Las Vegas, NV
(702) 644-0000

🍴 **Outback Steakhouse**
4243 Las Vegas Boulevard N.
Las Vegas, NV
(702) 643-3148

🍴 **Pizza Hut**
6895 E. Lake Mead Boulevard,
  Suite 100
Las Vegas, NV
(702) 453-9011

🍔 **Popeye's**
4200 N. Washington Boulevard,
  Suite 429
Nellis Air Force Base, NV
(702) 643-3365

🥪 **Port of Subs**
6895 E. Lake Mead Boulevard,
  Suite 10
Las Vegas, NV
(702) 437-5900

🥪 **Quiznos Sub**
2595 E. Craig Road
North Las Vegas, NV
(702) 215-2116

R & B Deli
3603 Las Vegas Boulevard N.,
   Suite 103B
Las Vegas, NV
(702) 644-2020

Roberto's Taco Shop
4955 E. Craig Road, Suite 2
Las Vegas, NV
(702) 643-2305

Rubis Restaurant
2987 Las Vegas Boulevard N.
North Las Vegas, NV
(702) 657-9395

Siam Garden
3297 Las Vegas Boulevard N.,
   Suite 65
Las Vegas, NV
(702) 644-7770

Sonic Drive-In
2120 E. Craig Road
North Las Vegas, NV
(702) 643-1470

Star Pizza
3435 N. Nellis Boulevard
Las Vegas, NV
(702) 651-9515

Subway Sandwiches & Salads
4985 E. Craig Road
Las Vegas, NV
(702) 644-1038

Sully's Pub
1695 N. Nellis Boulevard
Las Vegas, NV
(702) 452-3236

Summit Grill
1100 E. Colton Avenue
North Las Vegas, NV
(702) 798-9494

Teriyaki Co.
719 N. Nellis Boulevard
Las Vegas, NV
(702) 438-1088

Thai Kitchen
1000 N. Nellis Boulevard, Suite I
Las Vegas, NV
(702) 453-9188

Viva Zapatas Mexican
   Restaurant
3826 E. Craig Road
North Las Vegas, NV
(702) 643-8888

Wendy's
3251 Las Vegas Boulevard N.
Las Vegas, NV
(702) 644-3510

Local Attractions

Below is a short list of things to do
and see in Vegas. This is one town
where you could never run out of at-

tractions. Make sure you check out the **Neon Garage,** a fan experience like no other. The Neon Garage is strategically placed in the infield of the track, allowing unprecedented access to the drivers and the teams. Entertainment is also provided on the Neon Garage stage. For more info on the Neon Garage, contact the track at 1-800-644-4444.

Desert Pines Golf Club
3415 E. Bonanza Road
Las Vegas, NV
(702) 388-4400

Desert Rose Golf Club
5483 Club House Drive
Las Vegas, NV
(702) 431-4653

Elvis-A-Rama Museum
3401 Industrial Road
Las Vegas, NV
(702) 892-0711

Fast Track Indoor Karting Center
5160 Las Vegas Boulevard
Las Vegas, NV
(702) 988-8747

Floyd Lamb State Park
9200 Tule Springs Road
Las Vegas, NV
(702) 486-5413

Guggenheim Hermitage Museum
3355 Las Vegas Boulevard S.
Las Vegas, NV
(702) 414-2440

Hoover Dam
4343 N. Rancho Drive
Las Vegas, NV
(702) 658-9820

Las Vegas Art Museum
9600 W. Sahara Avenue
Las Vegas, NV
(702) 360-8000

Las Vegas International Scouting Museum
2915 W. Charleston Boulevard, Suite 2
Las Vegas, NV
(702) 878-7268

Las Vegas Mini Gran Prix
1401 N. Rainbow Boulevard
Las Vegas, NV
(702) 259-7000

Lee Canyon
7501 Tule Springs Road
Las Vegas, NV
(702) 593-9500

Lied Discovery Children's Museum
833 Las Vegas Boulevard N.
Las Vegas, NV
(702) 382-3445

Mountasia Family Fun Center
2050 Olympic Avenue
Las Vegas, NV
(702) 898-7777

NASCAR Café at the Sahara
2535 Las Vegas Boulevard S.
Las Vegas, NV
(702) 734-7223

Neon Museum
821 Las Vegas Boulevard N.
Las Vegas, NV
(702) 387-6366

**Nevada State Museum & Historical
Society**
700 Twin Lakes Drive
Las Vegas, NV
(702) 486-5205

Red Rock Canyon
1000 Scenic Drive
Las Vegas, NV
(702) 363-1921

Scandia Family Fun Center
2900 Sirius Avenue
Las Vegas, NV
(702) 364-0070

Sega Gameworks
3785 Las Vegas Boulevard S.
Las Vegas, NV
(702) 432-4263

Speedworld at the Sahara
2535 Las Vegas Boulevard S.
Las Vegas, NV
(702) 737-2750

Spring Mountain Ranch State Park
6375 W. Charleston Boulevard
Las Vegas, NV
(702) 875-4141

Shopping

KEY

🚗 Automotive $ Discount
⊕ Pharmacy   🛍 Mall
☆ Specialty   ⛉ Department Store

☆ Bass
805 S. Grand Central Parkway, Suite
1933
Las Vegas, NV
(702) 383-9739

$ Big Lots
350 N. Nellis Boulevard
Las Vegas, NV
(702) 459-2345

$ Bonanza Discount
574 N. Eastern Avenue
Las Vegas, NV
(702) 388-0065

🛍 Boulevard Mall
3528 S. Maryland Parkway
Las Vegas, NV
(702) 732-8949

$ Family Dollar Store
3636 Las Vegas Boulevard N.
Las Vegas, NV
(702) 643-7201

🏬 Fashion Show Mall
3200 Las Vegas Boulevard S., Suite
600
Las Vegas, NV
(702) 369-8382

☆ Geoffrey Beene
705 S. Grand Central Parkway, Suite
1015
Las Vegas, NV
(702) 384-3034

☆ IZOD
855 S. Grand Central Parkway, Suite
1863
Las Vegas, NV
(702) 366-9051

$ Kmart
2671 Las Vegas Boulevard N.
North Las Vegas, NV
(702) 642-2183

🏬 Las Vegas Lam Center
3636 Las Vegas Boulevard N.
Las Vegas, NV
(702) 643-0275

$ Las Vegas Premium Outlets
875 S. Grand Central Parkway
Las Vegas, NV
(702) 474-7500

**🏬 Maryland Square Shopping
Center**
3993 Howard Hughes Parkway
Las Vegas, NV
(702) 369-4800

🏬 Meadows Mall
4300 Meadows Lane, Suite 10
Las Vegas, NV
(702) 878-4849

☆ Nellis Trail
755 N. Nellis Boulevard
Las Vegas, NV
(702) 531-1081

🏬 New Orleans Square
900 Karen Avenue
Las Vegas, NV
(702) 737-8551

$ 99 Cents Only Stores
1435 W. Craig Road, Suite C
North Las Vegas, NV
(702) 642-8299

🏬 Tower Shops at Stratosphere
2000 Las Vegas Boulevard S.
Las Vegas, NV
(702) 383-5319

🏬 Twain & PV Shopping Center
3930 S. Eastern Avenue
Las Vegas, NV
(702) 369-4950

▶︎ Village Center
1048 N. Rancho Drive, Suite B
Las Vegas, NV
(702) 648-8655

$ Wal-Mart Supercenter
4350 N. Nellis Boulevard
Las Vegas, NV
(702) 643-1884

Churches/
Worship Centers

Calvary Lutheran Church
800 N. Bruce Street
Las Vegas, NV
(702) 649-7788

Calvary Southern Baptist Church
1600 E. Cartier Avenue
North Las Vegas, NV
(702) 649-2644

**Catholic Apostolic Church
   International**
925 Felix Palm Avenue
North Las Vegas, NV
(702) 878-1006

Christ the Good Shepherd
930 Shades End Avenue
North Las Vegas, NV
(702) 242-2929

Church of Christ
2424 McCarran Street
North Las Vegas, NV
(702) 642-3141

**Church of Jesus Christ of Latter-
   Day Saints**
1825 N. Hollywood Boulevard
Las Vegas, NV
(702) 459-5254

First Presbyterian Church
1515 W. Charleston Boulevard
Las Vegas, NV
(702) 384-4554

Mountain View Assembly of God
3900 E. Bonanza Road
Las Vegas, NV
(702) 452-8400

New Horizon Christian Fellowship
2167 N. Walnut Road
Las Vegas, NV
(702) 437-5673

Redeemer Lutheran Church
1730 N. Pecos Road
Las Vegas, NV
(702) 642-7744

St. Christopher Catholic Church
1401 Flower Avenue
North Las Vegas, NV
(702) 657-0488

St. Luke's Episcopal Church
832 N. Eastern Avenue
Las Vegas, NV
(702) 642-4459

St. Michael's Orthodox Church
5719 Judson Avenue
Las Vegas, NV
(702) 452-1299

Zion Methodist Church
2108 Revere Street
North Las Vegas, NV
(702) 648-7806

Medical Centers

North Vista Hospital
1409 E. Lake Mead Boulevard
North Las Vegas, NV
(702) 649-7711

Sunrise Hospital
3601 Las Vegas Boulevard N.
Las Vegas, NV
(702) 642-2229

Pet Medical Center

Animal Kindness Veterinary
4910 E. Bonanza Road
Las Vegas, NV
(702) 453-2990

LOWE'S MOTOR SPEEDWAY— CHARLOTTE

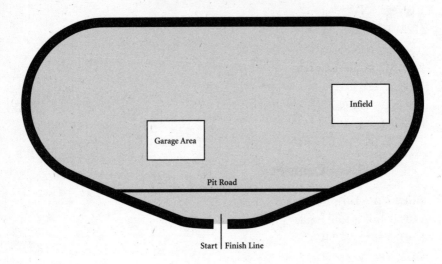

Track Information

Inaugural Year: 1960
Owner: SMI
City: Concord, North Carolina
Size: 1.5 miles
Banking: 24 degrees
Grandstand Capacity: 171,000

ADDRESS

Lowe's Motor Speedway
5555 Concord Parkway South
Concord, NC 28027
www.lowesmotorspeedway.com

TICKET INFORMATION

Phone: (800) 455-FANS
www.lowesmotorspeedway.com

About the Track

Lowe's Motor Speedway (LMS) is located right smack in the middle of the hub of NASCAR racing. Daytona Beach may be the home of NASCAR, but it's Charlotte where most of NASCAR's drivers have permanent addresses. For this very reason, racing at Lowe's is like a homecoming of sorts for most drivers and crew guys. Lowe's hosts two point NASCAR Sprint Cup events and the prestigious all-star event held in conjunction with the May race week. If you love Jimmie Johnson . . . this is your track. Ask any NASCAR driver out there who to beat at Lowe's and every one of them will tell you hands down . . . the number 48.

Track History

Bruton Smith (current owner of LMS) and the late Curtis Turner, a racing veteran and lumber industry businessman, partnered in 1959 to build the Charlotte Motor Speedway. The construction process took right over a year and cost the building duo approximately $1.25 million. The track emerged from a 1961 Chapter 11 and reorganization, but due to this fallout, Bruton Smith left the superspeedway in 1962 to pursue other business interests elsewhere, one of which was working with the Ford Motor Company in their dealership program. He quickly found financial success and began to purchase Charlotte Motor Speedway stock. By 1975, Smith had once again become majority owner in the track he and Turner built. Smith also took control of the day-to-day operations

and continues in that role even today. In 1998, Lowe's Home Improvement bought the naming rights to the North Carolina superspeedway, changing the name to the Lowe's Motor Speedway.

Track Records

Most Wins: Bobby Allison and Darrell Waltrip (6)
Most Top Five Finishes: Bobby Allison and Richard Petty (23)
Most Lead Changes: 59—on 5/27/1979
Fewest Lead Changes: 2—on 5/21/1961
Most Cautions: 22—on 5/29/2005
Fewest Cautions: 0—on 5/21/1961
Race Record: Jeff Gordon—160.306 mph (3 hours, 7 minutes, 31 seconds) (10/11/1999)
Qualifying Record: Elliott Sadler— 193.216 mph (27.948 seconds) (10/15/2005)

Fast Facts

- The first NASCAR Sprint Cup race was run at Lowe's Motor Speedway on June 19, 1960, and was won by Joe Lee Johnson.
- Cale Yarborough is the oldest driver to have won at Lowe's Motor Speedway—winning in October 1985, he was forty-six years

old (plus six months and nine days).

- George Washington ate lunch and rested in a house that became the speedway office at one point.
- In 1992, Lowe's installed a $1.7 million permanent lighting system.
- Portions of motion pictures *Days of Thunder, Speedway,* and *Stroker Ace* were filmed at LMS.
- Country music veteran Tracy Lawrence filmed his number-one hit "If the Good Die Young" video at LMS.
- The land that Lowe's Motor Speedway sits on was once a Civil War working plantation.
- The Pixar movie *Cars* premiered at LMS on May 26, 2006.

Parking

LMS offers free parking surrounding the entire speedway for fans attending the race. All parking is on a first-come, first-served basis. Parking nearest the track fills up quickly. The track does offer tram service for the lots farthest from the track. Call the track at 704-455-3200 or check www.lowesmotorspeedway.com for up-to-date parking info.

Track Rules

According to the track's official web site at www.lowesmotorspeedway.com, the track's rules are as follows:

ITEMS ALLOWED IN THE GRANDSTANDS

- ✓ soft-and hard-sided coolers (no larger than 14″ × 14″ × 14″)
- ✓ alcoholic beverages (cans only)
- ✓ cameras
- ✓ binoculars
- ✓ scanners
- ✓ seat cushions

ITEMS *NOT* ALLOWED IN THE GRANDSTANDS

- ✗ glass bottles
- ✗ strollers
- ✗ bags/backpacks (over 14″ × 14″ × 14″)
- ✗ coolers (over 14″ × 14″)
- ✗ pets (unless they are service animals helping guests with disabilities)
- ✗ weapons including firearms or knives
- ✗ skateboards
- ✗ roller skates
- ✗ scooters
- ✗ bicycles
- ✗ mopeds
- ✗ golf carts
- ✗ beach balls or balloons

✗ signs or banners

✗ horns or whistles

✗ stadium seats with armrests

✗ umbrellas

🏁 **INSIDER TIP**—Lost and found is located in the ticket service department on the second floor of the Smith Tower in front of Lowe's Motor Speedway.

Special Needs and Services

LMS does provide seating and parking for those with special needs or needing accessibility. LMS allows one companion to accompany fans with special needs. Call the track at 704-455-3200 prior to arrival for up-to-date information. Always ask for your parking to be near your seats.

Track Tours

LMS offers both individual and group tours. The tour includes pit road, the Sprint Cup garage area, Victory Lane, and a van ride around the track. Tours are available on non-event days and begin in the LMS gift shop, located in the administration building at the main entrance of the track. Group tours are available by reservation only. Call the track at 704-455-3204 for more info or group reservations.

Souvenirs

Official LMS souvenirs and driver merchandise can be purchased in the track's gift shop, located in the administration building at the main entrance of the track. Souvenir stands are also located all around Speedway. Driver-specific merchandise can be purchased at Souvenir Village, located at the corner of Highway 29 and Speedway Boulevard Road.

🏁 **INSIDER TIP**—LMS offers a variety of premium seating options, all of which give race fans a VIP race day experience. For more info on VIP seating and prerace pit tours, call the track at 704-455-3240. Make sure you ask about the Speedway Club, prerace pit tours, and the luxury seating.

About the Area

The Charlotte area is home base for most of the NASCAR drivers. This is due largely in part to the fact that most race shops are located in and around Charlotte, making Charlotte the hub for NASCAR. Many fans come in to Charlotte a few days early, so they can take in the race shop tours and the bonus track times available to the fans, as in qualifying and practice. Bruton Smith and his staff at LMS always make the trip worthwhile for the fans. Always check the track website prior to arrival for musical entertainment and special events at the track. The May points race at LMS is perfect racing weather. Every NASCAR fan should plan to attend at least one all-star event. This high-profile nonpoints race is always held the week prior to the 600. The week in between the all-star event and the 600 is always filled with driver appearances and other special events. The October event is midway through the Chase for the Championship, which provides much heated racing on the track but not off. The weather in Charlotte this time of year is perfecto. You might even hit the fall leaves at their peak.

INSIDER TIP—In addition to Lowe's Motor Speedway, Concord is home to NASCAR's Research and Development Center. It is also home to several NASCAR race teams, including Hendrick Motorsports, Roush Fenway Racing, and Chip Ganassi Racing. Many of the race shops offer tours during race week at LMS. All shops offering open house will list the dates and times on their team website.

Here are a few of the most popular shops to visit:

1. Richard Childress Racing— www.rcrracing.com
2. Hendrick Motorsports—www .hendrickmotorsports.com
3. Roush Fenway Racing— www.roushracing.com
4. Dale Earnhardt Inc.—www .daleearnhardtinc.com
5. Joe Gibbs Racing—www.joe gibbsracing.com

CHAMBER OF COMMERCE

Charlotte Chamber of Commerce
330 S. Tryon Street
P.O. Box 32785
Charlotte, NC 28232
(704) 378-1300
www.charlottechamber.com

Transportation

AIRPORT

Charlotte Douglas International
  Airport (CLT)
5501 Josh Birmingham Parkway
Charlotte, NC
(704) 359-4910
(Approximately sixteen miles from
  the track.)

AIRLINES

American (800) 433-7300
Delta (800) 221-1212
JetBlue (800) 538-2583
Northwest (800) 225-2525
United (800) 241-6522
US Airways (800) 428-4322

RENTAL CARS

Alamo (800) 327-9633
Avis (800) 831-2847
Budget (800) 527-0700
Dollar (800) 800-4000
Enterprise (800) 325-8007
Hertz (800) 654-3131
National (800) 227-7368
Thrifty (800) 643-7368

Hotels

KEY
≈ Pet Friendly   ≈ Pool
✕ Restaurant

≈, ✕ **Ballantyne Resort Hotel**
10000 Ballantyne Commons
  Parkway
Charlotte, NC
(704) 248-4000

Best Value Inn
2451 Kannapolis Highway
Concord, NC
(704) 788-8550

≈ **Candlewood Suites**
8812 University E. Drive
Charlotte, NC
(704) 598-9863

≈, ≈ **Comfort Suites**
7735 University City Boulevard
Charlotte, NC
(704) 547-0049

≈ **Comfort Suites**
7800 Gateway Lane
Concord, NC
(704) 979-3800

Concord Hotel
14 Union Street N.
Concord, NC
(704) 782-2131

≈ **Country Inn & Suites**
131 McCullough Drive
Charlotte, NC
(704) 549-8770

≈ **Courtyard by Marriott**
333 West W. T. Harris Boulevard
Charlotte, NC
(704) 549-4888

♿, ≈ **Days Inn**
5125 Davidson Highway
Concord, NC
(704) 786-9121

♿, ≈, ✕ **Doubletree Guest Suites Charlotte/Southpark**
6300 Morrison Boulevard
Charlotte, NC
(704) 364-2400

≈, ✕ **Doubletree Hotel Charlotte Airport**
2600 Yorkmont Road
Charlotte, NC
(704) 357-9100

♿, ≈ **Drury Inn & Suites**
415 West W. T. Harris Boulevard
Charlotte, NC
(704) 593-0700

≈, ✕ **Embassy Suites Hotel Resort & Conference Center**
5400 John Q. Hammons Drive NW
Concord, NC
(704) 455-8200

♿, ≈ **Fairfield Inn by Marriott**
5415 N. Interstate 85 Service Road
Charlotte, NC
(704) 596-2999

≈ **Hampton Inn—Speedway Boulevard**
9850 Weddington Road Extension
Concord, NC
(704) 979-5600

≈ **Hampton Inn & Suites South Park**
6700 Phillips Place Court
Charlotte, NC
(704) 319-5700

≈, ✕ **Hilton Charlotte Executive Park**
5624 Westpark Drive
Charlotte, NC
(704) 527-8000

≈, ✕ **Hilton—Charlotte University Place**
8629 J. M. Keynes Drive
Charlotte, NC
(704) 547-7444

♿, ≈, ✕ **Holiday Inn**
8520 University Executive Park Drive
Charlotte, NC
(704) 547-0999

≈ **Holiday Inn Express—I-85**
7772 Gateway Lane
Concord, NC
(704) 979-7900

≈ **Homewood Suites**
8340 N. Tryon Street
Charlotte, NC
(707) 549-8800

≈ **Hyatt Place**
4119 S. Stream Boulevard
Charlotte, NC
(704) 357-8555

⌂, ≈, ✕ **Marriott Charlotte
  Southpark**
2200 Rexford Road
Charlotte, NC
(704) 364-8220

⌂ **Mayfair Motel**
1516 Highway 29 N.
Concord, NC
(704) 786-1175

Microtel Inn & Suites
132 McCullough Drive
Charlotte, NC
(704) 549-9900

≈ **Relax Inn**
6426 N. Tryon Street
Charlotte, NC
(704) 921-9123

⌂, ≈ **Residence Inn**
8503 N. Tryon Street
Charlotte, NC
(704) 547-1122

≈ **Rodeway Inn**
1416 W. Sugar Creek Road
Charlotte, NC
(704) 597-5074

≈ **Sleep Inn and Suites**
7821 Gateway Lane
Concord, NC
(704) 979-8800

⌂, ≈ **Sleep Inn University Place**
8525 N. Tryon Street
Charlotte, NC
(704) 549-4544

≈ **Springhill Suites**
7811 Gateway Lane
Concord, NC
(704) 979-2500

⌂, ≈ **Suburban Extended Stay
  Hotel**
7725 Sossaman Lane
Concord, NC
(704) 979-5555

⌂ **Super 8 Motel**
4930 Sunset Road
Charlotte, NC
(704) 598-7710

⌂, ≈ **Towneplace Suites—
  University Research Park**
8710 Research Drive
Charlotte, NC
(704) 548-0388

≈ **Wingate Inn**
7841 Gateway Lane
Concord, NC
(704) 979-1300

≈ **Wingate Inn**
6057 Nations Ford Road
Charlotte, NC
(704) 523-3366

Camping

ON-SITE AND TRACK-OWNED CAMPING

LMS offers a variety of camping options for race fans. It is advisable to contact the track at 704-455-4445 for updated camping fees and information. Always ask for the rules of the specific area you choose to camp in; it is not uncommon for each camping area to have its own set of rules.

Fleetwood RV Camping Resort This is LMS's luxury camping at its best. This area has full hookups for fans choosing to pay the higher price for a VIP camping experience. This area is in walking distance of the track.

Rock City, Peninsula, Morehead Farms, Country Crock, and Tim Flock These areas are all dry camping. The track shuttle runs fans to and from the track. Portable toilets are provided for fans staying in these areas.

OFF-SITE CAMPING

Adkins Tent Rentals & Sales
2730 S. Ridge Avenue
Concord, NC
(704) 786-7032

Camp Thunderbird
1 Thunderbird Lane
Charlotte, NC
(704) 716-4100

McDowell Nature Reserve and Campground
6300 Morrison Boulevard
Charlotte, NC
(704) 364-2400

Tom Johnson Camping Center
6700 Speedway Boulevard
Concord, NC
(704) 455-1440

Restaurants

KEY
🍔 Fast Food   🪑 Sit Down
🥡 Takeout   ☎ Reservations

Must Eats

Boardwalk Billy's Raw Bar
9005 J. M. Keynes Drive
Charlotte, NC
(704) 503-7427

This is where all the locals eat, which tells you how good the food is. Stick around after dinner, and wait for the party to get started. The music goes on until the wee hours of the morning.

Ciro's Italian Restaurant
8927 J. M. Keynes Drive
Charlotte, NC
(704) 510-0012

Unlike Boardwalk Billy's, this is a quiet and relaxing atmosphere. The spaghetti is just like what would be served in southern Italy. There is lots of great vino to go around. This is a must stop for Italian food lovers.

Applebee's
8018 Concord Mills Boulevard
Concord, NC
(704) 979-1190

Avenue's Restaurant
172 Cabarrus Avenue W.
Concord, NC
(704) 782-0599

Bob Evans
7791 Gateway Lane
Concord, NC
(704) 979-8080

Bojangles' Famous Chicken
750 Cabarrus Avenue W.
Concord, NC
(704) 788-9131

Burger King
260 Concord Parkway N.
Concord, NC
(704) 788-8424

Carrabba's Italian Grill
7900 Lyles Lane NW
Concord, NC
(704) 979-3224

Casa Grande
1 Concord Commons Place SW
Concord, NC
(704) 782-6659

Christo's Family Restaurant
235 Branchview Drive SE
Concord, NC
(704) 262-7700

Cracker Barrel
7809 Lyles Lane
Concord, NC
(704) 979-0404

Danny's Place
300 Church Street N.
Concord, NC
(704) 788-7900

Dave and Buster's
8361 Concord Mills Boulevard
Concord, NC
(704) 979-1700

Dragon Palace
76 Spring Street SW
Concord, NC
(704) 785-8888

El Vallarta Mexican Restaurant
1445 Concord Parkway N., Suite 10
Concord, NC
(704) 792-2020

Emma's Carolina Cuisine
11 Union Street S., Suite 108
Concord, NC
(704) 788-1098

Golden Corral
1540 Highway 29 N.
Concord, NC
(704) 782-0044

Hardee's
547 Church Street N.
Concord, NC
(704) 786-2815

Hooters
9807 South Boulevard
Charlotte, NC
(704) 643-2044

Kabuto Japanese Steakhouse
1001 East W. T. Harris Boulevard
Charlotte, NC
(704) 548-1219

Kentucky Fried Chicken
258 Concord Parkway S.
Concord, NC
(704) 721-0114

Krispy Kreme Doughnuts
315 Wilshire Avenue SW
Concord, NC
(704) 782-2113

Macaroni Grill
8620 Research Drive
Charlotte, NC
(704) 595-9696

Mayflower Seafood
8480 NW Pit Stop Court
Concord, NC
(704) 510-2240

McDonald's
730 Cabarrus Avenue W.
Concord, NC
(704) 788-2701

🪑 **Moe's Southwest Grill**
2215 Ayrsley Town Boulevard,
   Suite D
Charlotte, NC
(704) 714-4566

🪑 **Olive Garden Italian Restaurant**
8010 Concord Mills Boulevard
Concord, NC
(704) 979-1130

🪑 **Onemor Restaurant Bar & Grill**
846 Union Street S.
Concord, NC
(704) 788-8874

🪑 **Outback Steakhouse**
1015 Chancellor Park Drive
Charlotte, NC
(704) 598-7727

🥡 **Paluso's Pizzeria**
10106 Johnston Road
Charlotte, NC
(704) 542-4511

🪑 **Quaker Steak and Lube**
7731 Gateway Lane
Concord, NC
(704) 979-5823

🪑 **Red Lobster**
8012 Concord Mills Boulevard
Concord, NC
(704) 979-1160

🪑 **Red Rocks Cafe Bar & Bakery**
4223 Providence Road
Charlotte, NC
(704) 364-0402

🪑 **Restaurant Acapulco**
274 Cabarrus Avenue W.
Concord, NC
(704) 789-9300

📞 **Ruth's Chris Steak House**
6000 Fairview Road
Charlotte, NC
(704) 556-1115

🪑 **Ryan's Steakhouse**
8601 Concord Mills Boulevard
Concord, NC
(704) 979-1055

🥡 **Subway Sandwiches & Salads**
856 Union Street, Suite 2
Concord, NC
(704) 782-0027

🪑 **Smokey Bones Barbeque and
   Grill**
8760 J. M. Keynes Drive
Charlotte, NC
(704) 549-8282

🥡 **Starbucks**
8111 Concord Mills Boulevard,
   Suite 745
Concord, NC
(704) 979-1555

🪑 **Stonehouse Grille**
Rocky River Golf Clubhouse
6900 Bruton Smith Boulevard
Concord, NC
(704) 455-1200

🪑 **Sullivan's Cafeteria**
87 McCachern Boulevard SE
Concord, NC
(704) 788-1403

🍔 **T & J's Deli**
30 Church Street SE
Concord, NC
(704) 784-3414

🪑 **Texas Roadhouse**
7801 Gateway Lane
Concord, NC
(704) 979-0390

🍔 **Troutman's Bar-B-Q Pit**
362 Church Street N.
Concord, NC
(704) 786-5213

🪑 **Two Leaves and a Bud**
11 Union Street S., Suite 100
Concord, NC
(704) 788-8327

🪑 **Union Street Bistro**
48 Union Street S.
Concord, NC
(704) 795-4902

🪑 **Upstream**
6902 Phillips Place Court
Charlotte, NC
(704) 556-7730

🍔 **Whataburger**
34 Church Street SE
Concord, NC
(704) 786-1618

🪑 **Yellow Rose Cafe & Billiards**
7631 Sharon Lakes Road, Suite L
Charlotte, NC
(704) 556-1992

Local Attractions

The **LMS Dirt Track,** located at Lowe's, is an exciting thing to do while in town for the Cup race. This is dirt track racing at its best and so much fun. Many of the NASCAR drivers sneak over on Friday or Saturday night of race weekend to catch all the action. For more info on the dirt track, call 1-800-455-3267. The **NASCAR Hall of Fame,** new in 2010, is worth the time and effort. This is a must stop for every race fan. The exhibits are priceless and many have never been on display before. Fans of all ages will love this. For more info on the Hall of Fame, go to www.nascar hall.com.

Balloons Over Charlotte
3709 Sweetgrass Lane
Charlotte, NC
(704) 541-7058

Discovery Place
301 N. Tryon Street
Charlotte, NC
(704) 372-6261

Cannon Village Visitor Center
200 West Avenue
Kannapolis, NC
(704) 938-3200

Hendrick Motor Sports
5315 Stowe Lane
Harrisburg, NC
(704) 455-3400

Charlotte's Botanical Forest
4700 Hoyt Hinson Road
Charlotte, NC
(704) 599-2600

Historic Rosedale
3427 N. Tryon Street
Charlotte, NC
(704) 335-0325

Charlotte Museum of History
3500 Shamrock Drive
Charlotte, NC
(704) 568-1774

Joe Gibbs Racing
13415 Reese Boulevard W.
Huntersville, NC
(704) 944-5000

Charlotte Nature Museum
301 N. Tryon Street
Charlotte, NC
(704) 337-2671

Reed Gold Mine
9621 Reed Mine Road
Midland, NC
(704) 721-4653

Charlotte Sports Center
8626 Hankins Road
Charlotte, NC
(704) 596-9009

Renaissance Park Golf Course
1525 W. Tyvola Road
Charlotte, NC
(704) 357-3375

Concord Zoo
1643 Simplicity Road
Concord, NC
(704) 782-3149

Richard Petty Driving Experience
6022 Victory Lane
Concord, NC
(704) 455-9443

Roush Racing, Inc.
4101 Roush Place NW
Concord, NC
(704) 720-4100

Skatelane USA
2790 Poplar Tent Road
Concord, NC
(704) 782-5513

USA Canoe/Kayak
301 S. Tryon Street
Charlotte, NC
(704) 348-4330

Shopping

KEY
🚗 Automotive $ Discount
⊕ Pharmacy   🏬 Mall
☆ Specialty   ⛫ Department Store

⛫ Belk
7115 Northlake Mall Drive
Newell, NC
(704) 598-2771

$ Best Buy
6390 Bayfield Parkway
Concord, NC
(704) 782-9401

$ Big Lots
280 Concord Parkway S., Suite 10
Concord, NC
(704) 262-7760

$ BJ's Wholesale Club
7905 Lyles Lane
Concord, NC
(704) 979-3900

☆ Burlington Coat Factory
8141 Concord Mills Boulevard
Concord, NC
(704) 979-3600

🏬 Carolina Mall
1480 Concord Parkway N.
Concord, NC
(704) 786-1185

🏬 Concord Mills
8111 Concord Mills Boulevard
Concord, NC
(704) 979-5000

$ Dollar General
501 Warren Coleman Boulevard
Concord, NC
(704) 262-7692

$ Dollar Tree
65 Concord Commons Place SW
Concord, NC
(704) 782-3355

🏬 Eastland Mall
5471 Central Avenue
Charlotte, NC
(704) 568-1263

☆ **Eddie Bauer**
8111 Concord Mills Boulevard
Concord, NC
(704) 979-0051

$ **Family Dollar Store**
40 Branchview Drive NE
Concord, NC
(704) 788-2806

$ **Famous Mart**
6600 N. Tryon Street
Charlotte, NC
(704) 596-3132

$ **Goody's Family Clothing**
170 Concord Commons Place SW
Concord, NC
(704) 721-7940

$ **Kmart**
8147 University City Boulevard
Charlotte, NC
(704) 599-1448

$ **Kmart**
545 Concord Parkway N.
Concord, NC
(704) 792-9600

♕ **Kohl's Department Store**
9315 N. Tryon Street
Charlotte, NC
(704) 593-1911

$ **Marshalls**
8215 University City Boulevard,
   Suite A
Charlotte, NC
(704) 597-2430

☆ **Pier 1 Imports**
8802 JW Clay Boulevard
Charlotte, NC
(704) 510-1042

☆ **Plato's Closet**
9630 University City Boulevard
Charlotte, NC
(704) 717-2972

$ **Ross Dress For Less**
8058 Concord Mills Boulevard
Concord, NC
(704) 979-0644

♕ **Saks Fifth Avenue**
8281 Concord Mills Boulevard
Concord, NC
(704) 979-6000

$ **Sam's Club**
8909 JW Clay Boulevard
Charlotte, NC
(704) 593-0227

☆ **S & K Famous Brand Menswear**
8821 JW Clay Boulevard, Suite 1
Charlotte, NC
(704) 593-0788

👕 **Sears**
600 Carolina Mall
Concord, NC
(704) 721-2100

☆ **Shoe Department**
8111 Concord Mills Boulevard
Concord, NC
(704) 979-0541

🛍 **Shoppers at University Place**
8929 J. M. Keynes Drive
Charlotte, NC
(704) 549-4811

☆ **Talbots**
8930 J. M. Keynes Drive
Charlotte, NC
(704) 549-9144

$ **Target**
3333 Cloverleaf Parkway
Kannapolis, NC
(704) 795-0555

$ **T.J. Maxx**
8221 Concord Mills Boulevard
Concord, NC
(704) 979-1020

☆ **Village Fudge & Candy Shop**
970 Branchview Drive NE, # 220
Concord, NC
(704) 792-1478

$ **Wal-Mart**
150 Concord Commons
Concord, NC
(704) 788-3138

$ **Wal-Mart**
8709 J. W. Clay Boulevard
Charlotte, NC
(704) 548-1168

Churches/
Worship Centers

Advent Lutheran Church
8840 University City Boulevard
Charlotte, NC
(704) 549-1555

All Saints Episcopal Church
6600 The Plaza
Charlotte, NC
(704) 536-4091

Cornerstone Presbyterian Church
401 Pitts School Road SW
Concord, NC
(704) 782-6824

Covenant Church of Harrisburg
6900 Hickory Ridge Road
Harrisburg, NC
(704) 455-5812

Crossroads United Methodist
220 George W. Liles Parkway NW
Concord, NC
(704) 795-0423

Ever Increasing Faith
555 Pitts School Road NW, Suite C
Concord, NC
(704) 784-8672

Gateway Church
4323 Concord Parkway S.
Concord, NC
(704) 784-4474

Harrisburg United Methodist
4560 Highway 49 S.
Harrisburg, NC
(704) 455-3544

Holly Grove Primitive Baptist
3033 Concord Parkway S.
Concord, NC
(704) 782-3081

King Way Baptist Church
7550 Ruben Linker Road NW
Concord, NC
(704) 721-5922

New Harvest Church
6481 Morehead Road
Harrisburg, NC
(704) 454-5533

Providence Presbyterian Church
551 Pitts School Road, Suite C
Concord, NC
(704) 788-8899

Roberta Church of God
4435 Roberta Road
Concord, NC
(704) 782-0743

St. James Catholic Church
139 Manor Avenue SW
Concord, NC
(704) 720-0600

**St. Thomas Aquinas Catholic
    Church**
1400 Suther Road
Charlotte, NC
(704) 549-1607

Sword of the Spirit
3318 Bogle Street
Concord, NC
(704) 782-5683

University City Fellowship
4010 Dearborn Place NW
Concord, NC
(704) 793-1823

University City Seventh Day
11431 University City Boulevard
Charlotte, NC
(704) 549-8007

West Cabarrus Church
7655 Speedway Boulevard
Concord, NC
(704) 455-2590

Medical Centers

Cabarrus Memorial Hospital
920 Church Street N.
Concord, NC
(704) 783-1645

Carolinas Medical Center
251 Eastway Drive
Charlotte, NC
(704) 446-9991

Carolinas Medical Center—
  University
Highway 29 and W. Harris
  Boulevard
Charlotte, NC
(704) 548-6000

Presbyterian Hospital
10030 Gilead Road
Huntersville, NC
(704) 316-4000

University Hospital
8800 N. Tryon Street
Charlotte, NC
(704) 548-6000

Pet Medical Centers

Banfield the Pet Hospital
8116 University City Boulevard
Charlotte, NC
(704) 599-3488

Hight Veterinary Hospital
9528 N. Tryon Street
Charlotte, NC
(704) 595-9377

Stoney Creek Animal Hospital
626 W. Mallard Creek Church Road
Charlotte, NC
(704) 717-0616

University Animal Clinic
4650 Highway 49 S.
Harrisburg, NC
(704) 455-5907

MARTINSVILLE SPEEDWAY

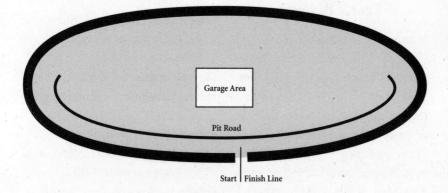

Track Information

Inaugural Year: 1949
Owner: ISC
City: Martinsville, Virginia
Size: 0.526 miles
Banking: 12 degrees
Grandstand Capacity: 65,000

ADDRESS
Martinsville Speedway
340 Speedway Road
Martinsville, VA 24112
(877) 722-3849
www.martinsvillespeedway.com

TICKET INFORMATION
Phone: (877) 722-3849
www.martinsvillespeedway.com

About the Track

Martinsville Speedway is a crown jewel in racing. Racing on this half-mile dual surface (asphalt and concrete) track is always great from beginning to end. For those fans who stick around for Victory Lane ceremonies, you won't have to squint—

Victory Lane at Martinsville is on the front straightaway at the start-finish line. Fans can see the action at Martinsville like no other track on the circuit.

Track History

Martinsville was constructed in 1947 by race promoter Clay Earles. Earles went way beyond his original building budget of $10,000 to construct the half-mile facility. By the time the first race was run in September 1947, Earles had plopped down $60,000 to complete his dream track. To date, Martinsville is the oldest track on the NASCAR Sprint Cup circuit and the shortest in length. ISC purchased the track in 2004 for $192 million from the joint ownership made up of Earles's family members and NASCAR's Bill and Jim France.

INSIDER TIP—Make sure you try one of the famous Martinsville hot dogs. Don't let the red color scare you . . . they are worth every fat gram.

Track Records

Most Wins: Richard Petty (15)

Most Top Five Finishes: Richard Petty (30)

Most Lead Changes: 25—on 9/28/1980

Fewest Lead Changes: 1—most recently on 4/9/1961 (total of 3 times)

Most Cautions: 19—on 10/23/2005

Fewest Cautions: 1—most recently on 4/25/1971 (total of 3 times)

Race Record: Jeff Gordon— 82.223 mph (3 hours, 11 minutes, 55 seconds) (9/22/1996)

Qualifying Record: Tony Stewart— 98.083 mph (19.306 seconds) (10/21/2005)

Fast Facts

- The first NASCAR Sprint Cup race was run at Martinsville Speedway on September 25, 1949, and was won by Red Byron.
- Harry Gant is the oldest driver to have won at Martinsville Speedway—winning in September 1991, he was fifty-one years old (plus eight months and thirteen days).
- Only four cars were still running at the end of the race on May 6, 1951—the fewest number of cars to complete the race at Martinsville.

Parking

Martinsville Speedway offers free parking to race fans attending the race. All parking is on a first-come, first-served basis. Call the track at 877-722-3849 for up-to-date traffic tips and parking info or go to www .martinsvillespeedway.com.

Track Rules

According to the track's official website at www.martinsvillespeedway. com, the track's rules are as follows:

ITEMS ALLOWED IN GRANDSTANDS

- ✓ one soft-sided bag/cooler (no larger than 6″ × 6″ × 12″, may contain ice)
- ✓ one clear plastic bag (no larger than 18″ × 18″ × 4″, may not contain ice)
- ✓ binoculars
- ✓ scanners
- ✓ headsets
- ✓ cameras
- ✓ seat cushions

ITEMS NOT ALLOWED IN THE GRANDSTANDS

- ✗ firearms
- ✗ scooters
- ✗ golf carts
- ✗ skateboards
- ✗ roller skates
- ✗ fireworks
- ✗ hard-sided coolers
- ✗ thermoses or insulated cups of any size
- ✗ pets (unless accompanying someone needing special assistance)
- ✗ strollers
- ✗ umbrellas

Special Needs and Services

Martinsville Speedway provides numerous accessible features for fans needing special assistance. Companion seating is also available for those in need of this service. Contact the track at 276-956-3151, extension 224, prior to arrival for up-to-date info. Always ask for your parking to be near your seats.

INSIDER TIP—Guest Information Centers are scattered around the facility. These very helpful centers can give you tips on track activities, guest amenities, access to disabled assistance carts, and directions to various areas of the track.

Track Tours

Martinsville does not currently offer individual track tours. Tours are only available as part of certain package deals and large groups. Call the track's sales office at 877-722-3849 to arrange a group tour or to get more info on the packages that include track tours.

Souvenirs

Official Martinsville track souvenirs and driver-specific items can be purchased at Souvenir Alley, which is located in the Exhibit Pavilion near the main entrance to the track. Track items can also be purchased at Martinsville's online store at www.martinsvillespeedway.com.

About the Area

After traveling the circuit for over twenty years now, I can honestly tell you that Martinsville Speedway and the area surrounding the track has become one of my top favorite stops on the NASCAR Sprint Cup tour. I am always amazed at how well kept the track is and just how beautiful the town is. It reminds me of a Norman Rockwell setting. Pulling up to the main entrance of Martinsville Speedway is like taking in a breath of fresh air. This track reminds me of how racing was twenty-five years ago. The driver accessibility is like no other track, and the race action feels like it is an arm's length away. There is not a bad grandstand seat in the house at this little gem. If you have never been to Martinsville, do yourself a favor and make the trip. It is advisable to dress in layers when attending either the spring or the fall race. The weather in Martinsville both seasons can be tricky. You never know if you will need sunscreen or a jacket. The fall race is a beautiful time of year to visit the area due to the fall colors.

INSIDER TIP—Free child safety and identification wristbands (with space to list the child's name, your preselected meeting location, the parent/guardian's name and telephone number, medical and other key information) are available at the Guest Information Centers, the Main Ticket Office, Pavilion Ticket Booth, the Security Office, and raceway ministry locations.

CHAMBER OF COMMERCE

Martinsville-Henry County
  Chamber of Commerce
115 Broad Street/P.O. Box 709
Martinsville, VA 24114
(276) 632-6401
www.mhcchamber.com

Transportation

AIRPORTS

**Piedmont Triad International
  Airport (GSO)**
6415 Bryan Boulevard
Greensboro, NC
(336) 665-5600
(Piedmont Triad International
  Airport is approximately forty
  miles from the track.)

Roanoke Regional Airport (ROA)
5202 Aviation Drive NW
Roanoke, VA
(540) 362-1999
(Roanoke Regional Airport is
  approximately forty-three miles
  from the track.)

AIRLINES

American (800) 433-7300
Delta (800) 221-1212
Northwest (800) 225-2525
United (800) 241-6522
US Airways (800) 428-4322

RENTAL CARS

Alamo (540) 366-6210
Avis (336) 665-5700
Budget (540) 265-7328
Dollar (866) 776-6667
Enterprise (336) 855-6464
National (336) 668-7657
Thrifty (336) 605-6017

Hotels

KEY
🐾 Pet Friendly   ≈ Pool
✗ Restaurant

🐾 **Best Lodge**
1985 Virginia Avenue
Martinsville, VA
(276) 647-3941

🐾, ≈, ✗ **Best Western Martinsville
  Inn**
1755 Virginia Avenue
Martinsville, VA
(276) 632-5611

Boxley Inn
117 E. Hunter Street
Madison, NC
(336) 445-0030

🐾 **Budget Host Inn**
18059 Virgil H Goode Highway
Rocky Mount, VA
(540) 483-9757

Budget Inn
1681 U.S. Highway 29 Business
Reidsville, NC
(336) 349-6540

Budget Inn
3980 U.S. Highway 220
Madison, NC
(336) 548-6011

🛏, ≈ **Comfort Inn**
1730 N. Main Street
Rocky Mount, VA
(540) 489-4000

🛏, ≈ **Days Inn—Martinsville**
3841 Greensboro Road
Ridgeway, VA
(276) 638-3914

Days Inn Eden
115 W. Kings Highway
Eden, NC
(336) 623-1500

🛏 **Econo Lodge**
110 E. Arbor Lane
Eden, NC
(336) 627-5131

Economy Inn
3050 W. Main Street
Danville, VA
(434) 792-3622

Executive Inn
2660 W. Main Street
Danville, VA
(434) 793-1244

≈ **Hampton Inn**
50 Hampton Drive
Martinsville, VA
(276) 647-4700

🛏, ≈ **Hampton Inn**
724 S. Van Buren Road
Eden, NC
(336) 627-1111

🛏, ≈ **Holiday Inn Express**
1895 Virginia Avenue
Martinsville, VA
(276) 666-6835

🛏, ≈ **Holiday Inn Express**
395 Old Franklin Turnpike
Rocky Mount, VA
(540) 489-5001

🛏, ≈ **Jameson Inn**
378 Commonwealth Boulevard W.
Martinsville, VA
(276) 638-0478

🛏, ≈ **Jameson Inn**
716 Linden Drive
Eden, NC
(336) 627-0472

King's Court Motel
6570 Greensboro Road
Ridgeway, VA
(276) 956-3101

🛏, ≈ **Knights Inn**
2357 Virginia Avenue
Collinsville, VA
(276) 647-3716

🛏 **Mar Gre Motel**
213 S. Van Buren Road
Eden, NC
(336) 623-9161

❉, ≈, ✗ **Quality Inn Dutch Inn**
2360 Virginia Avenue
Collinsville, VA
(276) 647-3721

❉ **Redwood Motel**
18021 Virgil H Goode Highway
Rocky Mount, VA
(540) 483-5238

❉ **Super 8 Motel**
1044 Memorial Boulevard N.
Martinsville, VA
(276) 666-8888

≈ **Travel Inn**
4520 Greensboro Road
Ridgeway, VA
(276) 956-3141

❉ **Virginian Motel**
105 W. Blue Ridge Street
Stuart, VA
(276) 694-4244

Camping

ON-SITE AND TRACK-OWNED CAMPING

Martinsville Speedway offers various camping options for race fans. It is always best to contact the track at 877-722-3849 prior to your arrival for up-to-date camping info and fees. It is also a good idea to request the rules for the specific area you choose to camp in—it is not uncommon for each area to have its own set of rules.

Backstrech Reserved Camping Lot This self-contained area, adjacent to the backstretch, is available only to season ticket holders.

Campground Reserved Camping This self-contained area is located near the entrance to the campground; also reserved for season ticket holders.

General Camping This area allows camping of all sorts. Everyone in the camping area must have a single event ticket.

North Reserved Camping This self-contained area is for fans who have purchased a single event race ticket. This reserved area is located on the main campground road.

Third Turn Reserved Camping This self-contained area, located outside of turn 3, is reserved for season ticket holders.

OFF-SITE CAMPING

D & J RV Park
265 D and J Park Drive
Axton, VA
(276) 632-6856

Dan River Campground
724 Webster Road
Stoneville, NC
(336) 427-8530

Deer Run Camp Grounds
1098 Deer Run Road
Ferrum, VA
(276) 930-1235

Fairystone State Park
967 Fairystone Lake Drive
Stuart, VA
(276) 930-2424

Goose Dam Campground
1155 Goose Dam Road
Rocky Mount, VA
(540) 483-2100

H & M RV Park
16576 Martinsville Highway
Axton, VA
(276) 650-1155

Horseshoe Point Park
934 Old Henry Road
Henry, VA
(540) 365-7385

Indian Heritage RV Park
184 Tensbury Drive
Martinsville, VA
(276) 632-9500

Salthouse Branch Park
620 Salthouse Branch Road
Henry, VA
(540) 365-7005

Restaurants

KEY

🍔 Fast Food   🪑 Sit Down
🥡 Takeout   🍷 Reservations

Must Eats

Hillbilly Hideaway Restaurant
4335 Pine Hall Road
Walnut Grove, VA
(336) 591-4861

This is a far piece out in the woods, but it is worth every minute of the drive. A family-style restaurant, it has great country food and the best iced tea around. Make sure you leave room for the desserts!

Texas Steakhouse of Martinsville
283 Commonwealth Boulevard
Martinsville, VA
(276) 632-7133

The cooked-to-order steaks are famous way beyond the Martinsville city limits. The appetizers are mouthwatering, too. Make sure you arrive hungry!

🥡 **Aloha Wok Chinese Restaurant**
3424 Virginia Avenue
Collinsville, VA
(276) 647-1443

Angela's Grill
5445 Figsboro Road
Martinsville, VA
(276) 638-1330

Applebee's
281 Commonwealth Boulevard W.
Martinsville, VA
(276) 638-2377

Arby's
972 Memorial Boulevard N.
Martinsville, VA
(276) 632-8504

Arts Etc. and Cafe
43 E. Church Street
Martinsville, VA
(276) 666-6655

Berta's Place
239 Broad Street
Martinsville, VA
(276) 632-9000

Bill & Tom's Restaurant
2446 Figsboro Road
Martinsville, VA
(276) 632-4688

Biscuitville
1121 Memorial Boulevard S.
Martinsville, VA
(276) 632-1079

Bojangles' Famous Chicken
1515 Virginia Avenue
Martinsville, VA
(276) 632-5830

Burger King
816 E. Church Street
Martinsville, VA
(276) 638-1270

Cafe Delight
60 Belmont Street
Collinsville, VA
(276) 647-2233

Captain Tom's Seafood
2615 Greensboro Road
Martinsville, VA
(276) 666-0326

Chicago Pizza
240 Commonwealth Boulevard W.
Martinsville, VA
(276) 632-9861

Chick-fil-A
240 Commonwealth Boulevard W.,
  Suite 30
Martinsville, VA
(276) 666-6740

China Buffet
1090 Memorial Boulevard N.
Martinsville, VA
(276) 632-8689

China Express
2906 Virginia Avenue
Collinsville, VA
(276) 647-4660

🪑 Clarence's Steak & Seafood House
6636 Greensboro Road
Ridgeway, VA
(276) 956-3400

🪑 Corona Restaurant
6254 Al Philpott Highway
Martinsville, VA
(276) 632-8480

🪑 Country Cookin
240 Commonwealth Boulevard W.
Martinsville, VA
(276) 666-0768

🍔 Dairy Queen
6690 Greensboro Road
Ridgeway, VA
(276) 956-1511

🍗 Dixie Pig Barbecue
817 Memorial Boulevard N.
Martinsville, VA
(276) 632-9082

🍗 Domino's Pizza
1102 Madison Street
Martinsville, VA
(276) 632-1811

🪑 Duffers
730 E. Church Street
Martinsville, VA
(276) 632-3837

🪑 El Parral Mexican Restaurant
670 Commonwealth Boulevard W.
Martinsville, VA
(276) 632-6408

🪑 El Ranchito
3069 Virginia Avenue
Collinsville, VA
(276) 647-4330

🪑 Elizabeth's Pizza
8500 Al Philpott Highway
Martinsville, VA
(276) 632-1366

🪑 Fridays Garden Deli
100 Commonwealth Boulevard E.
Martinsville, VA
(276) 638-6444

🪑 Garfield's Place
2670 Appalachian Drive
Martinsville, VA
(276) 632-9008

🪑 Globman's the Cafe
120 E. Main Street
Martinsville, VA
(276) 632-7472

🍗 Grandmas's Chicken
275 Riverside Drive
Bassett, VA
(276) 629-3131

Hardee's
547 Memorial Drive
Martinsville, VA
(276) 638-7056

Hazel's Place
124 E. Main Street
Martinsville, VA
(276) 666-4682

Henry Inn Restaurant
10 Broad Street
Martinsville, VA
(276) 632-5502

Heritage Cafe
10 E. Church Street
Martinsville, VA
(276) 638-8818

Hodge's Wings & More
716 Memorial Boulevard S.
Martinsville, VA
(276) 632-9497

Hometown USA
147 E. Main Street
Martinsville, VA
(276) 638-8930

Hurley's Uptown Pub
10 E. Church Street
Martinsville, VA
(276) 632-4444

Jerry's Pizza
2635 Greensboro Road
Martinsville, VA
(276) 638-3990

Kentucky Fried Chicken
18 Tensbury Drive
Martinsville, VA
(276) 638-2963

K-Wok
2796 Greensboro Road
Martinsville, VA
(276) 638-3888

Little Caesars Pizza
3404 Virginia Avenue
Collinsville, VA
(276) 647-8811

Long John Silver's
802 E. Church Street
Martinsville, VA
(276) 638-7300

Macarena's Seafood Bar & Grill
1755 Virginia Avenue
Martinsville, VA
(276) 638-5411

McDonald's
202 Commonwealth Boulevard W.
Martinsville, VA
(276) 638-4343

McMillan Family Restaurant
1620 Virginia Avenue
Martinsville, VA
(276) 632-8311

Michaels Steak & More
2089 Virginia Avenue
Collinsville, VA
(276) 647-3720

Mi Ranchito
1212 Memorial Boulevard S.
Martinsville, VA
(276) 632-6363

Nina's Italian Restaurant
1854 Virginia Avenue
Martinsville, VA
(276) 632-3800

Papa John's Pizza
639 E. Church Street
Martinsville, VA
(276) 634-5353

Pigs R US Barbecue
1014 Liberty Street
Martinsville, VA
(276) 632-1161

Pizza Hut
2550 Greensboro Road
Martinsville, VA
(276) 638-4514

Quiznos Sub
3627 Virginia Avenue
Collinsville, VA
(276) 647-7400

Rania's Italian Restaurant
147 E. Main Street
Martinsville, VA
(276) 638-4462

Roma Cafe
2280 Virginia Avenue
Collinsville, VA
(276) 647-7662

Ryan's Grill Buffet & Bakery
361 Commonwealth Boulevard W.
Martinsville, VA
(276) 634-5335

Sally's Family Restaurant
2628 Virginia Avenue
Collinsville, VA
(276) 647-8217

Shun Xing Chinese Restaurant
1101 Brookdale Street, Suite C
Martinsville, VA
(276) 632-8855

Skip's Restaurant
359 Patrick Avenue
Fieldale, VA
(276) 673-3855

🍔 **Sonic Drive-In**
410 Starling Avenue
Martinsville, VA
(276) 632-4114

🥪 **Subway Sandwiches & Salads**
937 E. Church Street
Martinsville, VA
(276) 634-5667

🍔 **Taco Bell**
8425 Al Philpott Highway
Martinsville, VA
(276) 632-2570

🍴 **Texas Steakhouse & Saloon**
283 Commonwealth Boulevard W.
Martinsville, VA
(276) 632-7133

🍴 **Third Bay Cafe**
1163 Spruce Street
Martinsville, VA
(276) 666-8414

🥪 **Tokyo Express**
1170 Memorial Boulevard
Martinsville, VA
(276) 632-7599

🥪 **Walsh's Chicken & More**
600 Starling Avenue
Martinsville, VA
(276) 632-1146

🍔 **Wendy's**
2801 Virginia Avenue
Collinsville, VA
(276) 647-7557

🍴 **Yamato**
810 Commonwealth Boulevard
Martinsville, VA
(276) 638-8188

Local Attractions

Martinsville is one of the race destinations where I do very little outside of catching all the racing at the track that is humanly possible. The track is open to the public Friday through Sunday with lots of on-track action to keep you occupied. I just love the old-fashioned feel of this track mixed in with great racing. I have listed other things to do while in Martinsville, but for me . . . the famous red Martinsville hot dogs, the beautiful track, and the terrific racing are what keep me trackside.

Beaver Hills Golf Course
325 Beaver Hills Club Drive
Martinsville, VA
(276) 632-1526

Colonial Downs
3951 Greensboro Road
Ridgeway, VA
(276) 632-0187

Eden Draper Recreation Center
308 E. Stadium Drive
Eden, NC
(336) 635-2268

Lake Sugar Tree Motor Sports
400 Movie Movers E.
Axton, VA
(276) 650-3378

Lynrock Golf Club
636 Valley Drive
Eden, NC
(336) 623-6110

Madison-Mayodan Recreation
300 S. Second Avenue
Mayodan, NC
(336) 548-9572

Patrick County Historical
116 W. Blue Ridge Street
Stuart, VA
(276) 694-2840

Piedmont Arts Association
215 Starling Avenue
Martinsville, VA
(276) 632-3221

Virginia Motorsports Museum
212 Johnson Street
Stuart, VA
(276) 694-5554

Virginia Museum of Natural History
1001 Douglas Avenue
Martinsville, VA
(276) 666-8600

Shopping

KEY

🚗 Automotive $ Discount
➕ Pharmacy   🛍 Mall
☆ Specialty   🏬 Department Store

🏬 **Belk**
240 Commonwealth Boulevard W.
Martinsville, VA
(276) 638-2471

$ **Big Lots**
604 S. Van Buren Road
Eden, NC
(336) 627-9711

☆ **Cox's Fashions**
455 Franklin Street
Rocky Mount, VA
(540) 483-5384

$ **Dollar General**
939 Fairystone Park Highway
Stanleytown, VA
(276) 629-2551

$ **Dollar Tree**
1009 Virginia Avenue, # 6
Martinsville, VA
(276) 632-5882

$ **Family Dollar Store**
730 E. Church Street
Martinsville, VA
(276) 632-1640

☆ **Fieldale Fashions**
4036 Appalachian Drive
Fieldale, VA
(276) 673-3440

$ **Goody's Family Clothing**
240 Commonwealth Boulevard W.
Martinsville, VA
(276) 656-1288

☆ **Greene Company**
2075 Stultz Road
Martinsville, VA
(276) 638-7101

⌂ **JC Penney**
240 Commonwealth Boulevard W.
Martinsville, VA
(276) 638-2401

$ **Kmart**
2876 Greensboro Road
Martinsville, VA
(276) 666-5964

🏬 **Liberty Fair Mall**
240 Commonwealth Boulevard W.
Martinsville, VA
(276) 632-9786

$ **Maxway**
57 Riverside Drive
Bassett, VA
(276) 629-5202

🏬 **Patrick Henry Mall**
26 W. Church Street
Martinsville, VA
(276) 632-5423

$ **Roses Stores**
600 Commonwealth Boulevard W.
Martinsville, VA
(276) 632-3036

⌂ **Sears**
240 Commonwealth Boulevard W.
Martinsville, VA
(276) 666-1300

☆ **Shoe Department**
812 Commonwealth Boulevard
Martinsville, VA
(276) 638-8020

☆ **Taylor 2 Fashions**
2440 Greensboro Road, # A
Martinsville, VA
(276) 670-2027

$ **Wal-Mart Supercenter**
976 Commonwealth Boulevard
Martinsville, VA
(276) 634-5393

Churches/
Worship Centers

Abundant Grace Church
1549 Daniels Creek Road
Collinsville, VA
(276) 647-2662

Abundant Life Fellowship
231 Ford Street
Collinsville, VA
(276) 647-5337

Agape Bible Christian Fellowship
240 E. Market Street
Martinsville, VA
(276) 634-5522

Alpha Apostolic Temple Church
1014 Jordan Street
Martinsville, VA
(276) 632-0148

ASK Church of God in Christ
69 Tanbark Place
Martinsville, VA
(276) 666-2447

Bible Baptist Church
316 Spring Drive
Collinsville, VA
(276) 647-8245

Broad Street Christian Church
106 Broad Street
Martinsville, VA
(276) 632-2609

Calvary Christian Church
515 Mulberry Road
Martinsville, VA
(276) 632-4577

**Calvary's Hill United Pentecostal
  Church**
4225 Mount Olivet Road
Martinsville, VA
(276) 632-0664

Charity Christian Church
915 Morgan Street
Martinsville, VA
(276) 632-0957

Chatham Heights Christian Church
4020 Sunset Drive
Martinsville, VA
(276) 632-5869

Chatham Heights Methodist Church
1817 Old Chatham Road
Martinsville, VA
(276) 638-2477

Christ Episcopal Church
311 E. Church Street
Martinsville, VA
(276) 632-2896

Clearview Wesleyan Church
925 Barrows Mill Road
Martinsville, VA
(276) 632-4435

Ephesus Seventh Day Adventist
8559 Al Philpott Highway
Martinsville, VA
(276) 632-0582

First Assembly of God
1002 Chatham Heights
Martinsville, VA
(276) 632-7902

First Baptist Church
23 Starling Avenue
Martinsville, VA
(276) 632-6336

First Presbyterian Church
1901 Patrick Henry Avenue
Martinsville, VA
(276) 632-3431

First United Methodist Church
146 E. Main Street
Martinsville, VA
(276) 638-8733

Holy Trinity Lutheran Church
1527 E. Church Street Extension
Martinsville, VA
(276) 632-4677

Hope Presbyterian Church
601 E. Church Street
Martinsville, VA
(276) 638-2050

Saint Joseph's Catholic Church
2481 Spruce Street
Martinsville, VA
(276) 638-4779

Medical Centers

Martinsville Memorial Hospital
320 Hospital Drive
Martinsville, VA
(276) 666-7200

Morehead Memorial Hospital
117 E. Kings Highway
Eden, NC
(336) 623-9711

**RJ Reynolds—Patrick County
   Memorial Hospital**
18688 Job Stuart Highway
Stuart, VA
(276) 694-8688

Pet Medical Centers

Henry County Animal Clinic
101 Veteran Road
Martinsville, VA
(276) 632-5262

King's Mountain Animal Clinic
5086 King's Mountain Road
Collinsville, VA
(276) 647-3714

Veterinary Services
9793 Virginia Avenue
Bassett, VA
(276) 629-4474

MICHIGAN INTERNATIONAL SPEEDWAY

Infield

Infield

Garage Area

Pit Road

Start | Finish Line

Track Information

Inaugural Year: 1969
Owner: ISC
City: Brooklyn, Michigan
Size: 2 miles
Banking: 18 degrees
Grandstand Capacity: 136,373

ADDRESS

Michigan International Speedway
12626 U.S. Highway 12
Brooklyn, MI 49230-9068
(517) 592-6666
www.mispeedway.com

TICKET INFORMATION

Phone: (800) 354-6666
www.mispeedway.com

About the Track

Michigan International Speedway (MIS) is known for its wide racing surface and high banking. In fact, the racing is so good at Michigan that California Speedway was built to mimic this superspeedway track. Michigan is also referred to as the "sister track" to Texas Motor Speedway. The racing is always exciting and the finishes are even better.

Track History

Michigan Speedway was designed by Charles Moneypenny, who also designed Daytona International Speedway. The initial building project took track owner and land developer Lawrence H. LoPatin just over a year and close to $6 million to complete. In June 1973, Roger Penske (Penske Corporation) purchased the Irish Hills track for a mere $2 million and later turned the track into a modern money-making venue. Penske retained ownership of MIS for over twenty-five years. In July 1999, the ownership switched hands and MIS became an ISC race facility.

Track Records

Most Wins: David Pearson (9)
Most Top Five Finishes: Cale Yarborough (21)
Most Lead Changes: 65—on 8/16/1981
Fewest Lead Changes: 7—on 8/12/1984
Most Cautions: 10—on 8/20/2006
Fewest Cautions: 0—most recently on 6/13/1999 (total of 3 times)
Race Record: Dale Jarrett—173.997 mph (2 hours, 17 minutes, 56 seconds) (6/13/1999)

Qualifying Record: Ryan Newman—194.232 mph (37.069 seconds) (6/19/2005)

Fast Facts

- The first NASCAR Sprint Cup race was run at Michigan International Speedway on June 15, 1969, and was won by Cale Yarborough.
- Harry Gant is the oldest driver to have won at Michigan International Speedway—winning in August 1992, he was fifty-two years old (plus seven months and six days).
- Ernie Irvan drove to victory in the Miller 400 at Michigan International Speedway on June 15, 1997. This is an especially sweet victory since it was this track that nearly took his life in August 1994. Ernie Irvan led the final twenty-one laps of the race.
- Michigan law enforcement officers have been using MIS for pursuit training since 2000.
- Current NASCAR car owner and retired Indy racer Chip Ganassi had his career-ending crash at MIS in 1984.
- Clifford Allison, the younger son of Bobby Allison and brother of the late Davey Allison, was killed at MIS in 1992.

Parking

MIS offers free parking for fans attending races. All parking is on a first-come, first-served basis. MIS does not allow overnight parking or camping in general parking areas. For up-to-date parking information, call the track at 517-592-6666 or visit www.mispeedway.com.

Track Rules

According to the track's official website at www.mispeedway.com, the track's rules are as follows:

ITEMS ALLOWED IN GRANDSTANDS

- ✓ one soft-sided cooler or bag (not to exceed 6" × 6" × 12")
- ✓ one clear plastic bag (not to exceed 18" × 18" × 4", no ice or freezer packs)
- ✓ binoculars
- ✓ scanners
- ✓ cameras (not in a bag)
- ✓ seat cushions or stadium seats (without armrests)
- ✓ video equipment

ITEMS *NOT* ALLOWED IN GRANDSTANDS

- ✗ hard-sided coolers
- ✗ thermoses or insulated cups of any size
- ✗ glass containers
- ✗ strollers
- ✗ umbrellas
- ✗ bicycles
- ✗ Rollerblades
- ✗ golf carts
- ✗ pets (with the exception of special service animals)
- ✗ banners or flags
- ✗ firearms
- ✗ knives
- ✗ fireworks

Special Needs and Services

MIS provides seating and parking for those needing special assistance or accessibility. One companion is allowed to accompany those with special needs. Call the track at 866-989-7223 prior to arrival for up-to-date information. Always ask for your seats to be near your parking.

Track Tours

MIS is not currently offering individual tours of the track. MIS does offer a track viewing area, which is open Monday through Friday from 9 a.m. to 4:30 p.m. Call the track at 517-592-6666 for additional information on track accessibility. Always call the track prior to your arrival for up-to-date information regarding the viewing area.

Souvenirs

MIS official track souvenirs and driver-specific items can be purchased at Souvenir Alley, which is located in the AAA Motorsports Fan Plaza and Infield Vendor Row. MIS track merchandise can also be purchased at the track's online store at www.mispeedway.com.

🏁 **INSIDER TIP**—ATMs are located at Souvenir Alley and the infield souvenir row.

About the Area

MIS is beautifully located in the Irish Hills area of southeastern Michigan. Motorsports run through the veins of this community. Many locals have provided for their families by working for either Penske or Ford, who both call Michigan their home state. The locals love racing and it shows. The area surrounding the track is lush, green, and dominated by big skies. The nearby lakes are as beautiful as great masses of water come. In fact, many drivers and crew members look for houses to rent on the water, so they can enjoy both the track and the massive waterfront. Detroit is a short drive away (fifty miles), which makes for lots of great shopping and awesome restaurants. When catching the races at MIS, pack for layers in the spring and bring along sunscreen and a hat for the summer event.

CHAMBER OF COMMERCE

Brooklyn-Irish Hills Chamber of
    Commerce
221 N. Main Street
Brooklyn, MI 49230
(517) 592-8907
www.brooklynmi.com

Transportation

AIRPORT

Detroit Metropolitan Wayne County
    Airport (DTW)
9000 Middlebelt Road
Romulus, MI
(734) 942-3550
(Detroit Airport is approximately
    forty-seven miles from the track.)

AIRLINES

AirTran (800) 247-8726
America West (800) 235-9292
American (800) 433-7300
Continental (800) 525-0280
Delta (800) 221-1212
Frontier (800) 432-1359
Northwest (800) 225-2525
Southwest (800) 435-9792
Spirit (800) 772-7117
United (800) 241-6522
USA 3000 (877) USA-3000
US Airways (800) 943-5436

RENTAL CARS

Alamo (800) 327-9633
Avis (800) 331-1212
Budget (800) 527-0700
Dollar (800) 421-6878
Enterprise (800) 325-8007
Hertz (800) 654-3131
National (800) 227-7368
Thrifty (800) 367-2277

Hotels

KEY
🐾 Pet Friendly ≈ Pool
✗ Restaurant

🐾 **Bavarian Inn Motel**
1728 Hudson Road
Hillsdale, MI
(517) 437-3367

🐾 **Baymont Inn & Suites**
2035 Holiday Inn Drive
Jackson, MI
(517) 789-6000

Cascades Motel
6745 Ann Arbor Road
Jackson, MI
(517) 764-1970

🐾 **Clearwater Resort Motel**
6150 U.S. Highway 223
Addison, MI
(517) 547-7472

🐾, ≈ **Comfort Inn**
1645 Commerce Park Drive
Chelsea, MI
(734) 433-8000

≈ **Comfort Inn & Suites**
2435 Shirley Drive
Jackson, MI
(517) 768-0088

Country Hearth Inn
1111 Boardman Road
Jackson, MI
(517) 783-6404

≈ **Country Inn & Suites**
3506 Oneil Drive
Jackson, MI
(517) 788-6400

≈ **Days Inn**
1575 W. Maumee Street
Adrian, MI
(517) 263-5741

≈ **Days Inn**
3241 W. Carleton Road
Hillsdale, MI
(517) 439-3297

≈ **Fairfield Inn**
2395 Shirley Drive
Jackson, MI
(517) 784-7877

≈ **Holiday Inn Express Adrian**
1077 E. U.S. Highway 223
Adrian, MI
(517) 265-5700

≈ **Holiday Inn Express Chelsea**
1540 Commerce Park Drive
Chelsea, MI
(734) 433-1600

☼, ≈, ✕ **Holiday Inn Jackson**
2000 Holiday Inn Drive
Jackson, MI
(517) 783-2681

Homestead Bed & Breakfast
9279 Macon Road
Saline, MI
(734) 429-9625

≈ **Jackson Hampton Inn**
2225 Shirley Drive
Jackson, MI
(517) 789-5151

☼, ≈ **Motel 6**
830 Royal Drive
Jackson, MI
(517) 789-7186

☼ **Super 8 Motel**
155 Wamplers Lake Road
Brooklyn, MI
(517) 592-0888

☼ **Super 8 Motel**
1091 W. U.S. Highway 223
Adrian, MI
(517) 265-8888

☼ **Super 8 Motel**
2001 Shirley Drive
Jackson, MI
(517) 788-8780

☼, ≈ **Travelodge**
901 Rosehill Road
Jackson, MI
(517) 787-1111

Camping

ON-SITE AND TRACK-OWNED CAMPING

MIS offers a variety of camping options for fans attending the race. Call the track at 517-592-6666 for up-to-date camping information and fees. Always ask for a set of rules for the specific area in which you choose to camp. It is not uncommon for each area to have its own set of rules.

Brookfest Campground The Brookfest Campground is located just outside of turn 4. This reserved area provides showers, portable restrooms, potable water, and a dump station.

Brooklyn Highway Campground
The Brooklyn Highway Campground is located across from the speedway. This reserved camping area provides a Buddy's Mini-Mart Convenience Store, showers, portable restrooms, potable water, and a dump station.

Graves Campground The Graves Campground is located on the south side of U.S. 12. This reserved area provides showers, portable restrooms, potable water, and a dump station.

Infield Campground Infield camping is on a first-come, first-served basis. All camping spots will be assigned. This area provides showers, portable restrooms, potable water, and a dump station.

M-50 Campground M-50 Campground is located behind turn 3. This reserved area provides showers, portable restrooms, potable water, and a dump station.

Northwoods Northfield Campground The Northwoods and Northfield Campgrounds are located across from the speedway, west of Brooklyn Highway. This reserved area is for tents and pop-up camping and provides showers, portable restrooms, potable water, and a dump station.

Pit Road Motorcoach Camping The Pit Road Motorcoach camping area is the track's premier camping area, with the lot located adjacent to pit road. Sites in this private camping area are sold as part of a package that includes up to four nights of camping (Thursday through Sunday), two pit road camping admissions, two prerace pit passes, and two Sunday morning champagne brunch tickets. This area's camping amenities include paving, reserved sites, water hookup, 50-amp electrical hookup, portable restrooms, dump station, and a private camping area.

Tree Farm Campground The Tree Farm Campground is located just outside of turns 3 and 4. This reserved area provides showers, portable restrooms, potable water, and a dump station.

Turn 2 Campground The Turn 2 Campground is located just outside of turn 2. The reserved sites in this area are equipped with water and electrical hookup (50-amp service) for self-contained units only (no buses, pop-ups, or tents). Portable restrooms and a dump station are also available.

OFF-SITE CAMPING

Apple Creek Campground
11185 Orban Road
Grass Lake, MI
(517) 522-3467

Greenbriar RV Park
14820 Wellwood Road
Brooklyn, MI
(517) 592-6952

Hayes State Park Headquarters
1220 Wamplers Lake Road
Onsted, MI
(517) 467-7401

Irish Hills Resort Campgrounds
16230 U.S. Highway 12
Cement City, MI
(517) 592-6751

Juniper Hills Campgrounds
13500 U.S. Highway 12
Brooklyn, MI
(517) 592-6803

Kooters Creek Side Camp Ground
13400 Taylor Road
Brooklyn, MI
(517) 592-8083

North Haven Resort
11400 Waterman Road
Brooklyn, MI
(517) 592-6170

Paradise Campgrounds
17864 U.S. Highway 12
Cement City, MI
(517) 592-5234

Shady Acres Campgrounds
100 Crispell Lake Road
Clarklake, MI
(517) 529-9031

Somerset Beach Campground
9822 Brooklawn Court
Somerset Center, MI
(517) 688-3783

Restaurants

KEY
🍔 Fast Food   🛏 Sit Down
🎁 Takeout   ☎ Reservations

Must Eats

Damon's Grill
3150 Boardwalk Street
Ann Arbor, MI
(734) 827-2277
This high-spirited sports bar–like restaurant has good food and lots of games to go along with it. You might just see your favorite crew guys grabbing a bite.

Tony Packo's
1902 Front Street
Toledo, OH
(419) 691-1953
This chain restaurant was made famous by Klinger in *MASH*. The pickle bar is a standout and the Hungarian hot dogs hit a home run.

Bob's Big Boy
329 S. Main Street
Brooklyn, MI
(517) 592-3212

Burger King
11299 S. Main Street
Brooklyn, MI
(517) 592-4076

Derosiles American Mexican Cuisine
145 Wamplers Lake Road
Brooklyn, MI
(517) 592-4033

Harold's Place
10625 U.S. Highway 12
Brooklyn, MI
(517) 467-2064

Hattie's Pizza & Subs
102 N. Main Street
Onsted, MI
(517) 467-2182

Hawkeye's Grill & Pub
11551 Brooklyn Road
Brooklyn, MI
(517) 592-8668

Hometown Pizza
193 S. Main Street
Brooklyn, MI
(517) 592-3267

Hungry Howie's Pizza
250 S. Main Street
Brooklyn, MI
(517) 592-2225

Irish Hills Pizza
8421 Sports Park Drive
Onsted, MI
(517) 467-7000

Kelly's On the Hill
8424 U.S. Highway 12
Brooklyn, MI
(517) 467-2850

Kentucky Fried Chicken
152 S. Main Street
Brooklyn, MI
(517) 592-4880

Marco's Pizza
145 Wamplers Lake Road
Brooklyn, MI
(517) 592-4444

McDonald's
306 S. Main Street
Brooklyn, MI
(517) 592-6134

Poppa's Place
208 S. Main Street
Brooklyn, MI
(517) 592-4625

RC's Clubhouse Pizza
8421 Sports Park Drive
Onsted, MI
(517) 467-6969

Spring City
307 S. Main Street
Brooklyn, MI
(517) 592-9393

Subway Sandwiches & Salads
311 S. Main Street
Brooklyn, MI
(517) 592-5994

Subway Sandwiches & Salads
7991 Onsted Highway
Onsted, MI
(517) 467-6658

Winners Circle Cafe
408 S. Main Street
Brooklyn, MI
(517) 592-4598

Local Attractions

WORTH THE TRIP

If you love motorsports, you have to visit the **Henry Ford Museum,** located in Dearborn, Michigan, an hour's drive from the track. The museum is rich in history and the exhibits are thrilling. For tour info call the museum at 1-800-835-5237 or go to www.hfmgv.org. Always call prior to arrival as these factory tours fill up fast.

Conklin Reed Organ & History
101 Fairview Street
Hanover, MI
(517) 563-8927

Deep Lake Recreational Park
147 Deep Lake
Brooklyn, MI
(517) 467-4200

Ella Sharp Museum
3225 Fourth Street
Jackson, MI
(517) 787-2320

Gauss's Green Valley Golf Course
5751 Brooklyn Road
Jackson, MI
(517) 764-0270

Henry Ford Museum
20900 Oakwood Boulevard
Dearborn, MI
(313) 271-1620

Hubbard Memorial Museum
317 Hanover Street
Concord, MI
(517) 524-8891

Hudson Museum
219 W. Main Street
Hudson, MI
(517) 448-8858

**Lenawee County Historical
    Museum**
110 E. Church Street
Adrian, MI
(517) 265-6071

Sharon Mills Park
5701 Sharon Hollow Road
Manchester, MI
(734) 971-6337

Tecumseh Area Museum
302 E. Chicago Boulevard
Tecumseh, MI
(517) 423-2374

Waterloo Farm Museum
9998 Waterloo Munith Road
Munith, MI
(517) 596-2254

Shopping

KEY
🚗 Automotive $ Discount
➕ Pharmacy   🛍 Mall
☆ Specialty   🏠 Department Store

🛍 Adrian Mall
1357 S. Main Street
Adrian, MI
(517) 263-0685

$ Big Lots
1370 S. Main Street
Adrian, MI
(517) 263-0203

$ Dollar General
4350 Page Avenue
Michigan Center, MI
(517) 764-2353

☆ Elder-Beerman
1357 S. Main Street
Adrian, MI
(517) 263-3313

$ Family Dollar Store
11441 Brooklyn Road
Brooklyn, MI
(517) 592-8223

🏬 **Jackson Crossing Mall**
1092 Jackson Crossing
Jackson, MI
(517) 783-4890

👕 **JC Penney**
1357 S. Main Street
Adrian, MI
(517) 263-0551

$ **Kmart**
3001 E. Michigan Avenue
Jackson, MI
(517) 787-3440

👕 **Kohl's Department Store**
2050 E. U.S. Highway 223
Adrian, MI
(517) 264-0750

☆ **Pamida**
400 S. Main Street
Brooklyn, MI
(517) 592-9550

$ **Sam's Club**
3600 Oneil Drive
Jackson, MI
(517) 788-6075

👕 **Sears**
1357 S. Main Street
Adrian, MI
(517) 265-0728

☆ **Shoe Department**
1720 W. Michigan Avenue
Jackson, MI
(517) 782-9694

$ **Target**
1076 Jackson Crossing
Jackson, MI
(517) 788-3900

$ **T.J. Maxx**
1152 Jackson Crossing
Jackson, MI
(517) 784-0285

$ **Wal-Mart**
1601 E. U.S. Highway 223
Adrian, MI
(517) 265-9771

🏬 **Westwood Mall**
1850 W. Michigan Avenue
Jackson, MI
(517) 787-1170

Churches/ Worship Centers

Abundant Life Assembly
130 S. Main Street
Brooklyn, MI
(517) 592-2232

All Saints Episcopal Church
151 N. Main Street
Brooklyn, MI
(517) 592-2244

Brooklyn Presbyterian Church
160 N. Main Street
Brooklyn, MI
(517) 592-2801

Cornerstone Community Church
126 N. Main Street
Brooklyn, MI
(517) 592-4657

Crosspointe Church
13191 M 50
Brooklyn, MI
(517) 592-2128

First Baptist Church
402 S. Mill Street
Brooklyn, MI
(517) 592-2240

Gateway Community Church
268 S. Main Street
Onsted, MI
(517) 467-2324

Heart of the Lakes Church
7031 Jefferson Road
Brooklyn, MI
(517) 592-8623

Irish Hills Community Church
399 Connor Street
Onsted, MI
(517) 467-2808

Springville United Methodist
10186 Springville Highway
Onsted, MI
(517) 467-4471

St. Joseph's Shrine
8743 U.S. Highway 12
Brooklyn, MI
(517) 467-2183

St. Mark's Lutheran Church
11151 U.S. Highway 12
Brooklyn, MI
(517) 467-7565

St. Rita's Catholic Church
10720 Hayes Road
Clarklake, MI
(517) 592-5470

Word-Life Fellowship Parsonage
8501 Marr Highway
Manitou Beach, MI
(517) 592-2128

Medical Centers

Chelsea Community Hospital
775 S. Main Street
Chelsea, MI
(734) 475-1311

Duane L Waters Hospital
3857 Cooper Street
Jackson, MI
(517) 780-5600

Herrick Memorial Hospital
500 E. Pottawatamie Street
Tecumseh, MI
(517) 424-3000

W A Foote Memorial Hospital
205 N. East Avenue
Jackson, MI
(517) 788-4800

Pet Medical Center

Columbia Animal Clinic
405 N. Main Street
Brooklyn, MI
(517) 592-6924

NEW HAMPSHIRE MOTOR SPEEDWAY

Infield

Garage Area

Pit Road

Start | Finish Line

Track Information

Inaugural Year: 1993
Owner: SMI
City: Loudon, New Hampshire
Size: 1.058 miles
Banking: 12 degrees
Grandstand Capacity: 91,000

ADDRESS

New Hampshire Motor Speedway
1122 Route 106 N.
Loudon, NH 03307
(603) 783-4931
www.nhms.com

TICKET INFORMATION

Phone: (603) 783-4931
www.nhms.com

About the Track

New Hampshire Motor Speedway (NHMS) is often referred to as simply Loudon for the town where it is located. The race at NHMS is always exciting. The track is very competitive and the fans always get a great show. The 1.5 mile northeastern track has seen its share of tragedy, as two young, up-and-coming drivers (Kenny Irwin Jr. and Adam Petty) lost their lives only months apart in 2000, leaving many to feel the track was jinxed. In fact, NASCAR issued restrictor plates on the Cup cars for the September race that same year to make sure the drivers were racing under the safest conditions. When the Cup series returned the following year, NASCAR decided not to use the plates. The fall race at Loudon kicks off the Chase for the Championship, which is a sellout every year.

Track History

New Hampshire Motor Speedway is a young track by racing standards. Groundbreaking took place in August 1989; the track opened in June 1990. The current site of NHMS is the former home of the Bryar Motorsports Park (1960-1989), a road-course circuit that hosted motorcycle and go-cart races. Bob Bahre purchased the track in 1990 and quickly transformed it to a multipurpose track. The New England track caught the attention of NASCAR, which awarded Bahre a pair of nationwide races in July 1990. It took another three years before NASCAR introduced the Sprint Cup to the oval speedway. Bruton Smith and SMI purchased the track from Bahre in

November 1997 for an astounding $340 million.

Track Records

Most Wins: Jeff Burton (4)

Most Top Five Finishes: Jeff Gordon (10)

Most Lead Changes: 23—most recently on 7/21/2002 (total of 2 times)

Fewest Lead Changes: 1—on 9/17/2000

Most Cautions: 17—7/10/1994

Fewest Cautions: 2—7/13/1997

Race Record: Jeff Burton—117.134 mph (2 hours, 42 minutes, 35 seconds) (7/13/1997)

Qualifying Record: Ryan Newman—133.357 mph (28.561 seconds) (9/12/2003)

Fast Facts

- The first NASCAR Sprint Cup race was run at New Hampshire Motor Speedway on July 11, 1993, and was won by Rusty Wallace.
- Dale Jarrett is the oldest driver to have won at New Hampshire Motor Speedway—winning in July 2001, he was forty-four years old (plus seven months and twenty-six days).
- The fewest number of cars to be running at the end of the race is

thirty—which has happened on three different occasions (as recently as 2003). Not all of these cars were on the lead lap, though.

- In 2000, this track was the site of a pair of fatal accidents which tragically took the lives of two promising young drivers, Adam Petty and Kenny Irwin Jr.

Parking

New Hampshire Motor Speedway provides a variety of parking for fans attending the race. All parking is first come, first served. NHMS does not allow overnight parking in their general parking areas. Call the track at 603-783-4931 or visit www.nhms .com for up-to-date parking information.

Track Rules

According to the track's official website at www.nhms.com, the track's rules are as follows:

ITEMS ALLOWED IN THE GRANDSTANDS
- ✓ coolers (14″ or under)
- ✓ cameras
- ✓ binoculars
- ✓ seat cushions (without armrest)
- ✓ scanners

ITEMS *NOT* ALLOWED IN THE GRANDSTANDS
- ✗ animals (except service animals assisting a guest)
- ✗ ATVs
- ✗ bicycles
- ✗ fireworks
- ✗ glass containers
- ✗ mopeds
- ✗ golf carts
- ✗ Rollerblades
- ✗ scaffolding
- ✗ skateboards
- ✗ stadium seats with arms
- ✗ umbrellas
- ✗ weapons (of any description)

Special Needs and Services

NHMS offers seating and parking for those needing special assistance or accessibility. One companion is allowed to accompany those with special needs. Call the track at 603-783-4931 prior to your arrival for up-to-date information and seating availability. Always ask for your parking to be near your seats.

Track Tours

NHMS does not currently offer individual or group track tours. Track tours are only given as a bonus to the Sunday suite pass holder. Call the track at 603-783-4931 for additional information regarding suite/tour packages.

Souvenirs

NHMS official track and driver-specific merchandise can be purchased at Souvenir Alley, which is located near the main entrance to the track. Track merchandise is also available at www.nhms.com.

About the Area

Loudon, New Hampshire, is what anyone might expect of a New England town: quaint and beautiful. The area surrounding the track is a bunch of little towns, one just as pretty as the next. One of my most favorite things to do while in New Hampshire is drive around and see the countryside. Being a southern girl myself, the landscape in the New England states is breathtaking. Even though Loudon is tucked away in a corner of New Hampshire, Boston is only a quick hour's drive away. When catching a race at Loudon, expect warm and comfortable temperatures. Summers in New Hampshire provide a nice break from the hot and humid temperatures of the deep South.

CHAMBER OF COMMERCE
Greater Concord Chamber of
    Commerce
40 Commercial Street
Concord, NH 03301
(603) 224-2508
www.concordnhchamber.com

INSIDER TIP—You can leave your car in Concord and get shuttled to the Speedway. Call the area chamber at 603-224-2508 for additional information and fees.

Transportation

AIRPORT
Manchester Airport (MHT)
1 Airport Road, # 300
Manchester, NH
(603) 624-6539
(Manchester Airport is
    approximately twenty-nine miles
    from the track.)

AIRLINES
ComAir (800) 354-9822
Continental (800) 525-0280
Delta (800) 221-1212
Manchester Air Canada
    (888) 247-2262
Northwest (800) 225-2525
Southwest (800) 435-9792

United (800) 241-6522
US Airways (800) 428-4322

RENTAL CARS
Alamo (800) 462-5266
Avis (800) 831-2847
Budget (800) 527-7000
Dollar (800) 800-4000
Enterprise (800) 736-8222
Hertz (800) 654-3131
National (800) 227-7368
Thrifty (800) 367-2277
USave (800) 880-4500

Hotels

KEY
☺ Pet Friendly   ≈ Pool
✕ Restaurant

Ames Farm Inn
2800 Lake Shore Road
Gilford, NH
(603) 293-4321

Anchorage on Lake Winnisquam
725 Laconia Road
Tilton, NH
(603) 524-3248

Bay Side Inn
86 Route 11D
Alton Bay, NH
(603) 875-5005

Bay Top Motel
1025 Weirs Boulevard
Laconia, NH
(603) 366-2225

Belknap Point Motel
107 Belknap Point Road
Gilford, NH
(603) 293-7511

☺, ≈ **Best Western Inn**
97 Hall Street
Concord, NH
(603) 228-4300

Birch Knoll Motel
867 Weirs Boulevard
Laconia, NH
(603) 366-4958

Centennial Inn
96 Pleasant Street
Concord, NH
(603) 227-9000

≈, ✕ **Christmas Island Motel**
630 Weirs Boulevard
Laconia, NH
(603) 366-4378

☺, ≈ **Comfort Inn**
71 Hall Street
Concord, NH
(603) 226-4100

⌂ **Country Lake Resort**
788 Laconia Road
Tilton, NH
(603) 524-6897

≈ **Courtyard by Marriott**
70 Constitution Avenue
Concord, NH
(603) 225-0303

⌂ **Daniel Webster Motor Lodge**
188 King Street
Boscawen, NH
(603) 796-2136

≈ **Days Inn**
406 S. Main Street
Concord, NH
(603) 224-2511

Ellacoya Resort & Cottages
110 Scenic Drive
Gilford, NH
(603) 293-7792

⌂ **Elmwood Motor Lodge**
200 King Street
Boscawen, NH
(603) 796-2411

≈ **Fairfield Inn**
4 Gulf Street
Concord, NH
(603) 224-4011

Ferry Point House B & B
100 Lower Bay Road
Sanbornton, NH
(603) 524-0087

⌂, ≈ **Fireside Inn & Suites**
17 Harris Shore Road
Gilford, NH
(603) 293-7526

Greystone Motor Inn & Motel
132 Scenic Drive
Gilford, NH
(603) 293-7377

≈, ✕ **Gunstock Inn & Fitness Center**
580 Cherry Valley Road
Gilford, NH
(603) 293-2021

≈ **Hampton Inn**
515 South Street
Bow, NH
(603) 224-5322

≈, ✕ **Holiday Inn Concord**
172 N. Main Street
Concord, NH
(603) 224-9534

Inn at Peyton Place
1785 New Hampshire Route 140
Gilmanton Iron Works, NH
(603) 364-7315

Inn at Smith Cove
19 Roberts Road
Gilford, NH
(603) 293-1111

≈, ✕ **Lake Opechee Inn & Spa**
62 Doris Ray Court
Laconia, NH
(603) 524-0111

Lake Shore Farm
275 Jenness Pond Road
Northwood, NH
(603) 942-5521

Lake Winnipesaukee Motel
350 Endicott N.
Laconia, NH
(603) 366-5502

Lakehouse Cottage
1144 Weirs Boulevard
Laconia, NH
(603) 366-5517

≈ **Landmark Inn**
480 Main Street
Laconia, NH
(603) 524-8000

Lazy E Motor Inn
808 Weirs Boulevard
Laconia, NH
(603) 366-4003

≈ **Lord Hampshire Motel &**
 Cottage
885 Laconia Road
Winnisquam, NH
(603) 524-4331

≈, ✕ **Margate Resort**
76 Lake Street
Laconia, NH
(603) 524-5210

Misty Harbor Resort Hotel
118 Weirs Road
Gilford, NH
(603) 293-4500

Northwood Motel
1130 First New Hampshire Turnpike
Northwood, NH
(603) 942-5476

Pine Bank Lodge
Daniel Webster Highway
Laconia, NH
(603) 366-4791

Quarterdeck Motel
832 Weirs Boulevard
Laconia, NH
(603) 366-4692

≈ **Red Roof Inn**
2 Staniels Road
Loudon, NH
(603) 225-8399

Riverview Motel
13 Suncook Valley Road
Alton, NH
(603) 875-5001

Sandy Point Beach
190 Mount Major Highway
Alton Bay, NH
(603) 875-6000

≈, ✕ **Shalimar Resort**
650 Laconia Road
Tilton, NH
(603) 524-1984

Silver Sands Motel
103 Weirs Road, # 11B
Gilford, NH
(603) 293-4481

Super 8 Motel
7 Tilton Road
Tilton, NH
(603) 286-8882

Tower Hill Cottages
107 Route 3
Laconia, NH
(603) 366-5525

Waters Edge Inn
16 Hill Road
Winnisquam, NH
(603) 524-0408

Webster Lake Inn
28 Pine Colony Road
Franklin, NH
(603) 934-1934

Weirs Beach Smoke House
38 Endicott Street N.
Laconia, NH
(603) 366-2400

Camping

ON-SITE AND TRACK-OWNED CAMPING

NHMS does not allow overnight camping in the infield. RV and camper spaces (no tents) are available on the exterior of the race surface (for a fee) for fans attending the race. This is a self-contained area. The track does not provide hookups or dumping stations. Call the track at 603-783-4931 for reservations and up-to-date information and fees.

OFF-SITE CAMPING

Cascade Campground
379 Route 106 S.
Loudon, NH
(603) 224-3212

Channahon State Park
25302 W. Story Street
Channahon, IL
(815) 467-4271

Granite State Campground
5 Ham Avenue
Belmont, NH
(603) 524-9460

Hillcrest Campground & Cabins
78 Dover Road
Chichester, NH
(603) 798-5124

Lazy River Family Campground
427 Goboro Road
Epsom, NH
(603) 798-5900

Love Inn Campground
190 Catamount Road
Pittsfield, NH
(603) 435-8802

Rocky Road Campground
1540 Route 106 N.
Loudon, NH
(603) 267-1956

Silver Lake Park Campgrounds
389 Jamestown Road
Belmont, NH
(603) 524-6289

**Thousand Acres Family
    Campground**
1078 S. Main Street
Franklin, NH
(603) 934-4440

Winnisquam Beach Campgrounds
Union Bridge Road
Belmont, NH
(603) 524-0021

Restaurants

KEY
🪑 Fast Food   🪑 Sit Down
🥡 Takeout   ☏ Reservations

Must Eats

The Puritan Backroom
245 Hooksett Road
Manchester, NH
(603) 669-6890
 This is a fun dining experience for the entire family. They are most famous for their ice cream.

Red Arrow Diner
61 Lowell Street
Manchester, NH
(603) 626-1118
 This all-American diner was featured on the Food Network's *Diners, Drive-ins and Dives.* The food is unbelievably good. Save room for the homemade twinkies! This is a must stop!

Alan's of Boscawen
133 N. Main Street
Boscawen, NH
(603) 753-6631

Amazon Cafe Steeple Gate Mall
270 Loudon Road
Concord, NH
(603) 415-2233

Applebee's
4 Sanborn Road
Tilton, NH
(603) 286-8844

Arnie's Place
164 Loudon Road
Concord, NH
(603) 228-3225

Blimpie Subs & Salads
135 Dover Road
Chichester, NH
(603) 798-3968

Bradley's Pizza
65 N. Main Street
Boscawen, NH
(603) 753-6368

Brookside House of Pizza
563 Route 106 N.
Loudon, NH
(603) 783-4550

Burger King
25 Tilton Road
Tilton, NH
(603) 286-8573

C C Tomatoes
217 Fisherville Road
Concord, NH
(603) 753-4450

Chiefs Place
348 Village Street
Penacook, NH
(603) 753-9500

Chili's Grill & Bar
18 Lowes Drive
Northfield, NH
(603) 286-8075

Constantly Pizza
W. Main Street
Tilton, NH
(603) 286-2229

D'Angelo Grilled Sandwiches
270 Loudon Road
Concord, NH
(603) 230-9901

Dairy Queen
585 W. Main Street
Tilton, NH
(603) 286-3205

Donatello's on the Green
133 Fisherville Road, # 1
Concord, NH
(603) 496-4192

Donatello's Pizza
15 Village Street
Penacook, NH
(603) 753-6000

Dunkin' Donuts
154 King Street
Boscawen, NH
(603) 796-2364

Egg Shell Restaurant
563 Route 106 N.
Loudon, NH
(603) 783-4060

Elias Pizza & Restaurant
99 Dover Road
Chichester, NH
(603) 798-3300

Food for Thought Cafe
14 Mill Street
Belmont, NH
(603) 267-1155

Fox & Hounds Pub
4 Sanborn Road
Tilton, NH
(603) 286-4204

GG's Deli & Specialty Foods
235 Main Street
Tilton, NH
(603) 266-1041

Godfather's Pizza
135 Dover Road
Chichester, NH
(603) 798-3345

Green Ginger
95 Laconia Road
Tilton, NH
(603) 286-9989

Greenside Restaurant
360 Tilton Road
Tilton, NH
(603) 528-7888

Hillcrest Pizza
296 Depot Street
Belmont, NH
(603) 267-7741

Jack's Pizza
11 Catamount Road
Pittsfield, NH
(603) 435-6500

Jim's Drive-In
143 Park Street
Northfield, NH
(603) 286-8533

Kalliopes Restaurant
4 Sanborn Road
Tilton, NH
(603) 286-7379

Kapelli's Pizzeria
203 King Street
Boscawen, NH
(603) 796-2727

Katie Flo's Café
Route 3, #4
Winnisquam, NH
(603) 524-4260

Kentucky Fried Chicken
41 Tilton Road
Tilton, NH
(603) 286-3331

Kings Chinese Restaurant
563 Route 106 N.
Loudon, NH
(603) 783-3316

Lochmere Golf & Country Club
360 Laconia Road
Tilton, NH
(603) 528-4653

Long Horn Steakhouse
217 Loudon Road
Concord, NH
(603) 228-0655

Loudon Road Restaurant
338 Loudon Road
Concord, NH
(603) 226-0533

Lun Hing Restaurant
887 Fisherville Road
Concord, NH
(603) 224-1025

M & J's Country Griddle
930 Laconia Road
Belmont, NH
(603) 267-8429

Makris Lobster & Steak House
354 Sheep Davis Road
Concord, NH
(603) 225-7665

Manchu Wok
270 Loudon Road, # 1022
Concord, NH
(603) 224-0385

McDonald's
5 Tilton Road
Tilton, NH
(603) 286-7332

Mulligan's Restaurant
41 Park Street
Northfield, NH
(603) 286-9365

🪑 **New Million Dragon Restaurant**
235 Main Street
Tilton, NH
(603) 286-9935

🪑 **Ninety Nine Restaurant & Pub**
154 Laconia Road
Tilton, NH
(603) 286-4994

🪑 **Old Friends Tavern**
927 Laconia Road
Tilton, NH
(603) 524-1777

🪑 **Olive Garden Italian Restaurant**
219 Loudon Road
Concord, NH
(603) 228-6886

🪑 **Parkers Roast Beef & Seafood**
345 Suncook Valley Road
Chichester, NH
(603) 435-5515

🪑 **Patriots Tavern**
255 Main Street
Tilton, NH
(603) 286-7774

🪑 **Pauli's Bakery & Restaurant**
175 E. Main Street
Tilton, NH
(603) 286-7081

🪑 **Ping Garden**
42 Main Street
Pittsfield, NH
(603) 435-8288

🪑 **Ruby Tuesday**
327 Loudon Road
Concord, NH
(603) 223-2505

🪑 **Shaker Table**
288 Shaker Road
Canterbury, NH
(603) 783-9511

🪑 **Smokey Bones BBQ & Grill**
317 Loudon Road
Concord, NH
(603) 224-6645

🥡 **Subway Sandwiches & Salads**
944 Laconia Road
Belmont, NH
(603) 267-6390

🥡 **Sukhothai Asian Gourmet**
120 Laconia Road
Tilton, NH
(603) 286-8888

🪑 **Szechuan Garden Restaurant**
108 Fisherville Road
Concord, NH
(603) 226-2650

Taco Bell
321 Loudon Road
Concord, NH
(603) 223-6908

TGIF Fridays
221 Loudon Road
Concord, NH
(603) 226-1012

Tilt'n Diner
61 Laconia Road
Tilton, NH
(603) 286-2204

Tilton House of Pizza
298 Main Street
Tilton, NH
(603) 286-7181

Town Pizza
27 Carroll Street
Pittsfield, NH
(603) 435-7144

Uno Chicago Grill
120 Laconia Road
Tilton, NH
(603) 286-4079

Upper Crust Pizzeria
65 Laconia Road
Tilton, NH
(603) 286-3191

Village Pizza
16 Elm Street
Pittsfield, NH
(603) 435-8585

Weathervane Seafood Restaurant
379 Dover Road
Chichester, NH
(603) 225-4044

Wendy's
196 Laconia Road
Tilton, NH
(603) 286-9644

Windmill Family Restaurant
172 Loudon Road
Concord, NH
(603) 225-0600

Yeti & Ayla's Breakfast & Lunch
8 Depot Street
Pittsfield, NH
(603) 435-7200

Yuen Sing Chinese Restaurant
630 W. Main Street
Tilton, NH
(603) 286-7777

Local Attractions

WORTH THE TRIP

The New England Aquarium is a fun-filled day and only an hour's drive from the track. For more info on the aquarium, call 617-973-5200 or visit www.neaq.org. While you are there, make sure you go on a search for the many ghosts of Boston. **Ghosts and Gravestones** offers a nighttime ghost tour like no other. I took my kids on this tour and they loved it. I would not suggest taking kids under five as the scare factor might be a bit much. For more info on the ghost tour, call 617-269-3626 or check out www.ghostsandgravestones.com.

Amalfi Racing Legends
29 Gilford East Drive
Gilford, NH
(603) 524-3056

Beaver Meadow Golf Course
1 Beaver Meadow Drive
Concord, NH
(603) 225-7033

Canterbury Shaker Village
288 Shaker Road
Canterbury, NH
(603) 783-9511

Christa McAuliffe Planetarium
2 Institute Drive
Concord, NH
(603) 271-7827

Gilman Museum
123 Main Street
Alton, NH
(603) 875-0201

Gunstock Ski Area
719 Cherry Valley Road
Gilford, NH
(603) 293-4341

Kaleidoscope Children's Museum
8 S. Main Street
Concord, NH
(603) 229-4526

New England Aquarium
1 Central Wharf
Boston, MA
(617) 973-5200

New Hampshire Historical Society
7 Eagle Square
Concord, NH
(603) 223-0627

Squam Lakes Tours
752 Daniel Webster Highway
Holderness, NH
(603) 968-7577

Weirs Railroad Station
211 Lakeside Avenue
Laconia, NH
(603) 366-5519

Shopping

KEY

🚗 Automotive $ Discount
➕ Pharmacy   🏬 Mall
☆ Specialty   🏯 Department Store

🏬 **Belknap Mall**
96 Daniel Webster Highway
Belmont, NH
(603) 524-5651

$ **Big Lots**
533 Mast Road
Goffstown, NH
(603) 627-4741

$ **BJ's Wholesale Club**
119 Laconia Road
Tilton, NH
(603) 286-3700

☆ **Bloom's Variety**
601 Main Street
Laconia, NH
(603) 524-0461

☆ **Bon-Ton**
270 Loudon Road
Concord, NH
(603) 227-9999

☆ **Burlington Coat Factory**
50 Storrs Street
Concord, NH
(603) 226-9683

$ **Cheapo Depot**
343 Court Street
Laconia, NH
(603) 528-3376

$ **Dollar Tree**
630 W. Main Street
Tilton, NH
(603) 286-2954

$ **Eddie Bauer Factory Outlet**
120 Laconia Road, # 225
Tilton, NH
(603) 286-7440

$ **Family Dollar Store**
108 Fisherville Road
Concord, NH
(603) 224-9329

☆ **Home Goods**
1458 Lake Shore Road
Gilford, NH
(603) 528-9601

🏯 **JC Penney**
25 Pleasant Street
Laconia, NH
(603) 528-4002

$ **Kmart**
1267 Hooksett Road
Hooksett, NH
(603) 625-5741

🏠 **Kohl's Department Store**
49 Lowes Drive
Northfield, NH
(603) 286-7071

$ **Marshalls**
50 Storrs Street
Concord, NH
(603) 223-6777

$ **Peebles**
96 Daniel Webster Highway
Belmont, NH
(603) 527-3780

$ **Sam's Club**
304 Sheep Davis Road
Concord, NH
(603) 226-1255

🏠 **Sears**
270 Loudon Road
Concord, NH
(603) 229-0195

☆ **Shoe Department**
270 Loudon Road
Concord, NH
(603) 224-2817

🏬 **Steeplegate Mall**
270 Loudon Road, # 1000
Concord, NH
(603) 224-1523

$ **Tanger Factory Outlet Center**
120 Laconia Road, # 134
Tilton, NH
(603) 286-7880

$ **Target**
80 Damante Drive
Concord, NH
(603) 227-0809

$ **T.J. Maxx**
12 Loudon Road
Concord, NH
(603) 228-0026

🏬 **Tower Village Mall**
1253 Hooksett Road
Hooksett, NH
(603) 622-8633

$ **Wal-Mart**
39 E. Main Street
Tilton, NH
(603) 286-7673

$ **Wal-Mart**
344 Loudon Road
Concord, NH
(603) 226-9312

$ Wardo's
38 New Hampshire Route 25
Meredith, NH
(603) 279-3399

Churches/
Worship Centers

Belmont Baptist Church
49 Church Street
Belmont, NH
(603) 267-8185

Chichester United Methodist
2 Canterbury Road
Chichester, NH
(603) 798-3220

**Community United Church of
Christ**
5 Center Road
Canterbury, NH
(603) 783-9365

Concordia Lutheran Church
211 N. Main Street
Concord, NH
(603) 224-0277

Faith Community Baptist Church
334 N. Village Road
Loudon, NH
(603) 783-4045

Gilmanton Community Church
1807 Route 107
Gilmanton, NH
(603) 267-6150

Grace Episcopal Church
30 Eastman Street
Concord, NH
(603) 224-2252

Grace Presbyterian Church
174 Province Street
Laconia, NH
(603) 528-4747

Living Word Assembly of God
1926 Stage Road
Gilmanton Iron Works, NH
(603) 364-5500

Loudon Congregational Church
7018 Church Street
Loudon, NH
(603) 783-9478

Loudon Ridge Church
694 Loudon Ridge Road
Loudon, NH
(603) 267-8066

St. Joseph Catholic Rectory
96 Main Street
Belmont, NH
(603) 267-8174

Sonlight Christian Fellowship
55 Wiggins Road
Loudon, NH
(603) 798-4339

**Tilton-Northfield United
   Methodist**
400 W. Main Street
Tilton, NH
(603) 286-4443

Trinity Episcopal Church
274 Main Street
Tilton, NH
(603) 286-3120

Universal Grace Church
275 Bear Hill Road
Loudon, NH
(603) 798-4560

Medical Centers

Concord Hospital
250 Pleasant Street
Concord, NH
(603) 225-2711

**Concord Hospital Walk-In Urgent
   Care Center**
60 Commercial Street
Concord, NH
(603) 230-1200

Franklin Regional Hospital
15 Aiken Avenue
Franklin, NH
(603) 934-2060

Lakes Region General Hospital
80 Highland Street
Laconia, NH
(603) 524-3211

New Hampshire Hospital
36 Clinton Street
Concord, NH
(603) 271-5300

Pet Medical Centers

Banfield the Pet Hospital
299 Loudon Road
Concord, NH
(603) 223-9648

Central NH Animal Care
4 King Road
Chichester, NH
(603) 798-3400

Concord Animal Hospital Pro
210 Loudon Road
Concord, NH
(603) 228-0107

Fisherville Animal Hospital
108 Fisherville Road
Concord, NH
(603) 229-0674

PHOENIX INTERNATIONAL RACEWAY

Start | Finish Line

Pit Road

Garage Area

Infield

Track Information

Inaugural Year: 1988
Owner: ISC
City: Avondale, Arizona
Size: 1 mile
Banking: 11 degrees in turns 1 and 2, 9 degrees in turns 3 and 4
Grandstand Capacity: 76,812

ADDRESS
Phoenix International Raceway
7602 S. Avondale Boulevard
Avondale, AZ 85323

(866) 408-7223
www.phoenixraceway.com

TICKET INFORMATION
Phone: (866) 408-7223
www.phoenixraceway.com

About the Track

Phoenix is flat and fast. The unique tri-oval shape makes Phoenix International Raceway (PIR) a track in a class all by itself. Look for action on the backstretch between turns 2 and 3, which is also referred to as the "dogleg." The hillside gives you a bird's-eye view of the action on the one-mile track. Legend has it the hill has to be raked clear of rattlesnakes before each event. Not sure how true that is, but the racing is great.

Track History

PIR was built in 1964, replacing the old Arizona State Fairgrounds track. The building process was tedious at best for the contractors due to the heavily rocked hillside of the Estrella Mountains. The track's unique shape is directly linked to the obstacles (rocks) the contractor had to overcome to build the Arizona track. The track was originally built with open wheel racing in mind. In fact, it was not until 1988 that NASCAR would host a Cup series event at PIR. Phoenix International Raceway suffered significant damage when lightning struck the main grandstands in 1987, burning the stands to the ground. The track has changed hands several times over the years. The first came in September 1985 when Buddy Jobe purchased the track from Dennis Wood. ISC purchased the track from Jobe in April 1999, adding to the ISC stable of tracks.

Track Records

Most Wins: Davey Allison, Jeff Burton, Dale Earnhardt Jr., and Kevin Harvick (2)

Most Top Five Finishes: Mark Martin (8)

Most Lead Changes: 23—on 11/5/2000

Fewest Lead Changes: 1—on 11/4/1990

Most Cautions: 11—11/7/2004

Fewest Cautions: 2—11/7/1999

Race Record: Tony Stewart—118.132 mph (2 hours, 38 minutes, 28 seconds) (11/7/1999)

Qualifying Record: Ryan Newman—135.854 mph (26.499 seconds) (11/5/2004)

Fast Facts

- The first NASCAR Sprint Cup race was run at Phoenix International Speedway on November 6, 1988, and was won by Alan Kulwicki.

- Rusty Wallace is the oldest driver to have won at Phoenix International Speedway—winning in October 1998, he was forty-two years old (plus two months and eleven days).

- Steve McQueen won a sports car race on the track's road course in October 1970.

- Alan Kulwicki won his first NASCAR Sprint Cup race at PIR on November 6, 1988. This was coincidentally the first NASCAR Sprint Cup race at PIR. This was also the first time Kulwicki would take the now-famous "Polish victory lap."
- In the winter 2004, PIR became a permanent lighted facility.
- In a *Sports Illustrated* poll, 12 percent of NASCAR drivers voted PIR as their favorite track, which gave PIR a second-place tie with Atlanta Motor Speedway.

Parking

PIR offers free parking to fans attending the race. All parking is on a first-come, first-served basis. PIR does not allow overnight parking in the general parking areas. For up-to-date parking and tram stop info, call the track at 623-463-5400 or visit www.phoenixraceway.com.

 INSIDER TIP—PIR offers a limited number of preferred parking spots to season ticket holders. For more info call the track at 623-463-5400.

Track Rules

According to the track's official website at www.phoenixraceway.com, the track's rules are as follows:

ITEMS ALLOWED IN THE GRANDSTANDS

- ✓ one soft-sided bag or cooler (no larger than 6″ × 6″ × 12″)
- ✓ one clear plastic bag (no larger than 18″ × 18″ × 4″)
- ✓ binoculars
- ✓ scanners
- ✓ headsets
- ✓ cameras
- ✓ seat cushions (no armrests)

Note: *All scanners, headsets, etc., must be worn around the neck or on the belt.*

ITEMS *NOT* ALLOWED IN THE GRANDSTANDS

- ✗ seat cushions with hollow tube construction
- ✗ firearms
- ✗ fireworks
- ✗ hard-sided coolers
- ✗ thermoses and insulated cups of any size
- ✗ strollers
- ✗ umbrellas
- ✗ scooters
- ✗ skateboards

✗ pets (unless assisting someone with special needs)

🏁 **INSIDER TIP**—One of the best seats in the house at PIR is the Hillside, located outside of turns 3 and 4. This general admission area is first come, first served. Children under twelve are free. Bring your lawnchair as there is no better way to watch the race at PIR.

Special Needs and Services

PIR offers seating and parking for those fans needing special assistance or accessibility. One companion is allowed to accompany those with special needs. Call the track at 623-463-5400 prior to arrival for up-to-date info. Always ask for your parking to be near your seats.

Track Tours

PIR offers individual and group tours at various times of the year. They do not offer tours on an ongoing basis. Call the track at 623-463-5400 for specific days and times of tours.

Souvenirs

PIR official track merchandise is available in the track's retail store, which is located behind the Bobby Allison Grandstands, outside of turn 2 between Gates 2 and 3, or on-line at www.phoenixraceway.com. Driver-specific merchandise can be purchased at Souvenir Alley, located near the main entrance to the track.

About the Area

The Phoenix area is quite different from other stops on the NASCAR Sprint Cup circuit. The races at Phoenix have become so popular to race fans not only for the great racing, but also due to the beauty of the countryside. Phoenix is another host city that really lends itself to an extra day of travel just to take in the attractions. In fact, many of the NASCAR drivers count Phoenix as one of their favorite golf destinations. NASCAR carefully selected the two race dates in Phoenix (April and November) as the weather in Phoenix is warm and sunny; whereas many other Cup host cities are battling colder temperatures during this time.

CHAMBER OF COMMERCE

Southwest Valley Chamber of
  Commerce
289 N. Litchfield Road
Goodyear, AZ 85338
(623) 932-2260
www.southwestvalleychamber.org

Transportation

AIRPORT

Phoenix Sky Harbor International
  Airport (PHX)
3400 E. Sky Harbor Boulevard
Phoenix, AZ
(602) 273-3300
(Approximately twenty-two miles
  from the track.)

AIRLINES

AirTran (800) 247-8726
American (800) 433-7300
ATA (800) 225-2995
Continental (800) 525-0280
Delta (800) 221-1212
Frontier (800) 432-1359
Great Lakes (800) 554-5111
JetBlue (800) 538-2583
Midwest (800) 452-2022
Northwest (800) 225-2525
Southwest (800) 435-9792
Sun Country (800) 359-6786
United (800) 241-6522
US Airways (800) 943-5436
WestJet (888) 937-8538

RENTAL CARS

Advantage (800) 777-5500
Alamo (800) 462-5266
Avis (800) 331-1212
Budget (800) 527-7000
Dollar (800) 800-4000
Enterprise (800) 736-8222
E-Z (800) 277-5171
Fox (800) 225-4369
Hertz (800) 654-3131
National (800) 227-7368
Payless (800) 729-5377
Thrifty (800) 847-4389

Hotels

KEY
🐾 Pet Friendly   ≈ Pool
✕ Restaurant

🐾, ≈, ✕ **Best Western Inn Phoenix**
55 N. Litchfield Road
Goodyear, AZ
(623) 932-3210

≈ **Comfort Suites**
8421 W. McDowell Road
Tolleson, AZ
(623) 936-6000

🐾 **Crystal Motel**
6352 NW Grand Avenue
Glendale, AZ
(623) 937-4166

≈ **Days Inn—I-10 W.**
1550 N. 52nd Drive
Phoenix, AZ
(602) 484-9257

🐾, ≈ **Econo Lodge**
1520 N. 84th Drive
Tolleson, AZ
(623) 936-4667

Glendale Gaslight Inn
5747 W. Glendale Avenue
Glendale, AZ
(623) 934-9119

≈ **Hampton Inn—I-10 W.**
5152 W. Latham Street
Phoenix, AZ
(602) 484-7000

🐾, ≈ **Holiday Inn Express—I-10 W.**
1313 N. Litchfield Road
Goodyear, AZ
(623) 535-1313

🐾, ≈ **Holiday Inn—West**
1500 N. 51st Avenue
Phoenix, AZ
(602) 484-7142

🐾, ≈, ✕ **Holiday Inn & Suites**
1188 N. Dysart Road
Goodyear, AZ
(623) 547-1313

In Town Suites Phoenix
1530 N. 50th Avenue
Phoenix, AZ
(602) 455-0191

In Town Suites McDowell Road
1530 N. 50th Avenue
Phoenix, AZ
(602) 455-3897

🐾, ≈ **La Quinta Inn & Suites**
4929 W. McDowell Road
Phoenix, AZ
(602) 595-7601

🐾, ≈ **Motel 6**
1530 N. 52nd Drive
Phoenix, AZ
(602) 272-0220

🐾, ≈ **Phoenix West Inn**
1241 N. 53rd Avenue
Phoenix, AZ
(602) 269-1919

🐾, ≈ **Red Roof Inn**
5215 W. Willetta Street
Phoenix, AZ
(602) 233-8004

Residence Inn—Phoenix Goodyear
2020 N. Litchfield Road
Goodyear, AZ
(623) 245-1414

🐾, ≈ **Super 8 Motel**
1242 N. 53rd Avenue
Phoenix, AZ
(602) 415-0888

🐾, ≈ **Super 8 Motel**
1710 N. Dysart Road
Goodyear, AZ
(623) 932-9622

෴, ≈ **Travelers Inn Phoenix**
5102 W. Latham Street
Phoenix, AZ
(602) 233-1988

≈ **Travelodge**
1424 N. 50th Avenue
Phoenix, AZ
(602) 455-3700

෴, ≈ **Value Inn**
1770 N. Dysart Road
Goodyear, AZ
(623) 932-9191

Vista Motel
6324 NW Grand Avenue
Glendale, AZ
(623) 937-6828

Camping

ON-SITE AND TRACK-OWNED CAMPING

PIR offers a limited number of on-site camping areas for fans attending the races. All camping in these areas is dry and must be self-contained. For more info, rules, and fees, call the track at 623-932-3651.

OFF-SITE CAMPING

Cotton Lane RV Resort
17506 W. Van Buren Street
Goodyear, AZ
(623) 853-4000

Covered Wagon RV Park
6540 N. Black Canyon Highway
Phoenix, AZ
(602) 242-2500

Destiny Phoenix West
416 N. Citrus Road
Goodyear, AZ
(623) 853-0537

Donorma RV Park
15637 N. Norma Lane
Surprise, AZ
(623) 583-8195

Pueblo El Mirage RV Resort
11201 N. El Mirage Road
El Mirage, AZ
(623) 583-0464

Sundial Mobile & RV Park
9250 N. 75th Avenue
Peoria, AZ
(623) 979-1921

Welcome Home RV Park
2501 W. Missouri Avenue
Phoenix, AZ
(602) 249-9854

White Tank Mountain Regional Park
13025 N. White Tank Mountain Road
Waddell, AZ
(623) 935-2505

Restaurants

KEY

🍔 Fast Food   🪑 Sit Down
📦 Takeout   ☎ Reservations

Must Eats

Pappadeaux Seafood Kitchen
11051 N. Black Canyon Highway
Phoenix, AZ
(602) 331-3434

This chain seafood restaurant is known for its great seafood and large portions. The soft-shell crabs are to die for and the banana pudding is a must!

T-Bone Steakhouse
19th Avenue
Avondale, AZ
(602) 276-0945

This old-time steakhouse serves up juicy steaks and all-you-can-eat salad bar. This is the only stop on the circuit with a bean bar.

🪑 **Ararat Restaurant**
10210 W. McDowell Road
Avondale, AZ
(623) 474-2252

🪑 **Bamboo Palace Buffet**
1461 N. Dysart Road
Avondale, AZ
(623) 932-0868

🪑 **Black Bear Diner**
1780 N. Dysart Road
Goodyear, AZ
(623) 932-2968

📦 **Blimpie Subs & Salads**
1595 N. Avondale Boulevard
Avondale, AZ
(623) 907-3909

🍔 **Burger King**
11445 W. Buckeye Road
Avondale, AZ
(623) 643-9451

🪑 **Ced's Fish & Chips**
11249 W. Buckeye Road
Avondale, AZ
(623) 643-9090

📦 **Del Taco**
1483 N. Dysart Road
Avondale, AZ
(623) 932-4438

📦 **Domino's Pizza**
11345 W. Buckeye Road, # B102
Avondale, AZ
(623) 388-5900

🪑 **Don Rafa Taqueria**
1467 N. Dysart Road
Avondale, AZ
(623) 882-3748

🪑 **Dragon Star Chinese Food**
13050 W. Rancho Santa Fe
   Boulevard, # 3
Avondale, AZ
(623) 935-2203

Golden Corral Buffet & Grill
420 N. Dysart Road
Goodyear, AZ
(623) 925-1112

Great China
1109 N. Dysart Road
Avondale, AZ
(623) 932-5711

IHOP Restaurant
1491 N. Dysart Road
Avondale, AZ
(623) 925-1260

Johnny Rockets
10220 W. McDowell Road
Avondale, AZ
(623) 643-9222

Kentucky Fried Chicken
1470 N. Eighth Street
Avondale, AZ
(623) 932-9040

Kyoto Bowl
10220 W. McDowell Road
Avondale, AZ
(623) 907-9877

Long John Silver's
1495 N. Dysart Road
Avondale, AZ
(623) 932-2065

Mariscos Las Playitas
10953 W. Buckeye Road
Avondale, AZ
(623) 907-1301

McDonald's
870 N. Dysart Road
Goodyear, AZ
(623) 932-2707

Native New Yorker
10220 W. McDowell Road
Avondale, AZ
(623) 907-8181

New York
11345 W. Buckeye Road
Avondale, AZ
(623) 907-9699

1 Brother's Pizza
11435 W. Buckeye Road
Avondale, AZ
(623) 936-9797

Panda Express
10110 W. McDowell Road
Avondale, AZ
(623) 907-1322

Peter Piper Pizza
1463 N. Dysart Road
Avondale, AZ
(623) 882-0020

Pizza Patron
1440 N. Dysart Road
Avondale, AZ
(623) 882-9494

Port of Subs
10220 W. McDowell Road
Avondale, AZ
(623) 907-0010

🍱 **Quiznos Sub**
10110 W. McDowell Road
Avondale, AZ
(623) 936-1410

🍗 **Red Robin Gourmet Burgers**
10240 W. McDowell Road
Avondale, AZ
(623) 907-3460

🍱 **Subway Sandwiches & Salads**
11435 W. Buckeye Road
Avondale, AZ
(623) 643-9371

🍔 **Taco Bell**
11325 W. Buckeye Road
Avondale, AZ
(623) 907-0160

🍗 **TJ's Homestyle Restaurant**
310 N. Eighth Street
Avondale, AZ
(623) 932-0309

🍗 **Waffle House**
1700 N. Dysart Road
Goodyear, AZ
(623) 932-9058

🍗 **Wendy Jack's**
1235 N. Eighth Street
Avondale, AZ
(623) 932-0032

🍔 **Wendy's**
900 N. 99th Avenue
Avondale, AZ
(623) 478-0990

🍱 **Whataburger**
1450 N. Dysart Road
Avondale, AZ
(623) 932-4934

🍗 **Wings Pizza & Things Bar**
965 E. Van Buren Street
Avondale, AZ
(623) 882-0335

Local Attractions

Phoenix is one of my favorite stops on the circuit due largely to the **Wigwam Resort and Golf Club.** This is truly a great escape. Not only does Wigwam have beautiful accommodations, the food is incredible and the driver spotting is at its best. In fact, this is one of the drivers' favorite places to golf. The late Benny Parsons considered this course one of the finest. If golfing is not your thing, the spa is wonderful. This resort is great for families as well. My kids love the pool!

Arizona Doll & Toy Museum
602 E. Adams Street
Phoenix, AZ
(602) 253-9337

Arizona Mining & Mineral Museum
1502 W. Washington Street
Phoenix, AZ
(602) 255-3791

Arizona Science Center
600 E. Washington Street
Phoenix, AZ
(602) 716-2000

Bead Museum Store
5754 W. Glenn Drive
Glendale, AZ
(623) 930-7395

Carnegie Center
1101 W. Washington Street
Phoenix, AZ
(602) 255-2110

Challenger Space Center
21200 N. 83rd Avenue
Peoria, AZ
(623) 322-2001

Children's Museum of Phoenix
1314 N. Third Street
Phoenix, AZ
(602) 253-0501

Coldwater Golf Club
100 N. Clubhouse Drive
Avondale, AZ
(623) 932-9000

Desert Star Park
8550 W. Encanto Boulevard
Phoenix, AZ
(602) 262-4539

Phoenix Art Museum
1625 N. Central Avenue
Phoenix, AZ
(602) 257-1222

Phoenix Museum of History
105 N. Fifth Avenue
Phoenix, AZ
(602) 253-2734

**Sonoran Desert National
  Monument**
222 N. Central Avenue
Phoenix, AZ
(602) 417-9200

State Capitol Museum
1700 W. Washington Street
Phoenix, AZ
(602) 542-4675

Wigwam Resort & Golf Club
451 N. Old Litchfield Road
Litchfield Park, AZ
(623) 935-9414

Shopping

KEY
🚗 Automotive $ Discount
✛ Pharmacy   🏬 Mall
☆ Specialty   🏫 Department Store

$ A K Big Dollar Store
6642 W. Maryland Avenue
Glendale, AZ
(623) 937-3470

☆ Back Alley
210 N. Central Avenue
Avondale, AZ
(623) 932-1488

☆ **BBB Fashion**
5251 W. Indian School Road
Phoenix, AZ
(623) 846-6000

$ Big Lots
7445 W. Indian School Road
Phoenix, AZ
(623) 848-2464

☆ **Burlington Coat Factory**
7611 W. Thomas Road
Phoenix, AZ
(623) 845-7277

$ Costco
10000 W. McDowell Road
Avondale, AZ
(623) 907-5668

Desert Sky Mall
7611 W. Thomas Road
Phoenix, AZ
(623) 245-1400

Dillard's
7621 W. Thomas Road
Phoenix, AZ
(623) 849-0100

$ Dollar Days Store
5030 W. McDowell Road, #25
Phoenix, AZ
(602) 352-6610

$ Dollar Depot
8206 W. Indian School Road
Phoenix, AZ
(623) 849-1680

$ Dollar Tree
1126 S. Litchfield Road
Goodyear, AZ
(623) 882-9123

$ Family Dollar Store
9602 W. Van Buren Street
Tolleson, AZ
(623) 478-5357

$ FP Stores
5239 W. Indian School Road
Phoenix, AZ
(623) 247-9328

Fry's Marketplace
4230 W. McDowell Road
Phoenix, AZ
(602) 415-5700

$ Giant Dollar Store
6628 W. Camelback Road
Glendale, AZ
(623) 247-0255

$ I-10 Discount Avenue
5118 W. McDowell Road
Phoenix, AZ
(602) 272-9445

JC Penney
13333 W. McDowell Road
Goodyear, AZ
(623) 535-7063

$ Kmart
8701 W. McDowell Road
Tolleson, AZ
(623) 936-1761

⛨ **Kohl's Department Store**
1611 N. Dysart Road
Avondale, AZ
(623) 536-2700

$ **L A Dollar & Discount**
5630 W. Camelback Road
Glendale, AZ
(623) 435-0955

$ **Marian One Dollar Store**
4151 N. 83rd Avenue
Phoenix, AZ
(623) 691-0260

⛨ **Mervyns**
7537 W. Thomas Road
Phoenix, AZ
(623) 849-8880

🏠 **Oregon Plaza**
5270 N. 59th Avenue
Glendale, AZ
(623) 934-6512

$ **Pay-N-Save**
7610 W. Indian School Road
Phoenix, AZ
(623) 247-2393

☆ **Pier 1 Imports**
1442 N. Litchfield Road
Goodyear, AZ
(623) 547-0206

$ **Ross Dress For Less**
1434 N. Litchfield Road
Goodyear, AZ
(623) 535-7242

$ **Sam's Club**
1459 N. Dysart Road
Avondale, AZ
(623) 882-3859

⛨ **Sears**
7611 W. Thomas Road
Phoenix, AZ
(623) 849-7984

$ **Target**
1515 N. Litchfield Road
Goodyear, AZ
(623) 935-3510

$ **Wal-Mart**
13055 W. Rancho Santa Fe
  Boulevard
Avondale, AZ
(623) 535-5557

$ **Wal-Mart Supercenter**
5010 N. 95th Avenue
Glendale, AZ
(623) 872-0292

Churches/ Worship Centers

Avondale Christian Assembly
541 E. Main Street
Avondale, AZ
(623) 932-1670

Bethesda Church of God and Christ
617 E. Doris Street
Avondale, AZ
(623) 932-3121

Blessed Sacrament Catholic Church
512 N. 93rd Avenue
Tolleson, AZ
(623) 936-7107

**Christ Community United
    Methodist Church**
104 W. Western Avenue
Avondale, AZ
(623) 932-3480

Christ Evangelical Lutheran
918 S. Litchfield Road
Goodyear, AZ
(623) 932-2394

Christ Gospel Church
16 N. Fifth Street
Avondale, AZ
(623) 932-5517

Christ Presbyterian Church
316 N. Central Avenue
Avondale, AZ
(623) 882-0721

Church of God
2605 N. 115th Drive
Avondale, AZ
(623) 478-0997

**Church of Jesus Christ of Latter-
    Day Saints**
701 N. 95th Avenue
Tolleson, AZ
(623) 936-3042

First Baptist Church Garden Lake
2517 N. 107th Avenue
Avondale, AZ
(623) 936-7148

Goodyear Church of Christ
807 N. La Jolla Boulevard
Goodyear, AZ
(623) 932-1094

Jehovah's Witnesses
14038 W. Yuma Road
Goodyear, AZ
(623) 932-1708

Litchfield Park First Baptist Church
901 E. Plaza Circle
Avondale, AZ
(623) 935-3163

Nazarene Church of Avondale
121 N. Central Avenue
Avondale, AZ
(623) 932-2733

Phoenix United Reformed Church
2418 N. 127th Lane
Avondale, AZ
(623) 935-2200

St. John Vianney Church
539 E. La Pasada Boulevard
Goodyear, AZ
(623) 932-3313

St. Peter's Episcopal Church
400 S. Old Litchfield Road
Litchfield Park, AZ
(623) 935-3279

St. Thomas Aquinas Church
13720 W. Thomas Road
Avondale, AZ
(623) 935-2151

Trinity Lutheran Church
830 E. Plaza Circle
Litchfield Park, AZ
(623) 935-4665

Truth Tabernacle Church
825 N. Central Avenue
Avondale, AZ
(623) 932-0893

Westridge Lutheran Church
8444 W. Encanto Boulevard
Phoenix, AZ
(623) 849-4327

Medical Centers

Boswell Memorial Hospital
10401 W. Thunderbird Boulevard
Sun City, AZ
(623) 977-7211

Phoenix Memorial Hospital
1201 S. Seventh Avenue
Phoenix, AZ
(623) 258-5111

West Valley Hospital
13677 W. McDowell Road
Goodyear, AZ
(623) 882-1500

Pet Medical Centers

Estrella Animal Hospital
10865 W. Indian School Road
Avondale, AZ
(623) 877-1088

Finlayson Animal Hospital
5036 N. 51st Avenue
Glendale, AZ
(623) 934-7284

Goodyear Animal Hospital Place
380 N. Estrella Parkway, # A6
Goodyear, AZ
(623) 882-9000

POCONO RACEWAY

Start | Finish Line

Pit Road

Garage Area

Infield

Track Information

Inaugural Year: 1974
Owner: the Mattioli family
City: Long Pond, Pennsylvania
Size: 2.5 miles
Banking: 14 degrees in turn 1, 8 degrees in turn 2, 6 degrees in turn 3
Grandstand Capacity: 76,812

ADDRESS

Pocono Raceway
Long Pond Road
Long Pond, PA 18334

(800) 722-3929
www.poconoraceway.com

TICKET INFORMATION
Phone: (800) 722-3929
www.poconoraceway.com

About the Track

Pocono Raceway is one of the most family-friendly tracks on the circuit. The Mattioli family would not have it any other way. Pocono can be tough on the drivers and crews due to the unique triangular design of the track—they either love it or hate it. The track design at Pocono is unique in that each turn was modeled after a different track: Trenton Speedway, the Milwaukee Mile, and Indianapolis Motor Speedway. Oddly enough, only one of these tracks (Indy) hosts the NASCAR Sprint Cup series. The race at this Pennsylvania track is a long five hundred miles; a bit too long for some while others feel the more laps at Pocono the better.

🏁 **INSIDER TIP**—Pocono offers premium tickets for those wanting the VIP race experience. For more info on Sky Box, Terrace Club, Club Pocono, Pacesetters Club, and Victory Circle Club seating packages, call the track at 1-800-722-3929.

Track History

Pocono Raceway was built in 1968 by the track's current owners, Doctors Joe and Rose Mattioli. NASCAR's premier series ran for the first time here in 1974, although the Indy series debuted on the track in 1971. The original track surface started showing so much distress after twenty-two years that the Mattiolis decided

to completely rebuild the track. Beginning in 1990 and extending over the next ten years, the Mattioli family spent $3 million a year to totally rebuild Pocono Raceway.

Track Records

Most Wins: Bill Elliott (5)

Most Top Five Finishes: Mark Martin (19)

Most Lead Changes: 56—on 7/30/1979

Fewest Lead Changes: 10—on 7/26/1998

Most Cautions: 13—most recently on 7/24/2005 (total of 2 times)

Fewest Cautions: 1—7/30/1978

Race Record: Rusty Wallace— 144.892 mph (3 hours, 27 minutes, 3 seconds) (7/21/1996)

Qualifying Record: Kasey Kahne— 172.533 mph (52.164 seconds) (6/11/2004)

Fast Facts

- The first NASCAR Sprint Cup race was run at Pocono Raceway on August 4, 1974, and was won by Richard Petty.
- Harry Gant is the oldest driver to have won at Pocono Raceway— winning in June 1990, he was fifty years old (plus five months and seven days).

- The fewest number of cars still running at the end of the race is eighteen—which happened on July 25, 1982.
- Pocono Raceway has a unique design. Each turn is modeled after turns at three different tracks. Turn 1 (14 degree banking) was modeled after the now defunct Trenton Speedway, turn 2 (sometimes referred to as "the Tunnel Turn") is like Indianapolis Motor Speedway (8 degree banking), and turn 3 (6 degree banking) is similar to the Milwaukee Mile.
- Bobby Allison suffered his career-ending accident at Pocono in June 1988.

INSIDER TIP—Pocono Raceway is located in the magic triangle, meaning Pocono Raceway, New York City, and Philadelphia are only ninety miles from each other.

Parking

Pocono Raceway offers free parking to fans attending the race. All parking is on a first-come, first-served basis. Pocono does not allow overnight camping in the general parking areas. For up-to-date parking information call the track at 1-800-722-3929 or visit www.poconoraceway.com.

Track Rules

According to the track's official website at www.poconoraceway.com, the track's rules are as follows:

ITEMS ALLOWED IN THE GRANDSTAND

- ✓ one cooler (not to exceed 12″ × 12″)
- ✓ plastic bags
- ✓ fanny packs
- ✓ backpacks
- ✓ purses
- ✓ diaper bags
- ✓ binoculars (and bag)
- ✓ scanners (and bag)
- ✓ seat cushions
- ✓ cameras

ITEMS *NOT* ALLOWED IN THE GRANDSTANDS

- ✗ glass containers
- ✗ skateboards
- ✗ golf carts
- ✗ roller skates

✗ firearms

✗ fireworks

✗ knives of any kind

✗ scooters

✗ pets (unless special assistance animals)

Special Needs and Services

Pocono Raceway offers seating and parking for those needing special assistance or accessibility. Pocono allows one companion to accompany those with special needs. For more information about the raceway's Disabilities Services, contact the ticket office prior to arrival at 1-800-722-3929 or 570-646-2300. Always ask for your parking to be near your seats.

Track Tours

Pocono Raceway offers free individual and group tours of the track six days a week from 10 a.m. to 3:30 p.m. from mid-April through late October (except race weeks). Tours can be scheduled prior to arrival by calling the Fan Store at 570-643-0273. It is always best to call in advance for larger groups.

Souvenirs

Official Pocono Raceway and driver-specific merchandise can be pur-chased at Souvenir Alley, which is located behind the grandstands adjacent to the Flag Pole. Souvenirs are also available at numerous free-standing booths scattered around the track and in the infield. Track merchandise is also available online at www.poconoraceway.com.

About the Area

Pocono is not only a racing retreat, it is also one of the most popular honeymoon spots in the United States. This is due largely in part to the beauty of the Pocono Mountains. Over the past several years, Pocono has also become a family-friendly vacation destination. In fact, many of the resorts and hotels are now offering kids' activities and even child care. The families of the drivers always make a point to tag along for Pocono race weekend. The weather in June and July is perfect racing weather with low humidity and lots of sunshine. Bring along a hat and sunscreen ... don't let the comfortable temperatures fool you.

Note: *Because this is a rural area, many places listed in this section do not have street numbers. I recommend calling the number listed for specific directions.*

CHAMBER OF COMMERCE

Pocono Mountains Chamber of
  Commerce
556 Main Street
Stroudsburg, PA, 18360
(570) 421-4433
www.poconochamber.net

Transportation

AIRPORTS

**Wilkes-Barre/Scranton
  International Airport (AVP)**
100 Terminal Road
Avoca, PA
(570) 602-2000
(Wilkes-Barre/Scranton
  International is twenty-three
  miles from the track.)

**Lehigh Valley International Airport
  (ABE)**
3311 Airport Road
Allentown, PA
(610) 266-6000
(Lehigh International is
  approximately thirty miles from
  the track.)

AIRLINES

Continental (800) 525-0280
Delta (800) 221-1212
Northwest (800) 225-2525
United (800) 241-6522
US Airways (800) 943-5436

RENTAL CARS

Alamo (800) 462-5266
Avis (800) 331-1212
Budget (800) 527-7000
Dollar (800) 800-4000
Enterprise (800) 736-8222
Hertz (800) 654-3131
National (800) 227-7368
Thrifty (800) 847-4389

Hotels

KEY
⌒ Pet Friendly   ≈ Pool
✕ Restaurant

Autumn View Lodge
140 Route 715 N., # C
Henryville, PA
(570) 629-4388

≈, ✕ **Bear Creek Mountain Resort
  and Spa**
101 Doe Mountain Lane
Macungie, PA
(866) 754-2822

⌒, ≈ **Best Western Inn**
State Highway 115
Blakeslee, PA
(570) 646-6000

✕ **Blakeslee Inn & Restaurant**
Route 940
Blakeslee, PA
(570) 646-1100

Blueberry Mountain Inn
Thomas Road
Blakeslee, PA
(570) 646-7144

Bon Air Motor Lodge
800 Route 940
Mount Pocono, PA
(570) 839-7789

≈, ✕ **Caesars Brookdale on the Lake**
Brookdale Road and Route 611
Scotrun, PA
(570) 839-8844

≈, ✕ **Caesars Paradise Stream Resort**
99 Route 940
Mount Pocono, PA
(570) 839-8881

≈, ✕ **Carriage House Country Club**
314 Pocono Manor Drive
Pocono Manor, PA
(570) 839-6761

≈, ✕ **Chateau Resort & Conference**
300 Camelback Road
Tannersville, PA
(570) 629-5900

Cloud Crest Motel
208 Robinson Avenue
Mount Pocono, PA
(570) 839-7741

≈ **Comfort Inn**
Route 611
Bartonsville, PA
(570) 476-1500

≈ **Comfort Inn**
800 Route 940
Mount Pocono, PA
(570) 839-9282

≈, ✕ **Crescent Lodge & Country Inn**
Route 191 and Route 940
Cresco, PA
(570) 595-7486

≈, ✕ **Days Inn—Tannersville**
Route 715 and Interstate 80
Tannersville, PA
(570) 629-1667

≈, ✕ **Great Wolf Lodge**
611 Scotrun Avenue
Scotrun, PA
(570) 688-9899

⋘ **Hampton Inn**
Route 940 E.
Mount Pocono, PA
(570) 839-2119

≈, ✕ **Howard Johnson**
63 Route 611
Bartonsville, PA
(570) 424-6100

≈ **Knights Inn—Poconos**
94 Route 611
Bartonsville, PA
(570) 629-8000

⋘ **Kuebler's Mountain Hotel**
Main Street
Tobyhanna, PA
(570) 894-8291

McGinley's Pocono Trail Lodge
Route 115
Blakeslee, PA
(570) 646-3015

Memorytown USA
Grange Road
Mount Pocono, PA
(570) 839-1680

≋ **Mount Pocono Motel**
17 Knob Road
Mount Pocono, PA
(570) 839-0700

Mountaintop Lodge B & B
Route 940
Pocono Pines, PA
(570) 646-6636

Penrose Cabins Homes Cottages
379 Hemlock Drive
Tobyhanna, PA
(570) 839-7237

Pinecrest Lake Rentals
Route 940
Pocono Pines, PA
(570) 646-1200

≋, ✕ **Pocono Manor Inn & Golf Resort**
Route 314
Pocono Manor, PA
(570) 839-7111

≋ **Quality Inn and Suites**
546 Pocono Boulevard
Mount Pocono, PA
(570) 839-3600

≋ **Ramada Inn**
Route 715 at Interstate 80, Exit 299
Tannersville, PA
(570) 629-4100

Ray's Cottages
1250 Neola Road
Stroudsburg, PA
(570) 619-5546

Sullivan Trail Motel
State Route 940
Pocono Lake, PA
(570) 646-3535

≋ **Super 8 Motel**
Route 611
Mount Pocono, PA
(570) 839-7728

Tudor Inn
Route 115
Blakeslee, PA
(570) 646-3300

⇌ **Whispering Hills Motel**
Grange Road
Mount Pocono, PA
(570) 839-9219

Camping

ON-SITE AND TRACK-OWNED CAMPING

Pocono Raceway offers a variety of camping options for those fans attending the race. For up-to-date camping info and fees call the track at 1-800-722-3929. Always ask for the rules for the specific area in which you choose to camp. It is not unusual for each camping area to have its own set of rules.

Family Grandstand RV Area This unreserved area is first come, first served. Anyone (including children) entering this area is required to have a race day ticket. This is a dry camping area.

Family Grandstand Tent Camping Area This nonreserved area is first come, first served. Anyone (including children) entering this camping area must have a race day ticket. Tents, minivans, and pop-ups are allowed in this dry camping area.

Trackside RV Area This area is for fans making reservations prior to arrival. The track does not allow drive ups in this reserved area. This area is normally sold out way in advance. It is best to call as early as possible to assure availability. This is for dry camping only.

OFF-SITE CAMPING

Four Seasons Campground
Babbling Brook Road
Scotrun, PA
(570) 629-2504

Hemlock Campground & Cottages
362 Hemlock Drive
Tobyhanna, PA
(570) 894-4388

Maple Rock Campsite
Route 715
Henryville, PA
(570) 629-0100

Mount Pocono Campground Inc.
30 Edgewood Road
Mount Pocono, PA
(570) 839-8950

Outdoor World Scotrun Resort
Route 611
Scotrun, PA
(570) 629-0620

Pennsylvania Commonwealth
Route 423
Mount Pocono, PA
(570) 894-8336

WT Family Camping
Route 115
Blakeslee, PA
(570) 646-9255

Restaurants

KEY
🍔 Fast Food   🪑 Sit Down
🥡 Takeout   🕯 Reservations

Must Eats

Nick's Lake House
110 S. Lake Drive
Lake Harmony, PA
(570) 722-2500

This is a very nice restaurant with a lovely lake view. The wine list is exceptional!

Shenanigans
130 S. Lake Drive
Lake Harmony, PA
(570) 722-1100

They do serve food here, but it is the party that draws the crowd. This is a hot spot for race teams.

🥡 **Amadeo's Pizza-Deli**
Route 940 and Route 423
Pocono Pines, PA
(570) 646-4540

🪑 **Blakeslee Diner**
State Highway 115
Blakeslee, PA
(570) 646-2800

🪑 **Blakeslee Inn & Restaurant**
Route 940
Blakeslee, PA
(570) 646-1100

🥡 **Brother Bruno's Pizza**
601 Route 940, # 18
Mount Pocono, PA
(570) 839-6477

🪑 **Copa Bar & Grill**
16 Fork Street
Mount Pocono, PA
(570) 839-1976

🥡 **Golden Dragon**
601 Route 940, # 26
Mount Pocono, PA
(570) 839-9780

🪑 **Junction**
Route 940
Pocono Pines, PA
(570) 646-4030

🥡 **La Roma Pizza**
Route 115
Blakeslee, PA
(570) 643-7000

🥡 **Mama Maria's Pizza Shop**
Route 115 off Interstate 80
Blakeslee, PA
(570) 646-1788

🪑 **Marita's II**
Route 940
Pocono Pines, PA
(570) 646-8958

McDonald's
Route 940 and Oak Street
Mount Pocono, PA
(570) 839-3290

Monty's Pizza
14 Route 115 and Route 940
Blakeslee, PA
(570) 643-8937

Murphy's Loft
Route 115
Blakeslee, PA
(570) 646-2813

Pangea Restaurant
Route 611
Scotrun, PA
(570) 629-0250

Papa Santo's Italian Restaurant
115 Route 940
Blakeslee, PA
(570) 643-7408

Peppino's Pizzeria & Deli
Route 940 E. and Township Road
Pocono Summit, PA
(570) 895-4453

Perkins Restaurant & Bakery
600 Route 940
Mount Pocono, PA
(570) 839-0300

Pizza Sicilia
State Route 611
Scotrun, PA
(570) 688-1204

Pocono Brewing Co.
Route 611
Swiftwater, PA
(570) 839-3230

Roberto's Restaurante
Route 940
Pocono Summit, PA
(570) 839-1661

Subway Sandwiches & Salads
601 Route 940
Mount Pocono, PA
(570) 839-5833

Tokyo Tea House
Route 940
Pocono Summit, PA
(570) 839-8880

Van Gilder's Jubilee Restaurant
Route 940
Pocono Pines, PA
(570) 646-2377

Village Squire Steakhouse
Route 115
Blakeslee, PA
(570) 646-3446

Woody's Country House
Route 115
Blakeslee, PA
(570) 646-9932

Local Attractions

WORTH THE TRIP

If you have an extra day or two in the Poconos, make sure you scoot down the road about thirty-five miles to the **Bear Creek Mountain Resort and Spa.** My kids love canoeing on their man-made pond and hitting the hiking trails. This is a great area for biking as well. I (of course) love the full-service spa located on the resort property. If you are looking for a place to stay overnight to get you away from the racetrack rush, the rooms are beautiful with awesome slope-side views. The food is delish, too.

Antoine Dutot Museum & Gallery
Main Street
Delaware Water Gap, PA
(570) 476-4240

Barrett Township Historical
Route 390 and Sand Spring Road
Cresco, PA
(570) 595-61572

Bear Creek Mountain Resort and Spa
101 Doe Mountain Lane
Macungie, PA 18062
(866) 754-2822

Bear Mountain Butterflies
18 Church Road
Jim Thorpe, PA
(570) 325-4848

Camelback Ski Area
1 Camelback Drive
Tannersville, PA
(570) 629-1661

Cresco Station Museum
Route 390 and Sand Spring Road
Cresco, PA
(570) 595-6157

Driebe Freight Station
537 Ann Street
Stroudsburg, PA
(570) 424-1776

Eckley Village
2 Eckley Main Street
Weatherly, PA
(570) 636-2070

Gouldsboro State Park
Route 423
Tobyhanna, PA
(570) 894-8336

Jim Thorpe River Adventures
624 North Street
Jim Thorpe, PA
(570) 325-2570

Mauch Chunk Museum & Cultural
41 W. Broadway
Jim Thorpe, PA
(570) 325-9190

**Monroe County Historical
  Association**
900 Main Street
Stroudsburg, PA
(570) 421-7703

Mountain View Park
Route 611
Tannersville, PA
(570) 629-7324

Mount Pocono Golf Course
10 Pine Hill Road
Mount Pocono, PA
(570) 839-1638

Old Jail Museum
128 W. Broadway
Jim Thorpe, PA
(570) 325-5259

Pocono Indian Museum
Route 209
Bushkill, PA
(570) 588-9164

Pocono Manor Inn & Golf Resort
Route 314
Pocono Manor, PA
(570) 839-7111

Tobyhanna State Park
Route 423
Tobyhanna, PA
(570) 894-8336

Toy Museum
1 Fenner Avenue
Sciota, PA
(570) 402-0243

Water Gap Trolley Sightseeing
Main Street
Delaware WaterGap, PA
(570) 476-9766

Shopping

KEY
🚗 Automotive $ Discount
➕ Pharmacy   🏬 Mall
☆ Specialty   🛍 Department Store

☆ A C Moore Arts & Crafts Store
1112 N. Ninth Street
Stroudsburg, PA
(570) 422-6860

☆ American Eagle Outfitters
156 Stroud Mall
Stroudsburg, PA
(570) 424-1028

**🛍 Ames Department Stores
  Valmont Plaza**
93 Valmont Parkway
Hazleton, PA
(570) 455-8711

$ Big Lots
751 Milford Road
East Stroudsburg, PA
(570) 424-3166

☆ **Bon-Ton**
Route 611 and Bridge Street
Stroudsburg, PA
(570) 424-7800

$ **Dollar General**
State Route 611
Tannersville, PA
(570) 629-6177

$ **Dollar Tree**
616 Stroud Mall, # 1393
Stroudsburg, PA
(570) 422-9500

☆ **Eddie Bauer**
417 Arena Hub Plaza
Wilkes Barre, PA
(570) 823-7002

$ **Family Dollar Store**
Route 115 and Route 940
Blakeslee, PA
(570) 643-7220

$ **Gap Outlet**
285 Crossing Outlet Square
Tannersville, PA
(570) 619-6530

🛈 **JC Penney**
N. Ninth and Bridge Street
Stroudsburg, PA
(570) 424-8620

$ **Kmart**
601 Route 940
Mount Pocono, PA
(570) 839-2277

🛈 **Kohl's Department Store**
200 Crossroads Mall
Stroudsburg, PA
(570) 421-1120

🛈 **Macy's**
59 Wyoming Valley Mall
Wilkes Barre, PA
(570) 823-4444

☆ **McCrory's**
64 Blue Valley Drive
Pen Argyl, PA
(610) 863-9900

☆ **N Style**
9 S. Robinson Avenue
Pen Argyl, PA
(610) 863-6428

☆ **Pier 1 Imports**
470 Pocono Commons
Stroudsburg, PA
(570) 476-0870

🛈 **Pomeroy's Department Store**
14 Wyoming Valley Mall
Wilkes Barre, PA
(570) 829-5751

$ **Ross Dress For Less**
100 Commerce Boulevard
Wilkes Barre, PA
(570) 822-2773

🛈 **Sears**
600 Stroud Mall
Stroudsburg, PA
(570) 420-4200

☆ **Shoe Department**
624 Stroud Mall
Stroudsburg, PA
(570) 424-4917

$ **Target**
350 Pocono Commons
Stroudsburg, PA
(570) 426-1050

$ **T.J. Maxx**
100 Pocono Commons
Stroudsburg, PA
(570) 476-1295

$ **Wal-Mart Supercenter**
500 Route 940
Mount Pocono, PA
(570) 895-4700

Churches/ Worship Centers

Blakeslee United Methodist Church
Route 115
Blakeslee, PA
(570) 646-7727

Christ King Family Center
Route 115
Blakeslee, PA
(570) 646-7456

Faith Lutheran Church
Route 940
Blakeslee, PA
(570) 646-0309

Glorious Church
Sullivan Trail
Pocono Pines, PA
(570) 643-2997

Grace United Church of Christ
Camelback Road
Tannersville, PA
(570) 629-3889

Kingdom Hall—Jehovah's Witness
Ward Avenue
Mount Pocono, PA
(570) 839-6852

Living Hope Baptist Church
Route 940
Mount Pocono, PA
(570) 839-5900

Lutheran Church of Our Savior
675 Belmont Avenue
Mount Pocono, PA
(570) 839-9868

Mount Pocono United Methodist Church
12 Church Avenue
Mount Pocono, PA
(570) 839-9902

Our Lady of the Lake Catholic Church
Sullivan Road
Pocono Pines, PA
(570) 646-6424

Pleasant Valley Presbyterian
Route 115
Brodheadsville, PA
(570) 992-0158

Pocono Community Church
4 Fork Street, # 2080
Mount Pocono, PA
(570) 839-3459

Pocono Mountain Bible Fellowship
Trinity Hill Road
Mount Pocono, PA
(570) 839-6922

Salem United Church of Christ
Old Route 940
Pocono Pines, PA
(570) 643-1411

St. Mary of the Mount
27 Fairview Avenue
Mount Pocono, PA
(570) 839-7138

St. Nicholas Byzantine Catholic
41 Fairview Avenue
Mount Pocono, PA
(570) 839-8090

St. Mark's Church
Miller Drive
Reeders, PA
(570) 629-4142

Saint Paul's United Church of Christ
Upper Swiftwater Road
Swiftwater, PA
(570) 839-0730

Trinity Episcopal Church
Trinity Hill Road
Mount Pocono, PA
(570) 839-9376

Wesleyan Church
Route 940 and Locust Ridge Road
Pocono Lake, PA
(570) 646-9181

Medical Centers

Gnaden Huetten Memorial Hospital
211 N. 12th Street
Lehighton, PA
(610) 377-1300

Pocono Medical Center
206 E. Brown Street
East Stroudsburg, PA
(570) 421-4000

Pet Medical Center

Pocono Lake Animal Clinic
Star Route 65
Pocono Lake, PA
(570) 839-2269

RICHMOND INTERNATIONAL RACEWAY

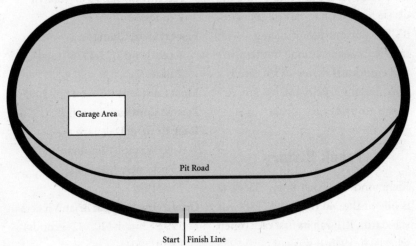

Garage Area

Pit Road

Start | Finish Line

Track Information

Inaugural Year: 1953
Owner: ISC
City: Richmond, Virginia
Size: 0.75 miles
Banking: 14 degrees
Grandstand Capacity: 112,029

ADDRESS

Richmond International Raceway
600 E. Laburnum Avenue
Richmond, VA 23222
(804) 228-7500
www.rir.com

TICKET INFORMATION

Phone: (866) 455-7223
www.rir.com

About the Track

You want some of the best racing on the circuit—well, here it is. Richmond is a guaranteed good race, year after year. This is one reason why Richmond sells out two races a year. Not only is the racing at its finest, but the races at Richmond are run under the lights in the evening after the sun goes down. This makes for an exciting race before the green flag even waves. The fall race at Richmond International Raceway (RIR) is by far one of the hottest tickets on the circuit. As the last race before the Chase for the Championship begins, it's "Katy, bar the door" racing—with trouble brewing among hot tempers and emotional drivers. This race is a must for any true NASCAR fan. Action is around every corner.

Track History

Richmond International Raceway is one of the old tracks by NASCAR standards. RIR ran its first race (open wheels) in 1946. It was not until 1953 that NASCAR's Grand National Division (NASCAR premier series) would race its way into the Virginia track. In 1955, Paul Sawyer and racing veteran Joe Weatherly purchased the Richmond Fairgrounds track. RIR has changed names probably more than any other track on the circuit. To date the half-mile facility has carried five different names; the most recent was made official in 1988. In 1999, ISC purchased the legendary track from Paul Sawyer.

Track Records

Most Wins: Richard Petty (13)
Most Top Five Finishes: Richard Petty (34)
Most Lead Changes: 25—most recently on 3/3/1996 (total of 2 times)
Fewest Lead Changes: 2—most recently on 2/23/1975 (total of 7 times)
Most Cautions: 15—on 5/3/2003
Fewest Cautions: 0—on 3/7/1976
Race Record: Dale Jarrett— 109.047 mph (2 hours, 45 minutes, 4 seconds) (9/6/1997)
Qualifying Record: Brian Vickers— 129.983 mph (20.772 seconds) (5/14/2004)

Fast Facts

- Harry Gant is the oldest driver to have won at Richmond International Raceway—winning in September 1991, he was fifty-one years old (plus seven months and twenty-eight days).
- The first NASCAR Sprint Cup race was run at Richmond International Raceway on April 19, 1953, and was won by Lee Petty.
- The king, Richard Petty, competed in his first race at Richmond on June 5, 1960, finishing sixth.

- Kyle Petty joins his father Richard and grandfather Lee as a winner at Richmond. Richmond International Raceway is the only track where all three have won races in NASCAR's top division.
- On April 19, 1953, only one car remained on the track at the end of the race.
- Richmond is often referred to as "America's Premier Short Track."

Parking

RIR provides free parking in lots located on its property for the fans attending the race. All parking is on a first-come, first-served basis. RIR does not allow overnight parking in the general parking areas. For up-to-date parking information call the track at 804-228-7500.

Track Rules

According to the track's official website at www.rir.com, the track's rules are as follows:

ITEMS ALLOWED IN THE GRANDSTANDS

- ✓ one soft-sided bag/cooler (no larger than 6″ × 6″ × 12″)
- ✓ one clear plastic bag (no larger than 18″ × 18″ × 4″, no ice)
- ✓ food and beverages (must fit in cooler)
- ✓ binoculars
- ✓ scanners
- ✓ headsets
- ✓ cameras
- ✓ seat cushions

ITEMS *NOT* ALLOWED IN THE GRANDSTANDS

- ✗ firearms
- ✗ fireworks
- ✗ glass containers
- ✗ pets (unless special assistance or Seeing Eye dog)
- ✗ beach balls
- ✗ hard-sided coolers
- ✗ insulated cups of any size
- ✗ strollers
- ✗ umbrellas
- ✗ flagpoles

Special Needs and Services

RIR offers seating and parking for those fans needing special assistance and accessibility. One companion may accompany those with special needs. For more info contact the track at 804-228-7500 prior to your arrival. Always ask for your parking to be near your seats.

Track Tours

RIR does not offer individual tours of the facility. Group tour requests should be made to the track at 804-228-7500.

Souvenirs

Official RIR track and driver-specific souvenirs can be purchased at Souvenir Alley on the Midway located outside the main grandstand, near the start-finish line.

 INSIDER TIP—To view the races at RIR in VIP fashion, check out the TORQUE, a members-only club. For more info on TORQUE, call the track at 804-228-7500.

About the Area

The area in and around RIR is great fun with lots of things to do and see. In fact, heading in to downtown Richmond is a must. Downtown Richmond gives you the big city, small town feel as soon as you arrive. The convenience of this track is up near the top of the list of NASCAR-sanctioned tracks. The airport, track, and downtown are all within a twenty-minute drive of one another. RIR currently hosts two NASCAR Sprint Cup races a year, one in May and the other in September, and both are run under the lights. Always dress in layers for the RIR races; it is not uncommon for the temps to cool down once the sun sets.

CHAMBER OF COMMERCE
Greater Richmond Chamber of
  Commerce
600 E. Main Street, Suite 700
Richmond, VA 23219
(804) 648-1234
www.grcc.com

Transportation

AIRPORT
Richmond International Airport
  (RIC)
1 Richard E. Byrd Terminal Drive
Richmond, VA
(804) 226-3000
(Approximately eleven miles from
  the track.)

AIRLINES
AirTran (800) 247-8726
American (800) 433-7300
Continental (800) 525-0280
Delta (800) 221-1212
JetBlue (800) 538-2583
Northwest (800) 225-2525
United (800) 241-6522

US Airways (800) 943-5436
WestJet (888) 937-8538

RENTAL CARS
Alamo (800) 462-5266
Avis (800) 331-1212
Budget (800) 527-7000
Dollar (800) 800-4000
Enterprise (800) 736-8222
Hertz (800) 654-3131
National (800) 227-7368
Thrifty (800) 847-4389

Hotels

KEY
☞ Pet Friendly   ≈ Pool
✕ Restaurant

☞ **Alpine Motel**
7009 Brook Road
Richmond, VA
(804) 261-7981

Belmont Motel
2301 Chamberlayne Avenue
Richmond, VA
(804) 329-0094

✕ **Berkeley Hotel**
1200 E. Cary Street
Richmond, VA
(804) 225-5105

☞ **Broadway Motel**
8302 Brook Road
Richmond, VA
(804) 261-0140

Budget Inn of Richmond
2201 N. Lombardy Street
Richmond, VA
(804) 321-6978

☞ **Cavalier Manor Motel**
8827 Brook Road
Glen Allen, VA
(804) 266-7671

Chamberlayne Motel
1002 Azalea Avenue
Richmond, VA
(804) 266-7641

☞, ≈ **Comfort Inn**
3200 W. Broad Street
Richmond, VA
(804) 359-4061

≈ **Courtyard by Marriott—West**
6400 W. Broad Street
Richmond, VA
(804) 282-1881

≈, ✕ **Crowne Plaza Richmond**
555 E. Canal Street
Richmond, VA
(804) 788-0900

⇔, ≈ **Days Inn**
5701 Chamberlayne Road
Richmond, VA
(804) 266-7616

⇔, ≈, ✕ **Doubletree Hotel**
301 W. Franklin Street
Richmond, VA
(804) 644-9871

⇔, ≈ **Econo Lodge**
1600 Robin Hood Road
Richmond, VA
(804) 353-1287

⇔ **Econo Lodge**
8350 Brook Road
Richmond, VA
(804) 262-7070

⇔ **Guest House Inn & Suites**
8901 Brook Road
Glen Allen, VA
(804) 553-8395

≈ **Hampton Inn**
7433 Bell Creek Road
Mechanicsville, VA
(804) 559-0559

≈, ✕ **Holiday Inn—I-64 W. End**
2000 Staples Mill Road
Richmond, VA
(804) 359-6061

≈, ✕ **Holiday Inn—Central**
3207 North Boulevard
Richmond, VA
(804) 359-9441

≈, ✕ **Holiday Inn—N I-95/
Parham Road**
801 E. Parham Road
Richmond, VA
(804) 266-8753

≈ **Holiday Inn Express—
Richmond**
7441 Bell Creek Road
Mechanicsville, VA
(804) 559-0022

Howard Johnson
8613 Brook Road
Glen Allen, VA
(804) 261-0188

Inns of Virginia
5215 W. Broad Street
Richmond, VA
(804) 288-2800

≈ **Knights Inn**
9002 Brook Road
Glen Allen, VA
(804) 266-2444

Linden Row Inn
100 E. Franklin Street
Richmond, VA
(804) 783-7000

↩, ✕ **Massad House Hotel**
11 N. Fourth Street
Richmond, VA
(804) 648-2893

↩, ≈, ✕ **Omni Richmond Hotel**
100 S. 12th Street
Richmond, VA
(804) 344-7000

↩ **Quality Inn**
201 E. Cary Street
Richmond, VA
(804) 788-1600

Red Carpet Inn
1501 Robin Hood Road
Richmond, VA
(804) 355-7979

≈, ✕ **Richmond Marriott**
500 E. Broad Street
Richmond, VA
(804) 643-3400

Richmond Motel
2600 Chamberlayne Avenue
Richmond, VA
(804) 321-7137

Sleep Inn
950 E. Parham Road
Richmond, VA
(804) 515-7800

↩ **Super 8 Motel**
5615 Chamberlayne Road
Richmond, VA
(804) 262-8880

Town Motel
5214 Brook Road
Richmond, VA
(804) 266-8781

≈ **Travelodge**
5221 Brook Road
Richmond, VA
(804) 266-7603

William Catlin House
2304 E. Broad Street
Richmond, VA
(804) 780-3746

Camping

ON-SITE AND TRACK-OWNED CAMPING

All on-site camping areas at RIR are currently sold out. There are no spots available in Richmond International Raceway's reserved overnight parking areas for RVs, oversized vehicles, or motor coaches. Call the track at 804-228-7500 to be placed on the waiting list.

OFF-SITE CAMPING

Kosmo Village
11197 Washington Highway
Glen Allen, VA
(804) 798-6689

Paramount's Kings Dominion
1600 Theme Park Way
Doswell, VA
(804) 876-5000

Pocahontas State Park
10301 State Park Road
Chesterfield, VA
(804) 796-4255

Roadrunner Campground
13900 Jefferson Davis Highway
Chester, VA
(804) 796-5160

Restaurants

KEY
🍔 Fast Food   🪑 Sit Down
🥡 Takeout   ☎ Reservations

Must Eats

Sam Miller's Restaurant
1210 E. Cary Street
Richmond, VA
(804) 644-5465
    Great bar food and cold beer.
Any race fan's dream!

Tobacco Co. Restaurant
1201 E. Cary Street
Richmond, VA
(804) 643-6560
    This is a true Richmond din-
ing tradition. The food is always
good, but expect to wait a few
extra minutes for a table on race
weekend.

🪑 **Anthony's Italian Restaurant**
4000 Mechanicsville Pike
Richmond, VA
(804) 321-5417

🍔 **Arby's**
5205 Brook Road
Richmond, VA
(804) 266-6579

🪑 **Bella Arte**
1223 Bellevue Avenue
Richmond, VA
(804) 515-9099

🍔 **Burger King**
3720 Mechanicsville Pike
Richmond, VA
(804) 329-2346

🪑 **Captain D's Seafood**
2701 Chamberlayne Avenue
Richmond, VA
(804) 321-8204

Chef's Island
2914 North Avenue
Richmond, VA
(804) 228-2101

Chicken Box Restaurant
3000 Third Avenue
Richmond, VA
(804) 228-2442

Chinatown Express
122 W. Brookland Park Boulevard
Richmond, VA
(804) 321-5893

Church's Chicken
550 E. Laburnum Avenue
Richmond, VA
(804) 329-0444

Club 181
113 W. Brookland Park Boulevard
Richmond, VA
(804) 321-3383

Coach B's Soul Food Take Out
410 W. Brookland Park Boulevard
Richmond, VA
(804) 329-3901

Dunn's Drive In Barbecue
3716 Mechanicsville Pike
Richmond, VA
(804) 329-4676

Family Secrets Restaurant
5310 Chamberlayne Road
Richmond, VA
(804) 515-8890

Flying Dragon
5314 Chamberlayne Road
Richmond, VA
(804) 553-1888

Friendly's Ice Cream Shop
5220 Brook Road
Richmond, VA
(804) 262-6868

Goal Post
2400 North Avenue
Richmond, VA
(804) 228-8237

Hardee's
3815 Mechanicsville Pike
Richmond, VA
(804) 329-5478

Ho-Ho Carry Out Restaurant
10 E. Laburnum Avenue
Richmond, VA
(804) 329-6709

Hunan Gourmet
3107 Mechanicsville Pike
Richmond, VA
(804) 644-8135

Kentucky Fried Chicken
1006 Azalea Avenue
Richmond, VA
(804) 266-3136

New York Fried Chicken
3000 Meadowbridge Road
Richmond, VA
(804) 321-1040

La Casita
5204 Brook Road
Richmond, VA
(804) 262-8729

Northside Grill
1215 Bellevue Avenue
Richmond, VA
(804) 266-4403

Little Caesars Pizza
4007 Mechanicsville Pike
Richmond, VA
(804) 321-2171

Pizza Hut
2204 E. Laburnum Avenue
Richmond, VA
(804) 321-3000

Long John Silver's
2206 E. Laburnum Avenue
Richmond, VA
(804) 321-9292

Pok Comb
2224 Chamberlayne Avenue
Richmond, VA
(804) 329-2344

Mama Mary's Sugar & Spice
3406 Mechanicsville Pike
Richmond, VA
(804) 321-1880

Popeye's Chicken & Biscuits
2709 Chamberlayne Avenue
Richmond, VA
(804) 228-8733

McDonald's
2011 Chamberlayne Avenue
Richmond, VA
(804) 321-3405

Red House II
1202 Azalea Avenue
Richmond, VA
(804) 266-8333

MD Chicken & Pizza
3113 Mechanicsville Pike
Richmond, VA
(804) 643-7777

Sandy's Restaurant & Lounge
2424 North Avenue
Richmond, VA
(804) 329-7263

Seafood House
5308 Chamberlayne Road
Richmond, VA
(804) 264-2429

Shenanigan's Eatery & Pub
4017 MacArthur Avenue
Richmond, VA
(804) 264-5010

Smitty's Frosty Freeze
3603 Mechanicsville Pike
Richmond, VA
(804) 329-1717

Stuart's Fresh Catch
2400 Mechanicsville Pike
Richmond, VA
(804) 643-3474

Subway Sandwiches & Salads
3135 Mechanicsville Pike
Richmond, VA
(804) 643-7514

Subway Sandwiches & Salads
5201 Chamberlayne Road
Richmond, VA
(804) 266-2242

Taco Bell
1208 Azalea Avenue
Richmond, VA
(804) 553-3177

A Taste of Heaven Restaurant
3096 Meadowbridge Road
Richmond, VA
(804) 321-3212

Top's China Restaurant
3820 Mechanicsville Pike
Richmond, VA
(804) 228-2266

Wendy's
2200 E. Laburnum Avenue
Richmond, VA
(804) 321-7421

Zorba's Pizza
4026 MacArthur Avenue
Richmond, VA
(804) 264-5370

Local Attractions

While in Richmond for the race, you must take time to tour **St. John's Church,** a National Historic Landmark. This is the original location of Patrick Henry's "Give Me Liberty or Give Me Death" speech. I love old churches and especially old graveyards. The historic graveyard at St. John's has many famous people buried in its 1,300 graves. St. John's offers tours seven days a week. Make sure you ask about their reenactment schedule. This is a great attraction for adults and kids.

American Civil War Center
490 Tredegar Street
Richmond, VA
(804) 788-6480

Beth Ahabah Museum & Archives
1109 W. Franklin Street
Richmond, VA
(804) 353-2668

Children's Museum of Richmond
2626 W. Broad Street
Richmond, VA
(804) 474-7000

Edgar Allan Poe Museum
1914 E. Main Street
Richmond, VA
(804) 648-5523

John Marshall House Museum
818 E. Marshall Street
Richmond, VA
(804) 648-7998

Lewis Ginter Botanical Garden
1800 Lakeside Avenue
Richmond, VA
(804) 262-9887

Museum of the Confederacy
1201 E. Clay Street
Richmond, VA
(804) 649-1861

Museum of Fine Arts
200 North Boulevard
Richmond, VA
(804) 340-1400

Old Dominion Railway Museum
102 Hull Street
Richmond, VA
(804) 233-6237

Richmond History Center
1015 E. Clay Street
Richmond, VA
(804) 649-0711

Richmond National Battlefield
3215 E. Broad Street
Richmond, VA
(804) 226-1981

Science Museum of Virginia
2500 W. Broad Street
Richmond, VA
(804) 864-1460

Shirley Plantation
501 Shirley Plantation Road
Charles City, VA
(804) 829-5121

St. John's Church
2401 E. Broad Street
Richmond, VA
(804) 648-5015

Virginia Center for Architecture
2501 Monument Avenue
Richmond, VA
(804) 644-3041

Virginia Holocaust Museum
2000 E. Cary Street
Richmond, VA
(804) 257-5400

Virginia House Museum
4301 Sulgrave Road
Richmond, VA
(804) 353-4251

Shopping

KEY
🚗 Automotive $ Discount
⊙ Pharmacy   🏬 Mall
☆ Specialty   🏫 Department Store

$ Ben Franklin
2036 Dabney Road, # B
Richmond, VA
(804) 353-6511

$ BJ's Wholesale Club
7260 Bell Creek Road
Mechanicsville, VA
(804) 559-9554

☆ Burlington Coat Factory
6303 W. Broad Street
Richmond, VA
(804) 288-2515

☆ Citi Trends
5208 Chamberlayne Road
Richmond, VA
(804) 515-9001

🏬 Cloverleaf Mall
7201 Midlothian Turnpike
Richmond, VA
(804) 276-8650

☆ Collector's Heaven
1601 Willow Lawn Drive
Richmond, VA
(804) 673-1127

$ Dollar General
3820 Mechanicsville Pike, # A
Richmond, VA
(804) 329-5407

$ Dollar Tree
7390 Bell Creek Road
Mechanicsville, VA
(804) 746-3535

🏬 Fairfield Commons
4869 Nine Mile Road
Richmond, VA
(804) 222-4167

$ Family Dollar Store
5236 Chamberlayne Road
Richmond, VA
(804) 266-5046

$ Kmart
4715 Nine Mile Road
Richmond, VA
(804) 222-5684

🏫 Kohl's Department Store
7390 Bell Creek Road
Mechanicsville, VA
(804) 559-4194

$ Maxway
4955 Nine Mile Road
Richmond, VA
(804) 222-2666

$ Peebles
4939 Nine Mile Road
Richmond, VA
(804) 226-9171

🛒 Port Walthall Shopping Center
15840 Port Walthall Drive
Richmond, VA
(804) 643-3187

🛒 River Road Shopping Center II
5029 Huguenot Road
Richmond, VA
(804) 282-0141

☆ S & K Famous Brands Menswear
5918 W. Broad Street
Richmond, VA
(804) 285-2244

🏠 Sears
100 Spotsylvania Mall
Richmond, VA
(804) 786-1607

🛒 Stony Point Fashion Park
9200 Stony Point Parkway
Richmond, VA
(804) 560-7467

$ Target
5401 W. Broad Street
Richmond, VA
(804) 285-3492

🛒 Virginia Center Commons
   Mall
10101 Brook Road
Glen Allen, VA
(804) 266-9000

$ Wal-Mart Supercenter
7430 Bell Creek Road
Mechanicsville, VA
(804) 730-8877

🛒 Willow Lawn Shopping Center
1601 Willow Lawn Drive
Richmond, VA
(804) 282-5198

Churches/
Worship Centers

Apostolic Faith Church
3801 Chamberlayne Avenue
Richmond, VA
(804) 329-5600

Church of Christ
3200 Dill Avenue
Richmond, VA
(804) 321-2479

**Concord Fellowship Baptist
Church**
3005 Enslow Avenue
Richmond, VA
(804) 329-1466

First Baptist Washington Park
720 Cheatwood Avenue
Richmond, VA
(804) 321-6645

First United Presbyterian Church
3401 North Avenue
Richmond, VA
(804) 321-5374

Fresh Anointing Cathedral Church
3001 Second Avenue
Richmond, VA
(804) 228-3738

Ginter Park United Methodist
1010 W. Laburnum Avenue
Richmond, VA
(804) 262-8651

Gospel Spreading Church
3800 Hawthorne Avenue
Richmond, VA
(804) 329-7684

Jerusalem Holy Church
2900 North Avenue
Richmond, VA
(804) 233-4048

Living Water Christian Fellowship
5108 Richmond Henrico Turnpike
Richmond, VA
(804) 497-7357

Meadowood Church of God
325 Azalea Avenue
Richmond, VA
(804) 321-1562

Muhammad's Temple of Islam
409 Crawford Street
Richmond, VA
(804) 228-8100

New Beginnings Church of God
3057 Meadowbridge Road
Richmond, VA
(804) 329-5700

New Canaan International Church
1708 Byron Street
Richmond, VA
(804) 329-1680

New Friendship Disciples
4322 North Avenue
Richmond, VA
(804) 321-7440

New Mount Olive Pentecostal Faith
126 W. Brookland Park Boulevard
Richmond, VA
(804) 329-8586

Northminster
2824 Second Avenue
Richmond, VA
(804) 321-2500

Resurrection Lutheran Church
2500 Seminary Avenue
Richmond, VA
(804) 321-7291

St. Elizabeth's Catholic Church
1301 Victor Street
Richmond, VA
(804) 329-4599

St. John's Baptist Church
4317 North Avenue
Richmond, VA
(804) 321-6691

St. Mark's Church of God in Christ
1100 E. Brookland Park Boulevard
Richmond, VA
(804) 329-6360

St. Thomas' Episcopal Church
3602 Hawthorne Avenue
Richmond, VA
(804) 321-9548

Medical Centers

Cumberland Hospital
2909 Moss Side Avenue
Richmond, VA
(804) 321-0510

Children's Hospital
2924 Brook Road
Richmond, VA
(804) 321-7474

Chippenham Medical Center
7605 Fourth Avenue, #303
Richmond, VA
(804) 323-8769

Pet Medical Centers

Animal Hospital
2412 N. Lombardy Street
Richmond, VA
(804) 321-7171

Farmers Veterinary Hospital
3311 Mechanicsville Pike
Richmond, VA
(804) 329-5553

Lakeside Animal Hospital
5206 Lakeside Avenue
Richmond, VA
(804) 262-8697

Hanover Green Veterinary Clinic
7273 Hanover Green Drive
Mechanicsville, VA
(804) 730-2565

TALLADEGA SUPERSPEEDWAY

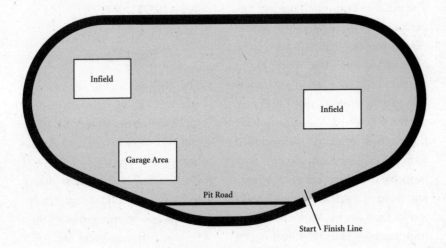

Track Information

Inaugural Year: 1969
Owner: ISC
City: Talladega, Alabama
Size: 2.66 miles
Banking: 33 degrees in turns; 18 degrees in tri-oval
Grandstand Capacity: 175,000

ADDRESS
Talladega Superspeedway
3366 Speedway Boulevard
Talladega, AL 35160
(877) 462-3342
www.talladegasuperspeedway.com

TICKET INFORMATION
Phone: (866) 989-7223
www.talladegasuperspeedway.com

About the Track

Talladega is superspeedway racing in its finest form. Talladega and Daytona are the only two tracks on the circuit where NASCAR mandates a restrictor plate, which basically slows the cars down and bunches them up in packs. This bunching together is what causes big pileups on the tracks, the kind of wreck referred to as "the big one." The racing is usually wild and fast paced for the entire event.

Track History

The massive 2.66-mile Talladega Superspeedway known today as simply "Dega" was originally planned to be constructed in Hillsborough, North Carolina, but local religious leaders opposed the project led by Bill France Sr. and Bill Ward. The duo quickly moved their sights to an abandoned airfield and farmland used for soybean fields located between Atlanta and Birmingham. The groundbreaking for the Alabama Motor Speedway took place in May 1968. Just over a year and $4 million later the sprawling Alabama track was complete. In 1989, ISC changed the track's name to the Talladega Superspeedway.

Track Records

Most Wins: Dale Earnhardt Sr. (10)
Most Top Five Finishes: Dale Earnhardt Sr. (23)
Most Lead Changes: 75—on 5/6/1984
Fewest Lead Changes: 13—on 5/6/1973
Most Cautions: 11—on 4/25/2004
Fewest Cautions: 0—most recently on 10/6/2002 (total of 3 times)

Race Record: Mark Martin— 188.354 mph (2 hours, 39 minutes, 18 seconds) (5/10/1997)
Qualifying Record: Bill Elliott— 212.809 mph (44.998 seconds) (4/30/1987)

Fast Facts

• The first NASCAR Sprint Cup race was run at Talladega Superspeedway on September 14, 1969, and was won by Richard Brickhouse.

• Harry Gant is the oldest driver to have won at Talladega Superspeedway—winning in May 1991, he was fifty-one years old (plus three months and twenty-six days).

• The fewest number of cars still running at the end of a race at Talladega is fourteen—this happened on July 27, 1986.

• Tiny Lund, 1963 Daytona 500 winner, was killed at Talladega in 1975.

• The late Dale Earnhardt made the "Slingshot" move famous at Talladega.

INSIDER TIP—The Kids Zone at Talladega Superspeedway is a must for kids spending the day at the racetrack! Located outside the track near the North Tunnel and Entrance Plaza 1, the area is full of activities for children and is open Saturday and Sunday. Admission to the area is free! Everyone entering the grandstands must have a ticket. Keep this in mind when taking the kids to the track.

Parking

Talladega Superspeedway offers free parking for those fans attending the races. All parking is on a first-come, first-served basis. Talladega does not allow overnight parking in the general parking areas. A limited number of reserved parking spots are also available for a fee. For up-to-date parking info call the track at 877-462-3342.

Track Rules

According to the track's official website at www.talladegasuperspeedway .com, the track's rules are as follows:

ITEMS ALLOWED IN THE GRANDSTANDS

- ✓ soft-sided coolers (not to exceed 6" × 6" × 12")
- ✓ clear plastic bags (not to exceed 18" × 18" × 4", no ice)
- ✓ food and beverages (no glass containers)
- ✓ binoculars
- ✓ radio scanners
- ✓ cameras
- ✓ seat cushions

ITEMS *NOT* ALLOWED IN THE GRANDSTANDS

- ✗ backpacks
- ✗ hard-sided coolers
- ✗ glass containers
- ✗ umbrellas
- ✗ folding chairs
- ✗ skateboards
- ✗ golf carts
- ✗ scooters
- ✗ baby seats
- ✗ strollers
- ✗ steel metal stadium seats
- ✗ flagpoles
- ✗ pets (unless service animal or Seeing Eye dog)
- ✗ bicycles
- ✗ Rollerblades

✗ fireworks
✗ firearms
✗ knives

Special Needs and Services

Talladega Superspeedway offers seating and parking for those needing special assistance or accessibility. One companion is allowed to accompany those with special needs. Call the track at 877-462-3342 prior to arrival for up-to-date info. Always ask for your parking to be near your seats.

Track Tours

Talladega offers both individual and group tours from 9 a.m. to 4 p.m. every day of the week, with the exception of holidays and race weekends. Tickets can be purchased in the Hall of Fame gift shop located at the main entrance to the track. The tour includes Victory Lane, the garage area, pit road, and a VIP suite. For more info on tours, call the track at 877-462-3342.

Souvenirs

Official Talladega Superspeedway merchandise can be purchased in the Hall of Fame gift shop located at the main entrance to the track or at the track's online store at www.talladegasuperspeedway.com. Driver-specific souvenirs can be purchased at Souvenir Alley located behind the Anniston, Lincoln, and Gadsden Grandstands.

About the Area

You will find out quickly that few cities and townships on the Sprint Cup circuit are as race country steadfast as Talladega. This small Alabama town is all about racing from one end of town to the other, and for good reason . . . NASCAR has hosted two events a year at Talladega since 1970. The city of Talladega is hopping on race weekend as are nearby cities Anniston and Birmingham. NASCAR has played with the race dates a bit over the years due to the intense, sizzling summer heat in Alabama. The current April and November dates have proved to be much more comfortable for the race fans and the drivers. This is a track to grab that rain gear for. Talladega has been known to rain in the mornings but then clear up for the race.

CHAMBER OF COMMERCE
Greater Talladega Area Chamber of
   Commerce
210 East Street S.
Talladega, AL 35160
(256) 362-9075
www.talladegachamber.com

Transportation

AIRPORT

Birmingham International Airport
  (BHM)
5900 Messer Airport Highway
Birmingham, AL
(205) 595-0533
(Approximately forty-two miles
  from the track.)

AIRLINES

American (800) 433-7300
Continental (800) 525-0280
Delta (800) 221-1212
Express Jet (888) 958-9538
Northwest (800) 225-2525
Southwest (800) 435-9792
United (800) 241-6522
US Airways (800) 943-5436

RENTAL CARS

Alamo (800) 462-5266
Avis (800) 331-1212
Budget (800) 527-7000
Dollar (800) 800-4000
Enterprise (800) 736-8222
Hertz (800) 654-3131
National (800) 227-7368

Hotels

KEY
🐾 Pet Friendly   ≈ Pool
✖ Restaurant

🐾 **American Inn & Suites**
36225 U.S. Highway 231
Ashville, AL
(205) 594-7080

🐾, ≈ **Baymont Inn**
1600 Alabama Highway 21 S.
Anniston, AL
(256) 835-1492

Big Bull Motel
Highway 231 S.
Pell City, AL
(205) 338-3344

Brothers 4 Motel
Highway 231 S.
Pell City, AL
(205) 338-3344

🐾, ≈ **Budget Inn & Suites**
65600 Alabama Highway 77
Talladega, AL
(256) 362-0900

🐾, ≈, ✖ **Cheaha State Park &**
  Restaurant
2141 Bunker Loop
Delta, AL
(256) 488-5115

≈ **Comfort Inn**
138 Elm Street
Oxford, AL
(256) 831-0860

≋ **Comfort Inn**
1951 Village Drive
Leeds, AL
(205) 640-6600

≋ **Comfort Suites**
125 Davis Loop
Oxford, AL
(256) 835-8873

↩ **Country Court Inn**
3425 U.S. Highway 78 E.
Anniston, AL
(256) 835-2224

↩ **Country Inn Motel**
83641 Highway 9
Ashland, AL
(256) 354-2191

≋ **County Inn & Suites**
100 Colonial Drive
Oxford, AL
(256) 241-0950

≋ **Courtyard by Marriott**
289 Colonial Drive
Oxford, AL
(256) 831-7995

↩, ≋ **Days Inn**
33669 U.S. Highway 280
Childersburg, AL
(256) 378-6007

↩, ≋ **Days Inn**
1835 Ashville Road
Leeds, AL
(205) 699-9833

↩, ≋ **Days Inn**
3 Recreation Drive
Oxford, AL
(256) 835-0300

↩ **Downtowner Inns**
300 Quintard Avenue
Anniston, AL
(256) 237-9777

↩, ≋ **Econo Lodge**
25 Elm Street
Oxford, AL
(256) 831-9480

≋ **Hampton Inn & Suites**
210 Colonial Drive
Oxford, AL
(256) 831-8958

Harpersville Motel
4941 Highway 280
Harpersville, AL
(205) 672-7038

≋ **Holiday Inn Express**
240 Vaughan Lane
Pell City, AL
(205) 884-0047

♿, ≈ **Jameson Inn**
161 Colonial Drive
Oxford, AL
(256) 835-2170

♿ **McClellan Inn**
5708 Weaver Road
Anniston, AL
(256) 820-3144

♿, ≈ **Keywest Inn**
32210 U.S. Highway 280
Childersburg, AL
(256) 378-0337

♿, ≈ **Motel 6**
202 Grace Street
Oxford, AL
(256) 831-5463

♿, ≈ **Lamplighter Inn**
33888 U.S. Highway 280
Childersburg, AL
(256) 378-5561

♿, ≈ **Oxford Western Inn**
U.S. Highway 78 and 21 S.
Oxford, AL
(256) 831-3410

≈ **Landmark Inn**
6210 McClellan Boulevard
Anniston, AL
(256) 820-1515

Red Carpet Inn
1007 Highway 21 S.
Anniston, AL
(256) 831-6082

≈ **Liberty Inn**
101 Highway 78 W.
Oxford, AL
(256) 831-3000

Rest Inn
3055 U.S. Highway 78 E.
Anniston, AL
(256) 831-3027

♿, ≈ **Long Leaf Lodge**
74 Exchange Avenue
Fort McClellan, AL
(256) 820-9494

≈ **Royal Inn Motel**
5618 McClellan Boulevard
Anniston, AL
(256) 820-5154

McCaig Motel
903 N. U.S. Highway 21
Talladega, AL
(256) 362-6110

≈ **Sleep Inn**
88 Colonial Drive
Oxford, AL
(256) 831-2191

⌂ **Super 8 Motel**
2451 Moody Parkway
Moody, AL
(205) 640-7091

⌂ **Super 8 Motel**
220 Haynes Street
Talladega, AL
(256) 315-9511

⌂ **Super 8 Motel**
6220 McClellan Boulevard
Anniston, AL
(256) 820-1000

⌂ **Super Value Inn**
104 Spring Branch Road
Oxford, AL
(256) 832-9480

Travelers Inn
1501 Barry Street
Oxford, AL
(256) 831-9500

Travelodge
1207 Alabama Highway 21 S.
Oxford, AL
(256) 835-0185

Tyler Hill Bed & Breakfast
402 E. Sixth Street
Anniston, AL
(256) 231-0066

⌂ **Vann Thomas Motel**
3002 McClellan Boulevard
Anniston, AL
(256) 238-6555

⌂, ≈, ✕ **Victoria Inn**
1604 Quintard Avenue
Anniston, AL
(256) 236-0503

≈ **Wingate Inn**
143 Colonial Drive
Oxford, AL
(256) 831-1921

Camping

ON-SITE AND TRACK-OWNED CAMPING

Talladega offers a variety of camping options for fans attending the race. For up-to-date info, waiting lists, and fees, call the track office at 877-462-3342. Always request the rules for the specific area in which you choose to camp. It is not uncommon for each area to have its own set of rules.

🏁 **INSIDER TIP**—Talladega is undoubtedly the wildest infield on the circuit. Talladega even houses a temporary "holding" cell for fans too intoxicated to drive or fans getting a bit too wild.

Frontrunners Club I This infield premium area is for motor homes only. All motor homes must be self-contained. This area is one of the most popular camping spots at Talladega.

Frontrunners Club II This infield premium area is for motor homes only. All motorhomes must be self-contained.

Reserved Infield Nongated Areas This infield area must be reserved in advance. Talladega will use a wait list if all spots are taken. All zones are dry camping.

The Blue and Yellow Zones are for tents, cars, pickups, and vans.

The Red and Green Zones are only for motorhomes, pull-behinds, fifth wheels, buses, and RVs.

Talladega and Eastaboga Boulevards This camping area is for cars, vans, RVs, and tents. This area is first-come, first-served. Dry camping only.

INSIDER TIP—The campgrounds at Talladega are no doubt the most heavily "camped" tracks on the circuit. The large number of campfires creates a haze over the track and the surrounding area. If you have allergies or are allergic to smoke, you might want to bypass this camping experience.

OFF-SITE CAMPING

Cheaha State Park & Restaurant
2141 Bunker Loop
Delta, AL
(256) 488-5115

Country Court RV Park
3459 U.S. Highway 78 E.
Anniston, AL
(256) 835-2045

Dabbs Landing
43708 U.S. Highway 78
Lincoln, AL
(205) 763-2064

DeSoto Caverns Park
5181 DeSoto Caverns Parkway
Childersburg, AL
(256) 378-7252

Lakeside Landing
4600 Martin Street S.
Cropwell, AL
(205) 525-5701

Logan Landing Campground
1036 Paul Bear Bryant Road
Alpine, AL
(256) 268-0045

Talladega Taz RV Park
4899 Speedway Boulevard
Lincoln, AL
(256) 832-4200

Restaurants

KEY
🍔 Fast Food   🪑 Sit Down
🥡 Takeout   🕯 Reservations

Must Eats

Dreamland BBQ
1427 14th Avenue S.
Birmingham, AL
(205) 933-2133
This is melt in your mouth southern BBQ. You will need lots of napkins and don't forget to leave room for dessert!

Surin West
19th Street and 11th Avenue
Birmingham, AL
(205) 324-1928
This is a great Thai restaurant. If you love spicy, this is your spot. Make sure to order a Monkey Business Martini. The wait can be a hassle, but the food is worth the extra time it takes to get a table.

🍔 **Arby's**
203 Battle Street E.
Talladega, AL
(256) 362-3986

🥡 **Beavers Bar-B-Q Place**
1762 Airport Road
Eastaboga, AL
(256) 831-0808

🥡 **Big Daddy's Bar-B-Q**
43121 Al Highway 21
Munford, AL
(256) 358-9005

🪑 **Buddy's**
313 Battle Street E.
Talladega, AL
(256) 362-8851

🍔 **Burger King**
318 Battle Street E.
Talladega, AL
(256) 362-7687

Cafe Royale
110 Court Square E.
Talladega, AL
(256) 362-3681

Captain D's Seafood
801 Battle Street E.
Talladega, AL
(256) 362-2851

Church's Chicken
806 Battle Street E.
Talladega, AL
(256) 761-0076

Clear Springs Marina Grill
121 Eureka Road
Lincoln, AL
(205) 763-1322

Country Folks
76746 Alabama Highway 77
Lincoln, AL
(205) 763-1448

Dairy Queen
5955 Speedway Boulevard
Eastaboga, AL
(256) 831-6400

Dairy Queen
103 Haynes Street
Talladega, AL
(256) 362-3962

**Diamond Lil's Restaurant &
Lounge**
108 Haynes Street
Talladega, AL
(256) 315-0620

Dinner Bell
76746 Alabama Highway 77
Lincoln, AL
(205) 763-1136

DJ's Diner
151 Stemley Bridge Road
Talladega, AL
(256) 761-0255

Domino's Pizza
201 Haynes Street
Talladega, AL
(256) 362-6800

Fincher's Real Delite
521 East Street N.
Talladega, AL
(256) 362-2174

First House Chinese Restaurant
107 Johnson Avenue N.
Talladega, AL
(256) 362-0505

Gator's BBQ
461 Battle Street W.
Talladega, AL
(256) 362-5454

Glass House Restaurant & Catering
21 Ashley Lane
Munford, AL
(256) 358-0093

Golden Eagle Restaurant
728 Battle Street E.
Talladega, AL
(256) 362-8383

Grill Barbeque
221 Haynes Street
Talladega, AL
(256) 362-0061

Hills Cafe & Deli
47720 U.S. Highway 78
Lincoln, AL
(205) 763-1900

Huddle House
722 Battle Street E.
Talladega, AL
(256) 362-8725

Huddle House
12153 Stemley Road, # B
Lincoln, AL
(205) 763-0892

Jack's Family Restaurant
601 Bankhead Boulevard
Talladega, AL
(256) 362-4761

Kathys Stampede Steakhouse
710 Battle Street E.
Talladega, AL
(256) 315-0600

Kentucky Fried Chicken
75835 Alabama Highway 77
Lincoln, AL
(205) 763-2545

Kentucky Fried Chicken
219 Haynes Street
Talladega, AL
(256) 362-5681

Longhorn Cafe
5120 Providence Road
Talladega, AL
(256) 315-9996

Margarita's
103 17th Street
Talladega, AL
(256) 315-9711

Matehuala Mexican Restaurant
114 Court Square S.
Talladega, AL
(256) 362-5754

McDonald's
110 Haynes Street
Talladega, AL
(256) 362-2448

McDonald's
75304 Alabama Highway 77
Lincoln, AL
(205) 763-0930

Miller's Barbeque
405 Fort Lashley Avenue
Talladega, AL
(256) 761-0187

Panos Italian Grill
709 Battle Street E.
Talladega, AL
(256) 362-3447

Parigi's Pizza
119 Court Square W.
Talladega, AL
(256) 362-3313

Rally's Hamburgers
117 Battle Street E.
Talladega, AL
(256) 362-6253

Sonic Drive-In
717 Battle Street E.
Talladega, AL
(256) 761-1950

Stemley Station Restaurant
7421 Stemley Bridge Road
Talladega, AL
(256) 268-2835

Subway Sandwiches & Salads
700 Battle Street E.
Talladega, AL
(256) 362-0741

Subway Sandwiches & Salads
214 Haynes Street
Talladega, AL
(256) 315-0191

Tabby's Family Restaurant
225 Sycamore Cemetery Road
Talladega, AL
(256) 207-3200

Taco Bell
215 Haynes Street
Talladega, AL
(256) 362-9200

Taco Bell
75835 Alabama Highway 77
Lincoln, AL
(205) 763-2545

Triangle Restaurant & Lounge
12 Fort Lashley Avenue
Talladega, AL
(256) 362-2771

Wendy's
824 Battle Street E.
Talladega, AL
(256) 362-4824

Local Attractions

Two must stops while catching a race at Talladega are the **Davey Allison Memorial Park** and the **International Motorsports Hall of Fame Museum.** The museum is located at the main entrance to the track. This museum houses cars and unique items (even airplanes) from the biggest names in motorsports, not just NASCAR. To be that close and not go would be a racing sin. The Davey Allison Memorial Park is very special to my family for obvious reasons. Located in the park is a Walk of Fame where NASCAR drivers are voted in each year by race fans. The park is a short drive from from the track in downtown Talladega.

Anniston Municipal Golf Course
1341 Johnston Drive
Anniston, AL
(256) 231-7631

**Anniston Museum of Natural
  History**
800 Museum Drive
Anniston, AL
(256) 237-6766

Berman Museum
840 Museum Drive
Anniston, AL
(256) 237-6261

Cheaha State Park
19644 Highway 281
Delta, AL
(256) 488-5111

Davey Allison Memorial Park
Coffee Street and Court Street
Talladega, AL
(256) 632-4261

DeSoto Caverns Park
5181 DeSoto Caverns Parkway
Childersburg, AL
(256) 378-7252

Kymulga Grist Mill Park
7346 Grist Mill Road
Childersburg, AL
(256) 378-7436

Lakeside Park
2801 Stemley Bridge Road
Cropwell, AL
(205) 884-3030

Talladega Municipal Golf Course
65130 Lincoln Highway 77 N.
Talladega, AL
(256) 362-8151

Ten Islands Historic Park
16157 Alabama Highway 144
Ragland, AL
(205) 472-0481

Shopping

KEY

🚗 Automotive $ Discount
⊕ Pharmacy   🏬 Mall
☆ Specialty   🏠 Department Store

Worth the Trip

Nearby Birmingham offers a very nice shopping experience. It is worth the forty-minute drive. The Summit is an outside shopping experience while the Galleria is an indoor mall with countless stores.

☆ **A J's Mens Fashions**
113 Court Square W.
Talladega, AL
(256) 761-0045

☆ **A J's Mens Fashions**
607 Snow Street
Oxford, AL
(256) 835-3660

☆ **Best Buy**
1100 Oxford Exchange Boulevard
Oxford, AL
(256) 832-0172

$ **Big Lots**
3222 McClellan Boulevard
Anniston, AL
(256) 236-9480

$ **Bill's Dollar Store**
121 Magnolia Street S.
Lincoln, AL
(205) 763-2595

$ **Bill's Dollar Store**
114 County Road 31
Ashland, AL
(256) 354-7122

$ **Bonus**
35754 U.S. Highway 231
Ashville, AL
(205) 594-7575

$ **Burkes Outlet**
100 Johnson Avenue N.
Talladega, AL
(256) 480-1523

☆ **Citi Trends**
3220 McClellan Boulevard
Anniston, AL
(256) 240-7013

🏠 **Dillard's**
700 Quintard Drive
Oxford, AL
(256) 835-2819

$ Dollar General
232 East Street N.
Talladega, AL
(256) 362-0160

$ Dollar Tree
726 Battle Street E.
Talladega, AL
(256) 362-5207

$ Family Dollar Store
106 17th Street
Talladega, AL
(256) 362-0592

$ Fred's Store
1881 U.S. Highway 78 W.
Oxford, AL
(256) 832-0340

$ Goody's Family Clothing
100 Johnson Avenue N., # 116A
Talladega, AL
(256) 761-1775

👕 JC Penney
815 S. Quintard Avenue
Anniston, AL
(256) 831-2144

$ Kmart
3101 McClellan Boulevard
Anniston, AL
(256) 236-5681

👕 Martin's Department Store
3100 McClellan Boulevard
Anniston, AL
(256) 237-0349

$ Peebles
100 Johnson Avenue N., # 115
Talladega, AL
(256) 362-4165

$ Ross Dress For Less
130 Oxford Exchange Boulevard
Oxford, AL
(256) 835-7890

👕 Sears
700 Quintard Drive
Oxford, AL
(256) 741-8393

☆ Shoe Department
101 Johnson Avenue N.
Talladega, AL
(256) 315-0149

$ Super Ten Stores
605 Fort Lashley Avenue
Talladega, AL
(256) 362-2151

$ Target
400 Oxford Exchange Boulevard
Oxford, AL
(256) 231-2900

☆ **Taylor Co.**
8029 Parkway Drive
Leeds, AL
(205) 699-8527

$ **T.J. Maxx**
300 Oxford Exchange Boulevard
Oxford, AL
(256) 831-1023

☆ **Wakefield's**
1212 Quintard Avenue
Anniston, AL
(256) 237-9521

$ **Wal-Mart**
214 Haynes Street
Talladega, AL
(256) 761-1681

Churches/ Worship Centers

Bethel United Methodist Church
1101 Stemley Bridge Road
Talladega, AL
(256) 362-2315

Church of Christ
416 East Street N.
Talladega, AL
(256) 362-2320

Cole Temple Church of God
349 Davis Street
Talladega, AL
(256) 315-9922

First Presbyterian Church
130 North Street E.
Talladega, AL
(256) 362-6191

House of Prayer of God
4540 Shocco Springs Road
Talladega, AL
(256) 362-4549

Kingdom Hall—Jehovah's Witness
900 South Street E.
Talladega, AL
(256) 362-6637

Limbaugh Chapel
1036 New Lincoln Road
Talladega, AL
(256) 249-3426

Mount Zion Seven Day
1 Church Street
Talladega, AL
(256) 362-8671

New Jerusalem Episcopal Church
307 Spring Street N.
Talladega, AL
(256) 761-9301

Pine Grove CME Church
4835 Speedway Boulevard
Eastaboga, AL
(256) 832-4009

Rocky Mount Baptist Church
13800 Jackson Trace Road
Talladega, AL
(256) 362-8691

**Rushing Springs Missionary
  Church**
9796 Stemley Bridge Road
Talladega, AL
(256) 268-9347

**St. Francis of Assissi Catholic
  Church**
722 East Street S.
Talladega, AL
(256) 362-5372

St. Peter's Episcopal Church
208 North Street E.
Talladega, AL
(256) 362-2505

Talladega Bible Methodist Church
120 Brecon Access Road
Talladega, AL
(256) 362-8446

Talladega Wesleyan
433 East Street N.
Talladega, AL
(256) 362-0750

Medical Centers

Clay County Hospital
83825 Highway 9
Ashland, AL
(256) 354-2131

St. Clair Regional Hospital
2805 Hospital Drive
Pell City, AL
(205) 338-3301

Stringfellow Memorial Hospital
301 E. 18th Street
Anniston, AL
(256) 235-8918

Pet Medical Center

Animal Care Associates
5090 U.S. Highway 78 W.
Oxford, AL
(256) 831-9256

TEXAS MOTOR SPEEDWAY

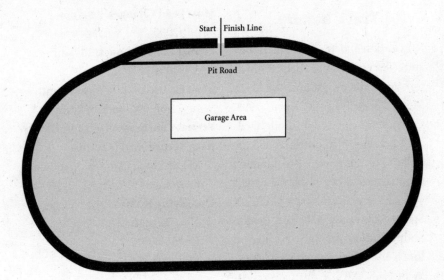

Start | Finish Line

Pit Road

Garage Area

Track Information

Inaugural Year: 1997
Owner: SMI
City: Fort Worth, Texas
Size: 1.5 miles
Banking: 24 degrees
Grandstand Capacity: 212,585

ADDRESS

Texas Motor Speedway
3545 Lone Star Circle
Fort Worth, TX 76177
(817) 215-8510
www.texasmotorspeedway.com

TICKET INFORMATION

Phone: (817) 215-8500
www.texasmotorspeedway.com

About the Track

Texas Motor Speedway is a fast 1.5-mile quad-oval deep in the heart of Texas. Many feel the racing at Texas is similar to that of Atlanta Motor Speedway. The fact that Texas and Atlanta are similar is not a mistake, as Bruton Smith and SMI own both super-fast tracks. Fans love the Texas track. In fact, many fans feel Texas is the most fan-friendly track on the circuit. The racing is great and the hospitality is even better.

Track History

Jeff Gordon and Texas natives Bobby and Terry Labonte helped Bruton Smith break ground for Texas Motor Speedway in April 1995. Construction of the 1.5-mile facility took eleven months and $250 million to complete. The building process turned out to be the easiest part of the plan to host a NASCAR Sprint Cup event. SMI and Bruton Smith had to get very creative to lure NASCAR into the state of Texas. With NASCAR's Sprint Cup schedule already full, SMI decided to buy up tracks currently with Cup dates in order to give Texas some dates. North Wilkesboro and Rockingham, both North Carolina short tracks, closed doors and handed over dates to Texas, which now has two Sprint Cup races a year.

Track Records

Most Wins: No one has won more than once.

Most Top Five Finishes: Jeff Gordon, Mark Martin (4)

Most Lead Changes: 29—on 4/2/2000

Fewest Lead Changes: 18—on 4/1/2001

Most Cautions: 12—most recently on 11/5/2006 (total of 2 times)

Fewest Cautions: 6—on 11/6/2005

Race Record: Carl Edwards— 151.055 mph (3 hours, 19 minutes, 0 seconds) (11/6/2005)

Qualifying Record: Brian Vickers— 196.235 mph (27.518 seconds) (11/5/2006)

Fast Facts

- The first NASCAR Sprint Cup race was run at Texas Motor Speedway on April 6, 1997, and was won by Jeff Burton.
- Dale Jarrett is the oldest driver to have won at Texas Motor Speedway—winning in April 2001, he was forty-four years old (plus four months and six days).
- Texas Motor Speedway has enough permanent lighting to illuminate eleven NFL football stadiums—an average of two million watts for a nighttime event.

A standard household plug is 120 volts—the speedway lights run on 480 volts each.

- The 1997 Countryfest took place at Texas Motor Speedway. Country artists Charlie Daniels, Vince Gill, Travis Tritt, LeAnn Rimes, Jo Dee Messina, Bryan White, Hank Williams Jr., and Wynonna Judd all performed for 185,000 country music fans.
- In 1997, 385,000 fans showed up for the sold-out Rockfest event featuring Matchbox Twenty, Jewel, Bush, Collective Soul, Counting Crows, No Doubt, and the Wallflowers.

Parking

General Parking at Texas Motor Speedway is free for all major race weekends. All parking is first come, first served. Texas Motor Speedway does not allow overnight parking in the general parking areas. VIP parking may be purchased in advance through the Speedway Main Ticket Office by calling 817-215-8500.

INSIDER TIP—If you want to view the race in high fashion at Texas, check out the Victory Lane Club and the Pit Stop Pavilion. The Victory Lane Club is premium luxury seating, which includes suite passes, parking, food and beverages, pit passes, and much more. The Pit Stop Pavilion is a step down but still offers the VIP experience, including pit passes, breakfast, and much more. For more info on both experiences, call the track office at 817-215-8500.

Track Rules

According to the track's official web site at www.texasmotorspeedway.com, the track's rules are as follows:

ITEMS ALLOWED IN THE GRANDSTANDS

- ✓ coolers (no larger than 14″ × 14″ × 14″)
- ✓ backpacks or fanny packs (no larger than 14″ × 14″ × 14″)
- ✓ binoculars
- ✓ scanners
- ✓ cameras
- ✓ alcoholic beverages (no glass containers)
- ✓ seat cushions

ITEMS *NOT* ALLOWED IN THE GRANDSTANDS

- ✗ glass
- ✗ strollers
- ✗ umbrellas
- ✗ skateboards
- ✗ scooters
- ✗ Rollerblades
- ✗ firearms
- ✗ fireworks
- ✗ illegal substances

Special Needs and Services

Texas Motor Speedway offers seating and parking for fans needing special assistance and accessibility. One companion is allowed to accompany those with special needs. Call the track at 817-215-8500 prior to your arrival. Always ask for your parking to be near your seats.

Track Tours

Track tours are available seven days a week at Texas, with the exception of race weekend when no tours are conducted. The tour includes a VIP suite, pit road, Speedway World gift shop, Victory Lane, and a van ride around the track. Group tours are only available by appointment. Call the track at 817-215-8565 for schedules and fees.

Souvenirs

Official track merchandise can be purchased in the Speedway World gift shop located on the southeast corner of the property off Victory Circle. Driver-specific merchandise can be purchased at Souvenir Alley located outside the frontstretch gates.

INSIDER TIP—ATMs are located at the Texas Motor Speedway dirt track, Speedway Club Lobby, Infield café, and Speedway World Lobby.

About the Area

Everything is big in Texas, including the Texas Motor Speedway fan base. Fans flock into the track twice a year for great racing, but make no mistake, the draw of the Dallas–Fort Worth area plays a big part in fans coming back year after year. The large metro area of Dallas–Fort Worth offers great shopping, entertainment, restaurants, and tourist attractions. Weather for both Texas dates is layer worthy. Both races tend to start out cool and warm up over the course of the day but cool off again in the late afternoon.

CHAMBER OF COMMERCE

Fort Worth Chamber of Commerce
777 Taylor Street, # 900
Fort Worth, TX 76102
(817) 336-2491
www.fortworthchamber.com

Transportation

AIRPORT

Dallas/Fort Worth International
   Airport (DFW)
3200 E. Airfield Drive
Dallas, TX
(972) 574-8888
(Approximately seventeen miles
   from the track.)

AIRLINES

AirTran Airways (800) 247-8726
America West (800) 235-9292
American (800) 433-7300
ATA (800) 225-2995
Champion Air (972) 574-3112
Continental (800) 525-0280
Delta (800) 221-1212
Frontier (800) 432-1359
Midwest (800) 452-2022
Northwest (800) 225-2525
Sun Country (800) 359-6786
Taca (800) 425-2479
United (800) 241-6522
US Airways (800) 943-5436

RENTAL CARS

Advantage (800) 777-5500
Alamo (800) 462-5266
Avis (800) 331-1212
Budget (800) 527-7000
Dollar (800) 800-4000
Enterprise (800) 736-8222
E-Z (800) 277-5171 or
   (972) 574-3360
Hertz (800) 654-3131
National (800) 227-7368
Thrifty (800) 847-4389

Hotels

KEY
🐾 Pet Friendly   ≈ Pool
✕ Restaurant

🐾, ≈ **Baymont Inn & Suites**
4681 Gemini Place
Fort Worth, TX
(817) 740-1046

🐾, ≈ **Baymont Inn & Suites**
301 Capitol Street
Grapevine, TX
(817) 329-9300

🐾 **Budget Host Inn**
3720 Tanacross Drive
Fort Worth, TX
(817) 222-1919

🐾 **Budget Inn**
7716 NE Loop 820
Fort Worth, TX
(817) 284-4004

🛏 **Candlewood Suites**
5201 Endicott Avenue
Fort Worth, TX
(817) 838-8229

🛏, ≈ **Comfort Inn**
801 W. Highway 114
Roanoke, TX
(817) 490-1455

🛏, ≈ **Comfort Inn**
4850 North Freeway
Fort Worth, TX
(817) 834-8001

🛏, ≈ **Comfort Inn**
5151 Thaxton Parkway
North Richland Hills, TX
(817) 577-4389

🛏, ≈ **Comfort Suites**
1100 N. Interstate 35 E.
Denton, TX
(940) 898-8510

🛏, ≈ **Comfort Suites**
3751 Tanacross Drive
Fort Worth, TX
(817) 222-2333

≈, ✕ **Dallas Marriott Solana**
5 Village Circle
Westlake, TX
(817) 430-5000

≈ **Days Inn**
601 Interstate 35 E.
Denton, TX
(940) 566-1990

≈ **Days Inn**
5370 Blue Mound Road
Fort Worth, TX
(817) 626-3566

≈, ✕ **Doral Tesoro Hotel & Golf
Club**
3300 Championship Parkway
Fort Worth, TX
(817) 961-0800

Elite Suites
2201 E. Continental Boulevard
Southlake, TX
(817) 251-0165

Extended Stay America
3804 Tanacross Drive
Fort Worth, TX
(817) 838-3500

≈ **Fairfield Inn & Suites Fort
Worth/Fossil Creek**
3701 NE Loop 820
Fort Worth, TX
(817) 232-5700

≈ **Fairfield Inn by Marriott**
3751 NE Loop 820
Fort Worth, TX
(817) 232-5547

Garden Manor
205 E. College Street
Grapevine, TX
(817) 424-9177

≈, ✗ Gaylord Texan Resort &
 Convention Center
1501 Gaylord Trail
Grapevine, TX
(817) 778-1000

Great Western Inn
5050 NE Loop 820
Fort Worth, TX
(817) 485-9828

Great Western Inn
5317 Blue Mound Road
Fort Worth, TX
(817) 625-6211

≈ Hampton Inn—Alliance
 Airport
13600 North Freeway
Fort Worth, TX
(817) 439-0400

≈ Hampton Inn—DFW Airport
1600 Hurst Town Center Drive
Hurst, TX
(817) 503-7777

≈ Holiday Inn Express—DFW
309 W. State Highway 114
Grapevine, TX
(817) 442-5919

⌂, ≈ Homewood Suites—North
 Fossil Creek
3701 Tanacross Drive
Fort Worth, TX
(817) 834-7400

Lakeview Inn
5500 NE Loop 820
Haltom City, TX
(817) 605-6200

⌂ Landmark Motel
405 N. Saginaw Boulevard
Saginaw, TX
(817) 232-8931

⌂, ≈ La Quinta Inn
4715 Meandering Way
Colleyville, TX
(817) 399-0918

⌂, ≈ La Quinta Inn—North
4700 North Freeway
Fort Worth, TX
(817) 222-2888

≈ Microtel Inn & Suites
337 Dorman Road
Roanoke, TX
(817) 490-9595

≈ Microtel Inn & Suites
3740 Tanacross Drive
Fort Worth, TX
(817) 222-3740

🛏, ≈ **Motel 6**
7804 Bedford Euless Road
North Richland Hills, TX
(817) 485-3002

🛏, ≈ **Mustang Inn & Suites**
5330 Blue Mound Road
Fort Worth, TX
(817) 624-1989

🛏, ≈, ✗ **Radisson Hotel Denton**
2211 N. Interstate 35 E.
Denton, TX
(940) 565-8499

≈ **Residence Inn—Airport**
13400 North Freeway
Fort Worth, TX
(817) 750-7000

≈ **Residence Inn—Fossil Creek**
5801 Sandshell Drive
Fort Worth, TX
(817) 439-1300

🛏, ≈ **Royal Hotel Suites**
1210 N. Interstate 35 E.
Denton, TX
(940) 383-2007

🛏, ≈ **Speedway Sleep Inn & Suites**
13471 Raceway Drive
Roanoke, TX
(817) 491-3120

🛏, ≈ **Super 8 Motel**
250 E. Highway 114
Grapevine, TX
(817) 329-7222

🛏, ≈ **Super 8 Motel**
5225 N. Beach Street
Fort Worth, TX
(817) 222-0892

🛏, ≈ **Super 8 Motel**
4665 Gemini Place
Fort Worth, TX
(817) 222-3220

Camping

ON-SITE AND TRACK-OWNED CAMPING

Texas Motor Speedway offers a variety of camping options for fans attending the race. Many of these areas are sold out due to the popularity of the track. Texas Motor Speedway fills its open spots by random drawing. Call the tract at 817-215-8500 for random drawing info, fees, and rules for each camping area.

Blue Ox Campgrounds This dry camping area is located outside of turn 3.

Blue Ox VIP This VIP infield camping area is sold out.

Hellmans Reserved Infield This reserved infield area is currently sold out. Open spaces are filled by a random drawing.

Lone Star Circle Reserved This reserved camping area is located near turn 3, between Harmonson Road and Lone Star Road.

Tent City This nonreserved area is for tent camping only. This camping area is filled on a first-come, first-served basis.

Unreserved Camping This dry camping area is located on the west side of the speedway. All spots will be filled on a first-come, first-served basis.

Victory Circle Reserved This reserved area is located near turn 3. Victory Circle is sold on a race-by-race basis. It cannot be held year after year like many of the other areas at Texas.

OFF-SITE CAMPING

Boyd RV Park
538 E. Rock Island Avenue
Boyd, TX
(940) 433-9910

Destiny Dallas RV Resort
7100 S. Interstate 35 E.
Denton, TX
(940) 497-3353

Fowler's RV Park
12465 Business Highway 287 N.
Fort Worth, TX
(817) 439-3898

Jim's RV
604 Main Street
Lake Dallas, TX
(940) 497-5467

Lewisville Lake Park
5 Lake Park Road
Lewisville, TX
(972) 219-3742

Paradise RV Park
1217 FM 407 W.
Argyle, TX
(940) 648-3573

Pat's Court
3749 NE 28th Street
Haltom City, TX
(817) 222-9201

Post Oak Place RV Park
109 Massey Street
Denton, TX
(940) 387-8584

U.S. Army Corps of Engineers
110 Fairway Drive
Grapevine, TX
(817) 481-4541

Vineyards Campground
1501 N. Dooley Street
Grapevine, TX
(817) 488-1464

Restaurants

KEY

🍔 Fast Food   🪑 Sit Down
📦 Takeout   📞 Reservations

Must Eats

Big Buck Brewery and Steakhouse
2501 Bass Pro Drive
Grapevine, TX
(214) 513-2337

This dining experience is like eating in an old hunting lodge. The food is great and the atmosphere is quite unique.

Saltgrass Steak House
102 State Highway 114 E.
Grapevine, TX
(817) 329-1900

You will think you have died and gone to steak heaven. You can eat these steaks with a spoon. This is by far one of the best restaurants on the circuit and hands down the best steak.

🪑 **A & W**
8121 Gasoline Alley
Roanoke, TX
(817) 491-3483

🪑 **Babe's Chicken Dinner House**
104 N. Oak Street
Roanoke, TX
(817) 491-2900

🪑 **Bludreaux Seafood Kitchen**
15306 Highway 114
Justin, TX
(817) 636-2406

🪑 **Blue Hangar Cafe**
700 Boeing Way
Roanoke, TX
(817) 490-0058

🪑 **Buca di Beppo**
2701 State Highway 114 E.
Roanoke, TX
(817) 746-6262

🪑 **Cactus Flower Cafe Alliance**
2401 Westport Parkway
Roanoke, TX
(817) 491-3519

📦 **Chicken Express**
800 S. FM 156
Justin, TX
(940) 648-1180

Chili's Grill & Bar
113 E. Highway 114
Roanoke, TX
(817) 490-6215

Chio's Mexican Grill
950 FM 156 S.
Justin, TX
(940) 648-3614

Classic Cafe
504 N. Oak Street
Roanoke, TX
(817) 430-8185

Don Mateo's Mexican Restaurant
200 N. Oak Street
Roanoke, TX
(817) 831-1122

Dove Creek Cafe
204 S. Highway 377
Roanoke, TX
(817) 491-4973

El Comalito Cafe
500 N. Highway 377
Roanoke, TX
(817) 491-4422

Fortuna Pizza & Pasta
2420 Westport Parkway
Fort Worth, TX
(817) 439-2292

Hong Kong Express
301 Trophy Lake Drive
Roanoke, TX
(817) 491-8806

Italian Bistro
501 E. Byron Nelson Boulevard
Roanoke, TX
(817) 491-9000

Italy Pasta & Pizza
4308 Bordeaux Way
Roanoke, TX
(817) 490-0666

Long John Silver's
8121 Gasoline Alley
Roanoke, TX
(817) 491-3483

McClure's Cafe
15306 Highway 114
Justin, TX
(817) 638-2208

Mom's Cafe
417 N. Sealy Avenue
Justin, TX
(940) 648-2581

Mr. Jim's Pizza
500 N. Highway 377
Roanoke, TX
(817) 491-4111

Popeye's Chicken & Biscuits
704 E. Byron Nelson Boulevard
Roanoke, TX
(817) 491-1002

Prairie House Restaurant
304 S. Highway 377
Roanoke, TX
(817) 430-0640

Schlotzsky's Deli
2410 Westport Parkway
Fort Worth, TX
(817) 439-1919

Snooty Pig Cafe
2401 Westport Parkway, Suite 120
Fort Worth, TX
(817) 837-1077

Sonic Drive-In
802 Highway 156
Justin, TX
(940) 648-1317

Sonny Bryan's Smokehouse
2421 Westport Parkway, Suite 100
Fort Worth, TX
(817) 224-9191

Speedway Donuts
950 S. FM 156
Justin, TX
(940) 648-3044

Subway Sandwiches & Salads
1224 N. Highway 377
Roanoke, TX
(817) 837-9996

Taco Bell
700 E. Byron Nelson Boulevard
Roanoke, TX
(817) 491-8530

Tortilla Flats
115 N. Oak Street
Roanoke, TX
(817) 490-8884

Waffle House
800 W. Highway 114
Roanoke, TX
(817) 490-6527

Wendy's
1204 N. Highway 377
Roanoke, TX
(817) 831-1533

Whataburger
605 E. Byron Nelson Boulevard
Roanoke, TX
(817) 490-1059

Wings21
1224 N. Highway 377
Roanoke, TX
(817) 831-1600

Local Attractions

WORTH THE TRIP

Two great attractions to make the time for are the **Texas Cowboy Hall of Fame** in Fort Worth and the **Dallas World Aquarium** in Dallas. Both are fun for the family and great afternoon getaways. The Cowboy Hall of Fame is fun and interesting if you are into the cowboy way of life, which I am. The aquarium is great for the kids, but be aware the ticket prices are a bit steep for an entire family. It is worth the drive and the facility is great, but check your budget before taking a family of eight.

Action Skate Parks
3000 Grapevine Mills Parkway,
   Suite 519
Grapevine, TX
(972) 724-4329

**Courthouse-on-the-Square
   Museum**
110 W. Hickory Street
Denton, TX
(972) 434-8809

Dallas World Aquarium
1801 N. Griffin Street
Dallas, TX
(214) 720-2224

Denton County Historical Museum
5800 N. Interstate 35, Suite 308
Denton, TX
(940) 380-0877

Doral Tesoro Golf Course
3300 Championship Parkway
Fort Worth, TX
(817) 497-2582

Gowns of the First Ladies of Texas
Texas Woman's University
303 Administration Drive, # 104
Denton, TX
(940) 898-3644

Grapevine Historical Museum
705 S. Main Street
Grapevine, TX
(817) 410-8145

Hangar Ten Flying Museum
1945 Matt Wright Lane
Denton, TX
(940) 565-1945

Integrity Park
9139 Highway 377
Argyle, TX
(940) 464-7177

**International Porcelain Artists and
   Teachers Museum**
204 E. Franklin Street
Grapevine, TX
(817) 251-1185

Pate Museum of Transportation
18501 Highway 377 S.
Fort Worth, TX
(817) 396-4305

Syncline Skatepark
11578 Airway Boulevard
Roanoke, TX
(817) 491-4512

Texas Cowboy Hall of Fame
128 E. Exchange Avenue
Fort Worth, TX
(817) 626-7131

Vintage Flying Museum
505 NW 38th Street
Fort Worth, TX
(817) 624-1935

Wildhorse Golf Club
9400 Ed Robson Boulevard, Suite A
Denton, TX
(940) 246-1001

Shopping

KEY

🚗 Automotive $ Discount
⊙ Pharmacy   📧 Mall
☆ Specialty   🏦 Department Store

☆ Bed Bath & Beyond
2930 E. Southlake Boulevard
Southlake, TX
(817) 748-3000

☆ Bealls
1651 W. Northwest Highway
Grapevine, TX
(817) 488-6025

$ Big Lots
6300 Rufe Snow Drive
Fort Worth, TX
(817) 581-8143

$ Costco
2601 E. State Highway 114
Southlake, TX
(817) 749-2809

$ Dollar General
825 W. First Street
Justin, TX
(940) 648-0997

$ Family Dollar Store
1587 FM 3433
Newark, TX
(817) 489-2304

📧 Golden Triangle Mall
2201 S. Interstate 35 E.
Denton, TX
(940) 566-6023

🏦 JC Penney
1701 Intermodal Parkway
Haslet, TX
(682) 831-1888

🏦 Kohl's Department Store
2001 S. Main Street
Keller, TX
(817) 431-4437

$ Marshalls
8028 Denton Highway
Watauga, TX
(817) 427-8750

**North East Mall Shopping
Center**
1101 Melbourne Road
Hurst, TX
(817) 284-3427

Northwest Crossing
431 E. Northwest Highway
Grapevine, TX
(817) 481-8843

☆ Once Upon a Child
2311 Cross Timbers Road
Flower Mound, TX
(817) 874-0779

☆ Pier 1 Imports
7608 Denton Highway, Suite 316
Watauga, TX
(817) 503-9295

☆ Plato's Closet
2311 Cross Timbers Road, Suite 317
Flower Mound, TX
(972) 691-8988

$ Ross Dress For Less
7612 Denton Highway
Watauga, TX
(817) 514-0581

$ Sam's Club
1701 W. State Highway 114
Grapevine, TX
(817) 416-0561

Southlake Town Square
1256 Main Street
Southlake, TX
(817) 329-5566

☆ Stein Mart
316 Grapevine Highway
Hurst, TX
(817) 281-6563

☆ Talbots
1430 Civic Place
Southlake, TX
(817) 421-5418

$ Target
8000 Denton Highway
Watauga, TX
(817) 427-8039

$ T.J. Maxx
3192 Justin Road
Lewisville, TX
(972) 317-4869

$ Wal-Mart Supercenter
8520 N. Beach Street
Fort Worth, TX
(817) 514-9793

Churches/
Worship Centers

Abundant Life
500 N. Highway 377
Roanoke, TX
(817) 490-0269

Alliance Church of Christ
127 Daisey Lane
Justin, TX
(940) 648-2888

Bible Baptist Church
415 Leuty Street
Justin, TX
(940) 648-3916

Christ's Haven Chapel
4150 Keller Haslet Road
Keller, TX
(817) 741-7613

Christian Faith Fellowship
500 N. Highway 377, Suite J
Roanoke, TX
(817) 491-0624

Church of Jesus Christ of Latter-Day Saints
300 Rusk Street
Roanoke, TX
(682) 831-1445

Church of the Resurrection
108 Pecan Street
Roanoke, TX
(817) 491-3590

First Baptist Church
209 N. Pine Street
Roanoke, TX
(817) 491-2656

Hilltop Church of Christ
341 Dorman Road
Roanoke, TX
(817) 491-4810

Justin Church of Christ
424 S. Snyder Avenue
Justin, TX
(940) 648-2482

Justin United Methodist Church
205 N. Jackson Avenue
Justin, TX
(940) 648-2594

Lakeside Fellowship
108 Pecan Street
Fort Worth, TX
(817) 491-3000

Roanoke Church of Christ
305 Rusk Street
Roanoke, TX
(817) 491-2388

Rockhaven Church
2297 Litsey Road
Roanoke, TX
(817) 430-0125

Sage Meadow Christian Fellowship
531 John Wiley Road
Justin, TX
(940) 648-2409

Southlake Boulevard Presbyterian
1452 W. Southlake Boulevard
Southlake, TX
(817) 442-8983

Speedway Christian Fellowship
211 W. Fifth Street
Justin, TX
(940) 648-1194

St. Barnabas Apostle Episcopal Church
4647 Shiver Road
Keller, TX
(817) 938-7131

St. Elizabeth Ann Seton Catholic Church
2016 Willis Lane
Keller, TX
(817) 431-3857

St. Nicholas Episcopal Church
4800 Wichita Trail
Flower Mound, TX
(972) 318-7070

St. Peter Lutheran Church
312 N. Highway 377
Roanoke, TX
(817) 491-2010

Tabernacle Baptist Church
512 N. Oak Street
Roanoke, TX
(817) 491-2180

Medical Centers

Baylor Medical Center
1650 W. College Street
Grapevine, TX
(817) 481-1588

EMC Express Care
8245 Precinct Line Road
North Richland Hills, TX
(817) 503-8800

Pet Medical Centers

Justin Animal Hospital
9849 S. FM 156
Justin, TX
(940) 648-0328

Keller Animal Clinic
221 S. Main Street
Keller, TX
(817) 431-1213

Keller Town Center Animal Hospital
901 E. Price Street
Keller, TX
(817) 431-2541

Roanoke Animal Clinic
513 E. Highway 114
Roanoke, TX
(817) 430-8989

WATKINS GLEN INTERNATIONAL

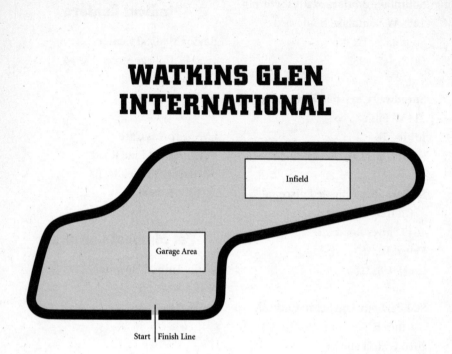

Infield

Garage Area

Start | Finish Line

Track Information

Inaugural Year: 1957
Owner: ISC
City: Watkins Glen, New York
Size: 2.45 miles
Banking: 60 to 10, variables
Grandstand Capacity: 85,000

ADDRESS
Watkins Glen International
2790 County Route 16
Watkins Glen, NY 14891
(607) 535-2481
www.theglen.com

TICKET INFORMATION
Phone: (866) 461-7223
www.theglen.com

About the Track

Watkins Glen is one of two (Infineon being the other) road courses on the NASCAR Sprint Cup circuit. The Glen's 2.45-mile course is the longer of the two. If you love road-course racing, you will love Watkins Glen. The track offers many left- and right-side turns that make for great road-course racing. Much like Infineon, only a handful of drivers seem to have a handle on the road-course events.

Track History

A young law student by the name of Cameron Argetsinger fell in love with Watkins Glen when he vacationed there in the summers. His love affair with the area and with auto racing became one in October 1948, when the combination road course of asphalt, cement, and dirt hosted its first event through the city streets. This historic event was the first post–World War II road-course race in U.S. history. The permanent track was not completed until 1956; the NASCAR series debuted at the Glen in 1957, crowning Buck Baker the race winner. NASCAR then decided to pull their elite series from the struggling track, leaving the Glen void of NASCAR races from 1965 to 1986. In 1983, ISC partnered with Corning Enterprises to purchase the sprawling road course in hopes of turning the track around. NASCAR returned to the Glen in 1986 and in 1997 took over total ownership of Watkins Glen International.

Track Records

Most Wins: Jeff Gordon (4)
Most Top Five Finishes: Mark Martin (12)
Most Lead Changes: 14—most recently on 8/13/2006 (total of 2 times)
Fewest Lead Changes: 0—on 8/4/1957
Most Cautions: 10—on 8/13/2006
Fewest Cautions: 0—on 7/18/1965
Race Record: Mark Martin— 103.300 mph (2 hours, 11 minutes, 54 seconds) (8/13/1995)
Qualifying Record: Jeff Gordon— 124.580 mph (70.798 seconds) (8/8/2003)

Fast Facts

- The first NASCAR Sprint Cup race was run at Watkins Glen International on August 4, 1957, and was won by Buck Baker.
- Geoffrey Bodine is the oldest driver to have won at Watkins Glen International—winning in August 1996, he was forty-seven years old (plus three months and twenty-four days).
- NASCAR driver J. D. McDuffie suffered fatal injuries at Watkins Glen in 1991.
- The track trophy is named after Cameron Argetsinger.

- Watkins Glen hosted the 1973 Summer Jam rock festival to over 600,000 rowdy fans.

🏁 **INSIDER TIP**—Free child safety and identification wristbands (with spaces to list a reserved seat or campsite and a contact number) are available at all Guest Services Information Tents located in the main grandstand area and in front of the ticket office.

Parking

Free parking is available for all fans attending the race. No overnight parking is allowed in the general parking areas. All parking is first come, first served.

🏁 **INSIDER TIP**—Shuttle buses are available during the NASCAR race weekend for transportation to and from outlying camping and parking areas around the track.

Track Rules

According to the track's official website at www.theglen.com, the track's rules are as follows:

ITEMS ALLOWED IN THE GRANDSTANDS

- ✓ one soft-sided bag/cooler (no larger than 6″ × 6″ × 12″)
- ✓ one clear plastic bag (no larger than 18″ × 18″ × 4″)
- ✓ binoculars
- ✓ scanners
- ✓ headsets
- ✓ cameras (worn separately over the neck or on a belt)
- ✓ seat cushions

ITEMS *NOT* ALLOWED IN THE GRANDSTANDS

- ✗ weapons of any description
- ✗ illegal drugs
- ✗ fireworks
- ✗ ATVs
- ✗ dirt bikes
- ✗ mopeds
- ✗ motorcycles
- ✗ bicycles
- ✗ water balloon launchers (or any other form of launching device)
- ✗ Super Soakers
- ✗ golf carts
- ✗ hard-sided coolers
- ✗ thermoses or insulated cups of any size

✗ strollers

✗ umbrellas

Special Needs and Services

Watkins Glen offers seating and parking for those needing special assistance or accessibility. One companion is allowed to accompany those with special needs. Call the track at 866-461-7223 prior to your arrival. Always ask for your parking to be near your seats.

Track Tours

Watkins Glen offers a tour for individuals and groups like no other track on the circuit. The Glen's track tour actually allows you (following the pace car) to drive three laps around the road course in your own vehicle. The tours are offered May through October, starting at noon each day. Tickets are available in the track gift shop, which is located in the village of Watkins Glen. For more info on tours and fees, call the track at 607-535-2338. Motorcycles are allowed on the track tour.

Souvenirs

Official Glen souvenirs are available at the Pyramid Souvenir Center, located in the infield, and the Shop, located at 2 N. Franklin Street in the village of Watkins Glen. Driver-specific souvenirs are available at Souvenir Alley along the Exhibitor's Midway located on Wedgewood Road.

INSIDER TIP—ATMs are located at the Shop in the village, the Pyramid Souvenir Center in the infield, and in the main concession area.

About the Area

Watkins Glen is something worth visiting if for no other reason than it is so different from the other host cities on the circuit. Located in the Finger Lakes area of New York, you can expect beautiful lakes, breathtaking hillsides, fabulous shopping, and countless wineries. In fact, the Watkins Glen area is home to over one hundred wineries, producing over forty million bottles of wine a year. This region is one of the largest wine producers in the country. When visiting the track, plan to pack for comfortable temps as Watkins Glen in August serves up beautiful fall weather conditions. You will be a little early for the fall color, but the scenery will not disappoint.

INSIDER TIP—The upper New York state area is beautiful! You will want to make sure to visit a winery or two.

CHAMBER OF COMMERCE

Schuyler County Chamber of
   Commerce
100 N. Franklin Street
Watkins Glen, NY 14891
(607) 535-4300
www.schuylerny.com

Transportation

AIRPORT
Elmira Corning Regional Airport
   (ELM)
276 Sing Sing Road
Horseheads, NY
(607) 739-5621
(Elmira/Corning Regional is
   approximately thirteen miles
   from the track.)

AIRLINES
Allegiant Air (702) 505-8888
Northwest (800) 225-2525
US Airways (800) 428-4322

RENTAL CARS
Avis (800) 331-1212
Hertz (800) 654-3131
National (800) 227-7368

Hotels

KEY
🐾 Pet Friendly   ≈ Pool
✕ Restaurant

🐾 **Anchor Inn & Marina**
3425 County Road 30
Watkins Glen, NY
(607) 535-4159

🐾, ≈ **Best Western Lodge**
3171 Canada Road
Painted Post, NY
(607) 962-2456

🐾, ≈ **Best Western Marshall
   Manor**
3527 Watkins Road
Horseheads, NY
(607) 739-3891

🐾 **Budget Inn**
435 S. Franklin Street
Watkins Glen, NY
(607) 535-4800

🐾 **Budget Inn**
135 E. Corning Road
Corning, NY
(607) 937-5686

Chalet Leon at Hector Falls
3835 State Route 414
Burdett, NY
(607) 546-7171

ᗕ **Chieftain Motel**
3815 State Route 14
Watkins Glen, NY
(607) 535-4759

Colonial Hotel
701 N. Franklin Street
Watkins Glen, NY
(607) 535-7545

≈ **Comfort Inn**
66 W. Pulteney Street
Corning, NY
(607) 962-15153

≈, ✕ **Corning Painted Post**
304 S. Hamilton Street
Painted Post, NY
(607) 962-5021

≈ **Country Inn & Suites**
105 E. Mall Road
Horseheads, NY
(607) 739-9205

≈, ✕ **Days Inn**
23 Riverside Drive
Corning, NY
(607) 936-9370

ᗕ **Econo Lodge**
871 County Road 64
Elmira, NY
(607) 739-2000

ᗕ **Econo Lodge**
200 Robert Dann Drive
Painted Post, NY
(607) 962-4444

≈ **Fairfield Inn**
3 S. Buffalo Street
Corning, NY
(607) 937-9600

Gate House Motel
11409 Lpga Drive
Corning, NY
(607) 936-4131

ᗕ **Glen Motor Inn Motel**
3380 State Route 14
Watkins Glen, NY
(607) 535-2706

ᗕ **Glen Way Motel**
212 S. Franklin Street
Watkins Glen, NY
(607) 535-4258

ᗕ **Golden Knight Inn**
4461 State Route 14
Rock Stream, NY
(607) 535-8012

≈ **Hampton Inn**
9775 Victory Highway
Painted Post, NY
(607) 936-3344

Highland Lodge
5176 Indian Fort Road
Trumansburg, NY
(607) 387-9333

≈ ✕ **Hilton Garden Inn Elmira**
35 Arnot Road
Horseheads, NY
(607) 795-1111

≈ **Holiday Inn Elmira-Horseheads**
2666 Corning Road
Horseheads, NY
(607) 739-3681

✕ **Inn at Glenora Wine Cellars**
5435 State Route 14
Dundee, NY
(607) 243-9500

⌂, ≈ **Knights Inn**
2707 Westinghouse Road
Horseheads, NY
(607) 739-3807

⌂, ≈ **Lodge on the Green**
196 S. Hamilton Road
Painted Post, NY
(607) 962-2456

⌂ **Madison Guest House**
413 S. Madison Avenue
Watkins Glen, NY
(607) 535-9096

Mark Twain Motor Inn
1996 Lake Street
Elmira, NY
(607) 733-9144

⌂ **Motel 6**
4133 Route 17
Horseheads, NY
(607) 739-2525

✕ **Park Inn**
35 Shether Street
Hammondsport, NY
(607) 569-9387

⌂, ≈, ✕ **Radisson Hotel Corning**
125 Denison Parkway E.
Corning, NY
(607) 962-5000

≈ **Red Carpet Inn**
3325 S. Main Street
Horseheads, NY
(607) 739-3831

⌂ **Relax Inn**
100 Clawson Boulevard
Montour Falls, NY
(607) 535-7183

⌂ **Relax Inn**
45 Fisherville Road
Elmira, NY
(607) 739-5611

Seneca Clipper Inn
436 S. Franklin Street
Watkins Glen, NY
(607) 535-2441

⌂, ≈ **Staybridge Suites Corning**
201 Townley Avenue
Corning, NY
(607) 936-7800

Stiles Motel
9239 Victory Highway
Painted Post, NY
(607) 962-5221

⛸ **Super 8 Motel**
255 S. Hamilton Street
Painted Post, NY
(607) 937-5383

Camping

ON-SITE AND TRACK-OWNED CAMPING

Watkins Glen offers both reserved and nonreserved camping on track property. Call the track at 866-461-7223 for up-to-date info on camping, including fees and camping rules. Always ask for the rules of the specific area in which you choose to camp. It is not uncommon for each area to have its own set of rules.

Non-Trackside Reserved This area is also for RVs, pop-ups, and tents. The only difference between this and the trackside reserved is location of the track and the view. It is dry camping only. This area is first come, first served.

Trackside Reserved This trackside view area is for RVs, pop-ups, and tents. No hookups are available. Dry camping only. This area can be reserved in advance.

OFF-SITE CAMPING

Cayuta Lake Camping
2457 County Road 6
Alpine, NY
(607) 594-2366

Clute Park & Campground
155 S. Clute Park
Watkins Glen, NY
(607) 535-4438

Cool-Lea Camp
2540 State Route 228
Odessa, NY
(607) 594-3500

Ferenbaugh Camping & Recreation Area
4826 State Route 414
Corning, NY
(607) 962-6193

KOA Campgrounds
1710 State Route 414
Watkins Glen, NY
(607) 535-7404

Paradise Park Campground
4150 Cross Road
Reading Center, NY
(607) 535-6600

Restaurants

KEY

🍔 Fast Food   🪑 Sit Down

🥡 Takeout   🕯 Reservations

Must Eats

Bully Hill Vineyards
8843 Greyton H Taylor Memorial Drive
Hammondsport, NY
(607) 868-3490

This is a restaurant located in the Bully Hill Vineyards way out in the rolling hills of New York. The food is quite fancy and even more tasty. The staff makes you feel like you are home. You have to try the Love My Goat wine.

Old Country Buffet
821 County Route 64
Elmira, NY
(607) 796-6369

This is a country-style buffet fit for a king. Everyone can find something they love. The dessert bar is awesome!

🍔 **Arby's**
120 Lembeck Lane
Watkins Glen, NY
(607) 535-9609

🥡 **Art & Nancy's Sub & Pizza Shop**
204 Ninth Street
Watkins Glen, NY
(607) 535-9714

🪑 **Bianco's Italian Restaurante**
401 E. Fourth Street
Watkins Glen, NY
(607) 535-2863

🪑 **Bleachers Sports Bar & Grill**
413 N. Franklin Street
Watkins Glen, NY
(607) 535-6705

🪑 **Blue Ribbon Diner**
139 N. Catherine Street
Montour Falls, NY
(607) 535-9004

🪑 **Buisch's Bullpen & Wing House**
229 S. Catherine Street
Montour Falls, NY
(607) 535-2215

🍔 **Burger King**
211 S. Franklin Street
Watkins Glen, NY
(607) 535-7280

🪑 **Captain Bill's Seneca Lake**
1 1/2 N. Franklin Street
Watkins Glen, NY
(607) 535-4541

🪑 **Cascata Winery**
3651 State Route 14
Watkins Glen, NY
(607) 535-8000

Castel Grisch Winery & Restaurant
3380 Irelandville Road
Watkins Glen, NY
(607) 535-9614

Chef's Diner
Watkins Montour Road Route 14 N.
Montour Falls, NY
(607) 535-9975

Country Side Grill
7534 Route 226
Bradford, NY
(607) 583-4513

Curly's Family Restaurant
2780 State Route 14
Montour Falls, NY
(607) 535-4383

Grist Mill Cafe
3825 Main Street
Burdett, NY
(607) 546-7770

Hickory House Restaurant
3543 Watkins Road
Horseheads, NY
(607) 739-2405

House of Hong
400 N. Franklin Street
Watkins Glen, NY
(607) 535-7024

Janet's Country Ranch Restaurant
Route 226
Bradford, NY
(607) 583-7977

Jerlando's Ristorante & Pizza Co.
400 N. Franklin Street
Watkins Glen, NY
(607) 535-4254

Jerlando's Ristorante & Pizza Co.
322 W. Main Street
Montour Falls, NY
(607) 535-8885

Kozy Korner
2801 State Route 226
Bradford, NY
(607) 583-7226

McDonald's
515 E. Fourth Street
Watkins Glen, NY
(607) 535-6119

Montage Restaurant
3380 State Route 14
Watkins Glen, NY
(607) 535-2706

Pizza Hut
412 S. Franklin Street
Watkins Glen, NY
(607) 535-4333

🪑 **Savard's Family Restaurant**
601 N. Franklin Street
Watkins Glen, NY
(607) 535-4538

🪑 **Seneca Harbor Station**
3 N. Franklin Street
Watkins Glen, NY
(607) 535-6101

🥡 **Smok'n Bones BBQ**
3815 Main Street
Burdett, NY
(607) 546-7999

🥡 **Subway Sandwiches & Salads**
800 N. Franklin Street
Watkins Glen, NY
(607) 535-4825

🪑 **Tobes**
135 E. Fourth Street
Watkins Glen, NY
(607) 535-4012

🥡 **Village Take Out Pizzeria**
110 Main Street
Odessa, NY
(607) 594-2268

🪑 **Wildflower Cafe**
301 N. Franklin Street
Watkins Glen, NY
(607) 535-9797

Local Attractions

WORTH THE TRIP
With over one hundred wineries in the area, what better to do while practice is going on at the track than hit the wine trail? If you only have time for one, make it the 2008 Top Winery of the Year, **Fox Run Vineyards.** For more info on winery hours and tastings, call Fox Run at 1-800-636-9786. The local chamber of commerce is a great place for a full list of all the wineries in the area.

Benjamin Patterson Inn Museum
59 W. Pulteney Street
Corning, NY
(607) 937-5281

Corning Museum of Glass
1 Museum Way
Corning, NY
(607) 937-5371

Greyton H. Taylor Wine Museum
8843 Greyton H. Taylor Memorial
 Drive
Hammondsport, NY
(607) 868-4814

Havana Glen Park
135 Havana Glen Road
Montour Falls, NY
(607) 535-9476

Hillendale Golf Course
218 N. Applegate Road
Ithaca, NY
(607) 273-2363

Mark Twain State Park
201 Middle Road
Horseheads, NY
(607) 739-0034

National Soaring Museum
51 Soaring Hill Drive
Elmira, NY
(607) 734-3128

National Warplane Museum
17 Aviation Drive
Horseheads, NY
(607) 796-6597

Rockwell Museum of Western Art
111 Cedar Street
Corning, NY
(607) 937-5386

Sciencenter
601 First Street
Ithaca, NY
(607) 272-0600

Watkins Glen Golf Course
3401 Route 14
Watkins Glen, NY
(607) 535-2340

Shopping

KEY
🚗 Automotive $ Discount
✚ Pharmacy   🏬 Mall
☆ Specialty   🏚 Department Store

🏚 **Ames Department Store**
100 Victory Highway
Painted Post, NY
(607) 937-54142

🏬 **Arnot Mall**
3300 Chambers Road
Horseheads, NY
(607) 739-8705

$ **Best Buy**
950 County Road 64
Elmira, NY
(607) 739-947

$ **Big Lots**
State Route 13 and Trimphammer
Road
Ithaca, NY
(607) 266-7066

$ **Dollar General**
142 N. Catherine Street, Suite 6915
Montour Falls, NY
(607) 535-2246

$ **Dollar Tree**
3159 Silverback Lane
Painted Post, NY
(607) 937-3751

✩ **Eddie Bauer**
40 Catherwood Road
Ithaca, NY
(607) 266-8080

$ **Family Dollar Store**
520 S. Franklin Street
Watkins Glen, NY
(607) 535-5476

👕 **JC Penney**
3300 Chambers Road
Horseheads, NY
(607) 739-3521

$ **Kmart**
1020 Center Street
Horseheads, NY
(607) 739-3661

🏬 **Lown's House of Shoppes**
131 Main Street
Penn Yan, NY
(315) 531-8343

👕 **Macy's**
3300 Chambers Road
Horseheads, NY
(607) 739-3717

✩ **Only One**
830 County Road 64
Elmira, NY
(607) 796-5371

✩ **Pier 1 Imports**
722 S. Meadow Street
Ithaca, NY
(607) 277-7987

🏬 **Pyramid Mall Ithaca**
40 Catherwood Road
Ithaca, NY
(607) 257-5337

✩ **Ray Jewelers**
1100 Clements Center Parkway
Elmira, NY
(607) 734-9400

$ **Sam's Club**
830 County Road 64
Elmira, NY
(607) 739-2883

👕 **Sears**
3300 Chambers Road
Horseheads, NY
(607) 739-6028

✩ **Shoe Department**
3300 Chambers Road
Horseheads, NY
(607) 795-1625

✩ **Talbots**
3343 Chambers Road
Horseheads, NY
(607) 795-1004

👕 **Tallman's Department Store**
150 Village Square
Painted Post, NY
(607) 962-2033

$ **Target**
40 Catherwood Road
Ithaca, NY
(607) 257-3387

$ T.J. Maxx
821 County Road 64
Elmira, NY
(607) 739-6429

$ Wal-Mart Supercenter
515 E. Fourth Street
Watkins Glen, NY
(607) 535-3108

Churches/
Worship Centers

**Beaver Dams United Methodist
  Church**
1285 County Road 19
Beaver Dams, NY
(607) 962-4567

Bethel Fellowship Church
2035 State Route 14
Montour Falls, NY
(607) 535-4492

Burdett Presbyterian Church
3995 Church Street
Burdett, NY
(607) 546-8560

Church of the Nazarene
405 S. Madison Avenue
Watkins Glen, NY
(607) 535-2313

First Baptist Church
213 Fifth Street
Watkins Glen, NY
(607) 535-7385

First Presbyterian Church
520 N. Decatur Street
Watkins Glen, NY
(607) 535-2377

Full Gospel Church
683 Backer Road
Beaver Dams, NY
(607) 962-2333

Glen Baptist Church
3311 Reading Road
Watkins Glen, NY
(607) 535-4802

Grace Lee Memorial Wesleyan
2075 Chambers Road
Beaver Dams, NY
(607) 962-3225

Jehovah's Witnesses
2590 State Route 414
Montour Falls, NY
(607) 535-7315

Lakeview Assembly of God
3601 State Route 14
Watkins Glen, NY
(607) 535-9730

**Montour Falls United Methodist
  Church**
124 Owego Street
Montour Falls, NY
(607) 535-7204

St. James Episcopal Church
112 Sixth Street
Watkins Glen, NY
(607) 535-2321

St. Mary's of the Lake Catholic Church
905 N. Decatur Street
Watkins Glen, NY
(607) 535-2786

St. Paul's Episcopal Church
112 S. Genesee
Montour Falls, NY
(607) 535-7234

United Methodist Church
127 E. Fourth Street
Watkins Glen, NY
(607) 535-4754

Medical Centers

Arnot Ogden Medical Center
100 John Roemmelt Drive
Horseheads, NY
(607) 796-4924

Corning Hospital
176 Denison Parkway E.
Corning, NY
(607) 937-7200

Schuyler Hospital
220 Steuben Street
Montour Falls, NY
(607) 535-7121

St. Joseph's Hospital
555 E. Market Street
Elmira, NY
(607) 733-6541

Pet Medical Centers

Corning Animal Hospital
11863 E. Corning Road
Corning, NY
(607) 962-5905

Lake Road Animal Hospital
3065 Lake Road
Horseheads, NY
(607) 733-6503

Mill Stone Veterinary Clinic
5923 State Route 14A
Dundee, NY
(607) 243-5298

Miracle Mile Animal Hospital
2501 Corning Road
Elmira, NY
(607) 796-4655

Rio Vista Veterinary Hospital
9765 Smith Hill Road
Painted Post, NY
(607) 962-0931

ABOUT THE AUTHOR

LIZ ALLISON has spent over twenty years at the race track as a driver's wife and, later, a member of the sports media covering NASCAR Sprint Cup events. Married to racing superstar Davey Allison until his untimely death in 1993, Liz's passion for the sport continues today as she covers the sport of stock car racing through many facets of the media.

A popular radio personality in Nashville on WGFX and WKDF, her NASCAR insight and top notch guests have made her NASCAR programming the #1 NASCAR show in Nashville. Liz was awarded the AIR Award for Best Midday Talk Show in 2007 for her role as host of the *Driver's Zone* radio show. In 2004, Liz joined the Nashville Super Speedway as announcer and host for the Speedway's four major race events, making her the first woman to serve the Nashville motorsports industry in this capacity.

Liz has covered NASCAR racing for TNT Sports as a pit road reporter and feature reporter. She has hosted such television shows as *Motoring Music City* on ESPN 2, has served as race analyst for ESPN's *Cold Pizza*, and has appeared on many national television and radio shows throughout her career, including the *Today* show, *Fox and Friends, 20/20*, and CNN.

The author of ten published books on the popular sport of NASCAR, Liz has served as a contributing author for FoxSports.com, Proctor and Gamble, AutoVantage, NASCAR.com, MSN.com, and various other publications.

Liz is remarried and lives in Nashville with her husband, Ryan, and children, Krista, Robbie, and Bella.